Trauma and Dreams

Trauma and Dreams

EDITED BY DEIRDRE BARRETT

HARVARD UNIVERSITY PRESS
Cambridge, Massachusetts
London, England
1996

Library of Congress Cataloging-in-Publication Data

Trauma and dreams / edited by Deirdre Barrett.
p. cm.
Includes bibliographical references and index.
ISBN 0-674-90552-0 (alk. paper)
1. Dreams. 2. Post-traumatic stress syndrome.
3. Psychic trauma. 4. Nightmares. 5. Dream interpretation. I. Barrett, Deirdre.
RC489.D74T73 1996
616.85'21—dc20   96-13023

*To our research subjects and psychotherapy clients,
whose collective experience may guide those who
cope with and treat trauma in the future*

Contents

Part Three　Traumas of Normal Living

Acknowledgments

The Association for the Study of Dreams introduced me to many of the authors in this book. The association's annual conferences provided an opportunity to hear of research and clinical findings that were not yet in print, and some of those now appear here.

I would like to thank Dan Brown and Bessel van der Kolk for reviewing an early proposal for this book and suggesting additional topics and chapter authors. G. William Domhoff read and commented on several of the chapters in progress.

At Harvard University Press the book was adeptly guided by Angela von der Lippe, and many graceful phrases owe their existence to Elizabeth Gretz's editing.

Portions of Chapter 6 first appeared in *Quadrant: The Journal of the C. G. Jung Foundation for Analytical Psychology,* published by the C. G. Jung Foundation of New York, © copyright, The C. G. Jung Foundation of New York, 1986, and in *Spring, A Journal of Archetype and Culture* (Putnam, Conn.) (1986): 47–61, and are reprinted by permission.

The material in Chapter 9 was originally presented at a symposium on dreams sponsored by the Department of Human Development and Health Sciences of the University of California, Los Angeles, and the Southern California Psychoanalytic Society and Institute. It appeared in another form as Chapter 13, "Dreaming Well: Frontiers of Form," in Robert Jay Lifton, *The Future of Immortality and Other Essays for a Nuclear Age,* © 1987 HarperCollins Publishers (New York: Basic Books, 1987), and is reproduced with permission.

Chapter 15 is an expanded version of an article that originally appeared as "Neurological Dreams," *MD Magazine,* February 1991.

Trauma and Dreams

Introduction

DEIRDRE BARRETT

All the things one has forgotten scream
for help in dreams.

ELIAS CANETTI

Dreams constitute a unique window on trauma and its effects. The window is not clear, however, but prismatic, showing us a changed version of events that is frequently distorted but can also bring chaos into resolution. This view can be both diagnostic and therapeutic.

From folklore of the dead visiting dreamers to Shakespeare's Lady Macbeth sleepwalking and trying to wash blood off her hands, people in centuries past have known of the special relationship between trauma and dreaming. The traumas could be forgotten, as Canetti describes, or only too well remembered, as in the perspective of Walt Whitman's soldier:

> In midnight sleep of many a face of anguish,
> Of the look at first of the mortally wounded, (of that indescribable look,)
> Of the dead on their backs with arms extended wide,
>   I dream, I dream, I dream
> . . . . .
> Long have they pass'd, faces and trenches and fields,
> Where through the carnage I moved with a callous composure, or away
>   from the fallen,
> Onward I sped at the time—but now of their forms at night,
>   I dream, I dream, I dream.
>
> "Old War-Dreams," 1865–66

As the formal Western disciplines of psychology and psychiatry developed, they to some extent lost touch with this awareness of trauma's impact on dreaming. Ironically, the most significant factor in turning away from the folk wisdom that sees dreams as haunted by remembered or unremembered horrors has been the Freudian idea of "wish fulfillment." Many traditional analysts to this day interpret even quite unpleasant dreams in terms of Freud's assertion that all dreams represent the fulfillment of wishes. The irony is that Freud himself in later writings clearly came to believe that this was not always the case. He stated that dreams in "war neuroses" were an exception and better viewed as fear enactments. And despite the concept of wish fulfillment for which he is better known, Freud was well aware that real childhood sexual traumas could show up quite realistically in dreams, as in the following case:

> One of my patients was presented in a dream with an almost undistorted reproduction of a [traumatic] sexual episode, which was at once recognizable as a true recollection. His memory of the event had, in fact, never been completely lost in waking life, although it had become greatly obscured, and its revival was a consequence of work done previously in analysis.   (Freud, [1900] 1965, p. 231)

Jung, in his writings on the symbolism in dreams and their parallels to myths and fairytales, also led most of his followers away from considering the involvement of literal trauma in dreams. But like Freud, Jung did recognize that these could be the primary source of a nightmare:

> Cases of severe shock were produced in abundance by the war, and here we may expect a large number of pure reaction-dreams in which the trauma is the determining factor. Although it is certainly very important for the over-all functioning of the psyche that the traumatic content gradually loses its autonomy by frequent repetition and in this way takes its place in the psychic hierarchy, a dream of this kind, which is essentially only a reproduction of the trauma, can hardly be called compensatory. (Jung, [1916] 1974, pp. 46–47)

For the first two thirds of this century little more was said about the role of trauma in dreaming. Wish fulfillment, metaphor, and symbolic interpretation became the focus of dream psychology. The psychology of trauma received remarkably little attention, with only minor renewal of interest following each war as society was challenged to integrate the survivors. In the late 1960s, however, veterans of the Vietnam War came home suffering even more severe Post-Traumatic Stress Disorder (PTSD) from close combat and guerrilla tactics than soldiers of previous wars. About the same time, feminism began to demand that society take seriously the domestic abuse of women and children. The modern study of psychological trauma began.

A connection between trauma and dreams now reappears in the recent literature on each, but the link is not usually developed further. Nightmares and recurring dreams are among the most common symptoms of PTSD.

One review of the disorder (Ross et al., 1989) even points to the disruption of rapid eye movement—REM or dreaming—sleep as the central defining characteristic of this syndrome. The authors suggest that PTSD symptoms such as extreme autonomic reactivity and vivid, even hallucinatory imagery of past events, "flashbacks," are normal phenomena for REM sleep and abnormally manifesting in the waking state. Nevertheless, in most trauma research or detailed PTSD reports, nightmares are often listed as a symptom without detail and without attention to their potential role in therapy. Similarly, dream studies consistently find stress and trauma to be much of what dreams focus on, and Domhoff (1993) goes so far as to suggest that this stress and trauma may be the central reason for dreams. Most dream theorists, however, continue to discuss even nightmares symbolically with only passing reference to the role of trauma.

Several studies have delineated a pattern of post-traumatic nightmares in which the initial dreams are fairly close to a literal reenactment of the trauma, sometimes with the twist that an additional horror, averted in real life, is added to the dream reenactment. Then, as time passes, and especially for those whose PTSD is gradually improving, the dream content begins to make the trauma more symbolic and to interweave it with concerns from the dreamer's daily life. Van der Kolk and colleagues (1984) found this to be true of Vietnam veterans' combat nightmares, in which the veteran's death, instead of his buddy's, was a common variant. Terr (1990) found that child survivors of the Chowchilla kidnapping dreamed at first of reenactments of the kidnapping and later of variations such as being buried alive in places other than the kidnappers' property or being grabbed by the kidnappers out of their current setting. Child sexual abuse survivors whom she studied reported similar patterns. When I visited Kuwait after the Iraqi occupation, Kuwaitis told me recurring dreams that followed this pattern— literal reenactments that were beginning to change into more metaphoric nightmares about being trapped by enemies or, in the case of children, about Saddam Hussein chasing them. These dreamers were not familiar with Western ideas about post-traumatic dreams, and Arabic folk beliefs focus on dreams as predictors of the future, minimizing their relation to past events. Reenactment nightmares in this setting are thus interpreted in ways that stir up even more fear than in other cultures that the trauma will happen again. But the dreams themselves look very similar to those dreamed by Vietnam veterans or the children of Chowchilla (Barrett and Behbehani, 1995).

In dissociative disorders and other amnestic syndromes, dreams may be the first clue in recovering repressed memories of trauma. Williams (1995) has carried out the best study to date on adult memory of childhood trauma by following women with a documented history of childhood hospital visits for sexual abuse. She found that a significant proportion of them repressed and then later remembered the abuse and that dreams were one of the modes in which these memories first returned. Proponents of the view that most recovered trauma is "false memory" are unaware of such findings. At the same time, enthusiasts who treat every sign of anxiety or depression as an indication of repressed trauma are unaware of the work of investigators such as Hall and Van de Castle (1966), who found that in their sample of thousands of dreams, the average dream's affect was the unpleasant side of neutral, or Hartmann (1984), who found that some frequent nightmare sufferers can be trauma free and that much horrific dream imagery can be purely metaphoric. How to distinguish between these etiologies of nightmares is one of issues this book addresses.

Even though much more clinical data relating dreams and trauma have been gathered in recent years, this information has for the most part been reported only in presentations at professional meetings, while little has been written on this topic. A tendency toward segregation is also evident, with half of the data presented to trauma societies and the other half to those for dreams. This book's purpose is to disseminate to dream analysts, trauma therapists, and other readers the work that exists at this interface.

The first two sections examine the catastrophic horrors of abnormal situations: combat, political torture, dramatic natural disasters, rape, and severe domestic abuse. Part I addresses encounters with these in childhood—the lasting effects on personality formation, the nature of memories for early trauma, and the development of defenses related to amnesia and dissociation. Nader discusses the way in which children dream of trauma directly at first, then more metaphorically as they begin to recover. Stoddard, Chedekel, and Shakun describe how the particular nature of traumatic burns during childhood results in nightmares struggling specifically with issues of damaged body image in addition to more general post-traumatic concerns. Belicki and Cuddy begin the important task of sorting how nightmares differ in populations with no history of abuse versus sexual abuse versus physical abuse, and find themes distinctive to each: the sexually abused women often dream of an evil presence entering their room or body, and their dreams have the most negative sexual content— especially that involving explicit anatomy—and the most content concerning others' dying; the women with a history of physical abuse report the most dreams about their own deaths. King and Sheehan describe a detailed psychotherapy protocol for using dreams to help diagnose and repair the damage of childhood incest. My own chapter focuses on patients with multiple personality and the ways in which their dissociative process gets intertwined with their dreams as alter personalities appear as dream characters, reminding the host of repressed memories via dreams, and sometimes are able to design dreams to influence the host.

Part II addresses the impact of catastrophic horrors on adults and their dream life. Here the clinical syndrome is more likely to be classic Post-Traumatic Stress Disorder with overly intrusive memories (usually including repetitive nightmares) as a more frequent problem than suppression of memory. Wilmer describes the dreams of Vietnam veterans about atrocities of which they could be either the victim or the perpetrator; these began to diminish only once they were able to share their stories in a supportive environment. Hartmann looks at the differences between personality profiles of combat veterans who developed PTSD nightmares and those who did not, finding that the very youngest recruits and those who had lost a best friend with whom they were highly identified were the most vulnerable. Lavie and Kaminer remind us that the whole point of repression is as an adaptive defense in their finding that the Holocaust survivors who have recovered best are the ones who hardly remember any dreams at all. Lifton takes another look at the Holocaust in the guilt of one Nazi doctor's dreams and compares these with reports of Vietnam vets. Aron describes the eerie similarity of Central American refugees' nightmares even when their individual traumas are quite different. Muller follows a long series of dreams from a rape survivor over the course of psychotherapy, from ones that are close to reenactment of the recent rape, to ones weaving in assailants from a previous rape, to ones of related early childhood traumas, to more optimistic, survival-oriented dreams. Siegel studies the evolution of dreams in survivors of the Oakland firestorm, underlining the way in which it reactivated symptoms and nightmares for those with childhood traumas as opposed to the quicker resolution experienced by those with happier histories.

Part III concerns the common "traumas" potentially—or in the case of bereavement, inevitably—encountered in the course of a normal life. In the trauma literature it is often considered incorrect to refer to events such as bereavement, divorce, or life-threatening illness as "traumas"; that term is reserved for catastrophic natural disasters and the result of human evil—abuse, rape, war. There is some validity to this view—the more common tragedies do not carry the stigma and prohibition against discussion that rape and domestic abuse do for the victim or even the marginalization by lack of identification that natural disasters and war do. But bereavement and similar experiences do share the characteristics of shock, grief, the destruction of security, and the induction of disturbing dreams—all reasons that they are often labeled "traumas" in common parlance. They are included in this separate section to examine not only what they have in common with the previous two parts' links between trauma and dreams, but also what may be different about the dreamings of people who have more societal support while working through normal grief and adjustment to major losses.

Cartwright follows subjects' dreams through divorce and finds that those who initially dreamed most about their ex-spouse and those with the most mastery dreams as opposed to simple repetition dreams are less prone to lasting depression. Garfield traces the Kubler-Ross-style stages that emerge in bereavement dreams. Sacks describes how dreams can be diagnostic of illness and recovery before these are clinically recognizable. Bosnak examines the ways in which dream work can aid the psychological adjustment of transplant patients to their new organ and speculates on the influence of incorporation dreams in preventing physiological rejection. Zadra explores the close relationship of trauma to recurring dreams and outlines the usefulness of lucid dreaming techniques for ending recurring nightmares or transforming them into an experience of empowerment.

Together, these accounts tell us in which ways different traumas are universal and in which ways they have unique effects on a survivor's functioning and dream life. The authors give guidance in discerning when nightmare content is metaphoric in origin and when it is literal. They help to answer the difficult questions posed by repression, which may help some dreamers to get on with their lives but prevent others from moving forward. Above all, these pages describe the rich variety of ways in which dreams can give voice to the unspeakable and begin to restore the savaged.

PART ONE

Dreams after
Childhood Trauma

Children's Traumatic Dreams

KATHLEEN NADER

After a traumatic event, the children and adolescents who have been af-fected—those with direct exposure, those in the community without direct exposure, and some outside of the community, especially those who have been previously traumatized or worried about someone who might be endangered by the event—often report dreams of some sort about their experiences. Night terrors or nightmares associated with traumatic response have been reported for children after hospitalizations (Levy, 1945; Stuber et al., 1991), natural and man-made disasters (Newman, 1976; Hanford et al., 1986; MacFarlane, 1987), animal attacks (Gislason and Call, 1982), kidnapping (Terr, 1979), child abuse or molestation (McLeer et al., 1988; Kiser et al., 1991), war exposure (Baker, 1990; Nader and Pynoos, 1993b), community violence (Burgess, 1975; Pruett, 1979; Pynoos et al., 1987), and witnessing harm, for example, rape (Pynoos and Nader, 1988a). Depression is an associated feature of post-traumatic stress response, and horrible dreams are one of the factors found to be closely associated with depressive symptoms (Kashani et al., 1989).

The content and nature of children's and adolescents' dreams following traumatic experiences are affected by many variables, including (1) aspects of the traumatic experience, such as the number of deaths and the extent of loss experienced; the degree to which threat, injury, blood, mutilation, and/or death are witnessed; the perception of personal threat and threat to significant others; and imagined, feared, or rumored events associated with the traumatic event; (2) the prominence of specific traumatic imagery; (3) the phase of recovery; (4) specific meanings attributed to aspects of the event; and (5) individual experience and personality. This chapter provides a preliminary look at the trauma-induced dreams of children and adolescents exposed to specific instances of violence, disaster, and catastrophic treatment for life-threatening illness.

Prevalence of Traumatic Dreams

The prevalence of dreaming may be affected by cultural factors. Levine (1991) compared the dreams of Irish, Israeli, and Bedouin children. Irish children exposed to media coverage were otherwise relatively isolated from the conflict in Northern Ireland. Israeli children were indirectly exposed to war; they had suffered bomb threats and had lost family members in combat. Bedouin children from Israel's Negev Desert complained of direct threats and intimidation from Israeli soldiers during relocation. Levine found that Israeli kibbutz children reported fewer dreams than either of the other two groups.

Within a single culture, the post-trauma frequency of traumatic dreams appears to increase with increased exposure and with greater severity of the traumatic response. Three to five weeks after a sniper attack on an elementary school playground ($N = 159$) (Pynoos et al., 1987), 63 percent of children on the playground during the attack, 56 percent of children inside the school, 42 percent of children not at school that day, and 33 percent of children on three-week vacation from this year-round school reported bad dreams. Children interviewed one and a half years after the 1988 Armenian earthquake (Pynoos and Goenjin, 1992) tended to report more frequent bad dreams the more severely traumatized they were.

The severity of the incident, including the degree of a sense of threat or horror, may increase traumatic dreaming. All of the twenty-three children kidnapped in Chowchilla from their school bus and buried in a truck trailer had dreams related to the kidnapping (Terr, 1979). One to three months after witnessing the rapes of their mothers, 80 percent of children ($N = 10$) reported dreams of the rape or bad dreams at least once per week. In half of the cases the children were made to watch, and in all other cases they were present at some point during the rape (Pynoos and Nader, 1988a). Prior to bone marrow transplantation, with its life-threatening and painful procedures, children aged three to six ($N = 6$) reported no bad dreams. Three months after transplantation, 67 percent of the children reported bad dreams, and six and twelve months after the transplant 83 percent did so (Stuber et al., 1991). In contrast, children exposed to the Three Mile Island nuclear power plant's partial meltdown and overflow of radioactive water in 1979 were not exposed to an immediate and direct life threat; nevertheless, 40 percent of the children interviewed reported dreams in which their families died or got cancer (Hanford et al., 1983).

Association of Dreams with Other Symptoms

More study is needed to determine how dreams occur in association with other symptoms. In a Factor Analysis from a study of children exposed to a sniper attack (Pynoos et al., 1987), bad or trauma-related dreams and sleep disturbance were associated with difficulty concentrating and memory difficulties. In an exploratory Factor Analysis with a small pilot study of Kuwaiti children, bad or trauma-related dreams were associated with difficulty concentrating and reduced enjoyment of activities (see Nader and Pynoos, 1993b). The impairment to concentration may be a result of the disturbance of restful sleep.

Night Terrors and Somnambulism

Parents have reported night terrors (instances in which their children scream or cry out in their sleep with no remembrance of the dream) and somnam-bulism infrequently for their children following traumatic exposure. On many nights after a sniper attack, a nine-year-old girl jumped up from bed screaming and ran for the door; she was stopped from leaving the house by her family members. She did not recall these occurrences in the morning. A sixteen-year-old girl whose father died tragically in an accident often ground her teeth, tossed and turned, and uttered distressed phrases in the night. She had no recollection of dreaming. Four years after a kidnapping, children who had night terrors (57 percent) often walked or talked in their sleep (Terr, 1983). One night, while asleep, one kidnap victim came into her parents' room, saying repeatedly, "I'm going to die" (p. 587); she did not remember the dream in the morning.

Age

Between the ages of three and seven, children report few dreams upon being awakened from REM sleep. Between the ages of three and five, their dreams typically lack a story line or plot, lack activity by a self character, and contain few human characters (they more often contain animals). There is generally little intercharacter interaction and no feeling states. Dreams begin to show active self-reference with thought and feeling between ages seven and nine. The accession of adultlike dream features increases with increased cognitive competency (Foulkes, 1990; Foulkes et al., 1990). At ages eleven to twelve, dreaming begins to approximate that of adulthood; children are able to construct a dream narrative (Westerlund and Johnson, 1989). A loss of innocence may occur in a variety of forms following children's traumatic experiences. Some traumatized preschool children have dreams more like those described for older children. Following bone marrow transplantation, a three-year-old girl dreamed of cutters coming to cut her and her efforts to get away. A five-year-old boy with leukemia who had relapsed after bone marrow transplantation began to dream of space men coming to take him to their planet. In his early dreams he was afraid of the space men. In later dreams he found them to be friendly, and decided it was safe to go with them. He died a few months after befriending them.

Monster dreams. Although school-age children and adolescents often have dreams of endangerment or dreams replicating the traumatic experience, young children often report monster dreams or dreams that symbolically represent their experiences, their fears, and their sense of vulnerability. Preschool children exposed to a hurricane dreamed of the hurricane, of being chased by an eye (they had heard of the eye of the hurricane), and of a variety of monsters. Headstart children exposed to the Los Angeles riots in 1992 dreamed of monsters, witches, fires, and guns. Preschool children undergoing bone marrow transplantation and medical procedures dreamed of ghosts coming to take them away, dragons threatening them, or being chased by mutilators. School-age children may replace ghosts and non-descript monsters with monsters from the movie screen, for example, in America, Freddie Krueger (the mutilator from Elm Street).

Monster dreams may occur at any age. Although less frequently, they have been reported by adults and adolescents after traumatic experiences. In older children and adults the monsters may represent some quality of the experience and/or of the perpetrator of harm. During a woman's experience of prolonged sexual and professional harassment, a short man made repeated inappropriate advances, slowed every task, and impeded goal accomplishment. Another professional was present but did not intervene. The woman dreamed of fighting off a shrimp-colored snail monster and a crab claw in a sewer while a man stood by on safe clean ground and watched. After a seventeen-year-old boy witnessed the attempted rape and knife assault of his mother, he ran to get a knife and attempted unsuccessfully to stab the assailant, discovering how much force it would take to penetrate the man's back with the knife. He dreamed repeatedly of a man-monster who would never die no matter how many times he stabbed him (Pynoos and Nader, 1988a).

Aspects of the Traumatic Experience

The content of children's post-traumatic dreams is affected by intrapersonal, interpersonal, and experiential factors. Among these factors are aspects of the traumatic experience and the child's personal response to them. Cultural factors may also shape the content of traumatic dreams (Levine, 1991). In the comparison of the dreams of Bedouin, Irish, and Israeli children, all three groups of children reported twice as many conflictual dreams (including conflicts regarding threats to integrity, threats to independence, social responsibility, material resources, relational resources, and status) as non-conflictual dreams (Levine, 1991; see also Bilu, 1989). Bedouin children were significantly more likely than the other two groups to be less personally active in the conflicts in their dreams, to have more realistic dreams, to dream of nonhuman opponents (for example, a wolf threatening the sheep), and to know or be related to their dream comrades. The Bedouin children were more exposed to warlike conditions than the other two groups, and they more often dreamed of threats to their physical survival (usually from the natural world). Irish and kibbutz children more often dreamed of interpersonal conflicts. Kibbutz children often dreamed of threats to their independence.

Exposure

Acutely, traumatic dreams may be related to the dreamer's actual or emotional proximity to the danger. One month after their exposure to a sniper attack, children in the direct line of fire more frequently reported dreams replicating aspects of the event with vivid action, little elaboration, and an accompanying sense of life threat. Less exposed children had fearful dreams that were more general, often without a direct image of life threat (Pynoos et al., 1987). Children may also have dreams of aspects of the traumatic experience based on their fears or on rumors that have elicited intense emotion. A boy who worried about his brother during a natural disaster and then discovered that his brother had died dreamed of seeing him smashed under the bricks of the building. Children evacuated from war zones dreamed, for example, of a body being torn apart by a bomb, of torture, and of having their or a family member's throat cut.

Emotional proximity also results in dreams of the traumatic action. A Kuwaiti boy in London during the 1990–91 Gulf Crisis worried about the harm that might come to his uncle who was a soldier in Kuwait. He watched the war on television during the day and in the evening and dreamed at night of his uncle being threatened by tanks and bullets.

Course

For some children, traumatic dreams disappear a few days to a few weeks after the event. For others the dreams persist or recur in response to traumatic reminders or changes in the phase or focus of recovery. One year after a sniper attack in a schoolyard, 42 percent of children under gunfire on the playground continued to report bad dreams (Nader et al., 1990). In addition to bad dreams or trauma-related dreams one year after the shooting, 24 percent of children on the playground at the time, 25 percent of children who knew the deceased well, 13 percent who knew her somewhat, and 5 percent who did not know her had dreams of her.

Although dreams replicating aspects of the exposed child's experience are initially common after a traumatic experience, the nature of the traumatic event, including the number of deaths, may affect the course of dream content. A tornado knocked down a school wall, killing nine children and injuring others. The number of deaths affected the course and nature of traumatic response. A preliminary hand tally of dream content suggests that there were more dreams about dead children one month after the event than one year later, and more dreams about the wall falling and about injury one year later than acutely. One year after the event, there were dreams that the dead had survived; none of these dreams was reported acutely.

Dreams may become more distorted or disguised over time. Children kidnapped in Chowchilla (Terr, 1979) had more dreams replicating aspects of the kidnapping or terror dreams in the early phase following the event. For example, Jackie dreamed that the two oldest kidnappers took her and Johnny and then shot and killed them. Months after the kidnapping, disguised dreams or modified kidnapping dreams were more common. Jackie dreamed she was a princess in a castle. A giant captured her and ripped off her shirt. Upon questioning, she realized that it was the same shirt that the kidnappers had taken from her during the kidnapping (Terr, 1979). The children still had repetitive nightmares four years after the kidnapping: 57 percent had night terrors (often with somnambulism or sleep talking), 30 percent had modified kidnapping dreams, and 52 percent had disguised dreams (Terr, 1983).

Dream distortions may also occur initially and are sometimes related to the difficulty in facing certain aspects of the event and their possible repercussions. During a tornado, one third grader saw a wall begin to fall. She started to run away from the wall, but her best friend grabbed her foot and she fell. Her foot was multiply fractured under a table collapsed by wall blocks. Her best friend had gone under the table for protection and probably was attempting to pull her to safety. The friend was badly injured, bloody and seemingly not breathing. Although she felt that her friend had not intended to harm her, the girl felt very angry toward her friend. She feared admitting or expressing this anger because she feared losing her friend. Instead she became verbally aggressive with her mother; she dreamed that a monster was grabbing her. After working through the anger toward her friend in a treatment session, her aggressiveness toward her mother and her monster dreams disappeared.

Although reexperiencing symptoms did not group with one another in either the sniper attack or the Kuwait pilot studies, clinical experience suggests that dreams and other reexperiencing phenomena do occur within the same period of time. Over time, some traumatic concerns may move from overt conscious reexperiencing to dreams or play. There is some evidence that as intrusive imagery decreases, traumatic play and/or unconscious reenactment behaviors increase (Nader and Fairbanks, 1994; Pynoos and Nader, 1993). After a kidnapping and burial underground, five children acutely and twelve children four years later dreamed of dying (Terr, 1983). Traumatic material may also appear in dreams when it is not overtly reexperienced in other ways or is not being openly processed. After a hurricane, an adolescent boy had hurricane nightmares for two months. During that time, his mother would not allow him to talk about the hurricane. In therapy,which provided the opportunity to discuss and process his experiences, the nightmares disappeared after the third session.

The Prominence of Specific Traumatic Imagery

The Traumatic Experience

One theory about the repetitive reexperiencing of traumatic imagery and thoughts attributes it to the failure of repression; another attributes it to a compulsion to repeat in the service of mastery. Both theories imply a need to process the traumatic material in order to reduce or eliminate traumatic repetition. Horowitz (1970) hypothesized that traumatic experiences entered into active (short-term) memory storage as visual images. Pressure continued until translation and codification of them was completed; then active memory terminated. Resistance to the reentry (and processing) of these images was related to, for example, the revival of unpleasant and potentially excessive emotions and/or to "dangerous, associated ideas" that might lead to painful feelings (for example, terror of being injured or guilt for remaining uninjured). Horowitz thus described two opposing processes: one favoring completion of the unfinished processing of memories through translation, codification, and permanent storage; the second, continued inhibition in order to avoid pain. With inhibition, "the traumatic perceptions remained repressed, but active and unmastered"—the person had not learned to cope with them. When repression failed despite inhibitory efforts, there were intrusive images (pp. 198–199).

Dreams may emphasize prominent traumatic imagery, such as bloody injury. For example, an eleven-year-old girl who witnessed the suicide of a woman who shot herself in the head and then bled profusely from head, nose, and mouth and a boy who, at twelve, had witnessed and been injured in a massacre both had very bloody Freddie Krueger dreams. At fifteen, after having these dreams, the boy began reading about mass killers and watching horror movies. He seemed to be attempting to desensitize himself to the blood and horror as well as to understand why someone would commit such acts.

Dreams as Replications

Throughout the phases of trauma recovery, children incorporate traumatic imagery into their dreams. Dreams may replicate visual, auditory, and/or kinesthetic experiences.

War. In Kuwait during the Gulf Crisis, Iraq invaded and occupied Kuwait. Buildings were damaged by bombing, burning, breaking holes in walls in order to fire guns, breaking windows, and leaving excrement. People were shot at, shot, captured, tortured, starved, injected, raped, and beaten. Children reported directly witnessing extreme tortures, for example, seeing a pregnant woman with her belly shot open or seeing soldiers slowly saw off the leg of a man or poke a pointed object into someone's eye. Adolescent boys especially were killed and/or tortured, and their bodies were sometimes hung in the streets. Croatian refugee children have spoken of similar atrocities suffered during their region's civil war. In addition, after fleeing areas under direct attack by the Serbian army, they often expressed concern about the loss of home and land. Kuwaiti and Croatian children both dreamed of people being tortured, having their throats slit, or being shot. They dreamed of being personally endangered by someone trying to kill them with a knife, a gun, or bare hands; of being captured and tortured; of destroyed buildings; of the damage to their beautiful seacoast (Kuwait) or their beautiful land (Croatia). Demoralization was a part of the attack against the Kuwaitis. One method was humiliation. A Kuwaiti child dreamed his whole family was captured and their heads shaved.

Other violence. After the Chowchilla kidnapping, children had terror dreams and replicated, modified, or disguised dreams of the kidnapping (Terr, 1979). In Los Angeles, children who witnessed the rapes of their mothers dreamed of the rapist returning, of being threatened, of being severely physically harmed, of directly confronting the assailant, or of taking revenge (Pynoos and Nader, 1988a).

Some children and adolescents dream of being chased by someone wanting to hurt them. For example, a girl who thought the bullet that killed the friend standing next to her was meant for her, a girl who ran for cover during a sniper attack, and a girl who was chased and groped by a man previously unknown to her all had recurrent chase dreams. The last girl was chased by people or animals in her dreams. Kuwaiti children dreamed of being chased by wolves or other wild animals (see Nader et al., 1993). Sexually abused children's dreams have included themes of being chased, punished, and isolated. The dreams of those studied often expressed fears of being controlled by a larger, faster, and more powerful person. Younger molestation victims often dreamed of concrete items such as snakes or bees going in and out of holes (Sebold, 1987).

Disaster. Children who were in a cafeteria when a tornado knocked the wall down, killing and injuring their some of their peers, watched the window blow out with glass flying, saw large blocks or bricks falling on top of children, and through the open wall viewed a strange-colored sky. They saw bloody children carried down the hallways or out to rescue vehicles; some saw adults attempting futilely to revive dead children. They dreamed of the wall falling again, of houses being destroyed by a tornado, of children dying or people being hurt, of "blood and skies," of branches falling, of being hit by glass, and of trying to find bandages for dead people. After a hurricane, parents and children dreamed of being threatened by winds or tornadoes coming directly at them.

Endangerment and Worry about Others

With or without replications of aspects of the original traumatic event, children of all exposures may have ongoing dreams of endangerment to self or others, of disasters, of being chased, or of monsters. Children who have experienced disaster or a violent event often dream of developing a severe or fatal disease or of being killed. The boy who had been shot twice in a massacre in which twenty-one people were killed, including his best friend and his best friend's mother, dreamed repeatedly that his family was endangered or killed in earthquakes, tornadoes, or hurricanes. After a tornado that caused the deaths of children, surviving children dreamed that they were killed, that injured children died, or that their families and neighbors were injured or killed. One child repeatedly dreamed of a baby crying sometimes when someone was dying. After the Gulf Crisis, Kuwaiti children dreamed of their brothers being hanged, of relatives being tortured and/or killed, of family members or friends being captured and taken away, and of relatives being killed or injured in accidents (for example, by being knocked off a bridge or falling down a deep hole).

The Phasic Nature of Traumatic Recovery

The child lends meaning to specific traumatic moments and puts them into the context of her or his life. During the course of recovery, there may be a reduction in numbing and a complimentary exacerbation of intrusive symptoms. Each child establishes his or her own rhythm of trauma review. Over time, a child may redefine individual traumatic moments or experiences and her or his own response to them. A change in the child's intervention fantasies or resolution of specific issues may permit the child's deeper focus on certain details (Nader, 1994).

Dreams may not occur or be remembered until after aspects of the trauma have been worked through or some amount of ego strength has been restored. After a public suicide, some children and adults had night terrors for one to two years, until after significant progress was made in treatment; then dreams were remembered. An adolescent whose family had been murdered had only grief dreams until a measure of trauma and then grief work was accomplished.

For adults, the need to refocus on specific traumatic issues may become easily apparent through examination of current intrusive imagery, selective attention, activities, and dreams. For example, a woman who attempted to assist a woman who had shot herself in the head began, two years later, to see guns in images on billboards, gas pumps, and specific license plates. It was apparent that she needed to reprocess the moments of fear related to the two guns the woman had waved at others before shooting herself. A woman who was robbed at gunpoint and had been molested as an eight-year-old began repeatedly to see the man holding the gun, with emphasis on his hands. The focus of her treatment became first the hands of the molester and then the hands of the gunman. When her dreams became various scenes of endangering others, she focused in treatment on her sense of isolation, her victim identity, and the sense that she attracted violence to herself, thereby endangering others.

As events and focus change in the course of trauma recovery, the dreams of children (especially those over the age of eight) and adolescents may both communicate their concerns and depict relevant issues for the focus of treatment. After making progress in her trauma treatment, an adolescent girl testified in court regarding her and her family's kidnapping and the murder of her family. When the man convicted for these crimes was scheduled for sentencing a few months later, she began to dream he was chasing her and that the trauma clinician and the girl's boyfriend did not know he was free. In the dream, the murderer caught up with her and grabbed her foot as she ran upstairs, and her clinician and boyfriend could not hear her calling for help. This dream not only depicted her fear of the assailant's release and possible ill intentions toward her for testifying but also made clear this extremely competent girl's sense of aloneness and need for protection.

To see the marked themes in young children's dreams is not always as easy. Foulkes (1990) observed that until the age of eight, children's dream reports are very brief. Preschool-age children may not be able to relate their dreams in enough detail to make clear their relationship to specific aspects of the traumatic experience. The child's sense of vulnerability and need for protection may be most prominent. Children aged six to eight may not report their dreams with sufficient detail, may omit details, or may fear telling their dreams at all.

Embedded Meanings

The recurrent themes found in preschool-age children's dreams can often be found in their play and drawings as well. A child whose home was badly damaged and whose toys were all lost in a hurricane dreamed of Franken- stein, vampires, ghosts, and "Faster Stockman" the fly-man. He drew mon- sters in response to an initial request to draw a picture of anything he wanted to and tell a story about it. He proceeded to play with puppet monsters until he became frightened during the play. He later found a good monster to get rid of the bad monsters. A fear of falling and injury recurred peri- odically throughout his interview. At the end of the play, his conversation drew closer to the real source of his fear. The child described the hurricane as a thing that twirled around. He talked of how the chair he was sitting in could twirl around and send him flying (like the fly-man) against the wall and kill him.

Monster dreams may reflect a form of condensation in which assailants and their perceived overwhelming animalistic nature are combined into one being. In a dream where "every step forward was a step backward," a preadolescent exposed to ongoing violent conflict dreamed of being scared to death when confronted by a huge animal with a lion's head, human hands, the legs of a beast, and the feet of a bear. The child could not escape and uttered a cry so intense that it "almost tears the slopes of the moun- tains" (Bilu, 1989, p. 386).

Dreams may both replicate aspects of the traumatic experience and in- corporate psychodynamic issues, for example, issues of protection, betrayal, loss, or accountability. A six-year-old boy whose mother attempted to stran- gle him but was foiled by his father had recurrent nightmares that replicated the murderous attack (Anthony, 1986). In one dream, his father drove his car up the driveway and hit the boy while the mother stood watching, making no attempt to stop the father. The boy woke up screaming, "You couldn't help it, you didn't do it on purpose. She did nothing about it. She should have stopped you" (p. 332). This dream incorporates the belief that parents should protect children and accuses both father and mother of this breach. It represents the culpability of one who could but does not prevent or stop the harm. It removes the act of direct harm from the hands of the now absent/lost mother but continues to hold her responsible for the harm done.

Issues at one point depicted in dreams may become a part of a post-traumatic life pattern. Between ages five and nine, a girl was molested by her father and felt unprotected by her mother. She was more caretaker to her parents than they to her. She described a scene of regularly being approached by her father with her back against the wall next to her bed, intense fear, a sense of aloneness and horror, and then a lack of memory of specific aspects of the experience. She repeatedly dreamed in blurred images of something dangerous coming down the river. The closer it came to her, the more frightened she became, until she awakened with a strange taste in her mouth, tightness in her throat, nausea, and trembling with fear. As an adult, she re-created the situation and emotions represented in the dreams. During the phase of her treatment that she recalled the dreams, she had chronic tightness of throat, nausea, fatigue, a sense of aloneness, a sense that she was having to take care of everyone else, and an inability to escape the circumstances of her life. She occasionally reexperienced the bad taste in her mouth. She did not remember before recalling the dreams in treatment that her father and other molesters had ejaculated in her mouth.

Fear of Recurrence

After a traumatic experience, exposed and unexposed children fear the recurrence of a traumatic event (Pynoos and Nader, 1988b). A girl who was chased and groped dreamed of getting away from someone chasing her, only to find an animal chasing her. This fear may be reinforced by external events. For example, Saddam Hussein continued to say that he would take Kuwait even after the war was over. Kuwaiti children dreamed that he returned and recaptured Kuwait.

Differing Agendas

Different family or group members may have different exposures and experiences and thus differing psychological agendas following traumatic exposure (Pynoos and Nader, 1990). These differences may be apparent in their dreams. One family with three different exposures to the same event had different symptom complexes and different acute phase dreams. The five-year-old daughter had watched helplessly while her sister, several feet away, was hit by a car. She dreamed that she was with her sister when the car came, but was still unable to prevent the tragedy. The dream allowed her to fulfill the wish to be close enough to help her sister but was thwarted by her intense fear and sense of helplessness. It replicated the sense of being frozen, unable to assist. The dream underscored that there was nothing that she could do to prevent the horror that she had witnessed.

The mother of the girl hit by the car had been nearby and had run to the place where her daughter had been. Not seeing her daughter, she feared she was under the car tire. She had recurring dreams that the car had actually rolled over her daughter.

Acutely, the latency-age injured child dreamed of what she was doing before the car hit her from behind. Because of her head injury, the doctor told her that she might not remember being hit by the car. She was happy, initially, to delay these memories, but remembered these lost moments during her treatment. After recalling her experiences, she dreamed of aspects of her experience, including the frightening look on her mother's face when her mother got to her.

Grief

There is both an independence and an interplay between children's traumatic and grief reactions. Coping with both is particularly demanding for children (Pynoos and Nader, 1990). An adolescent Croatian boy combined trauma and grief issues (the yearning for reunification) into one dream, in which he saw his father killed, then heard his dead father tell him that he would come back to him and the family.

Resolution of specific traumatic issues may necessarily precede grief resolution. The adolescent girl whose family was murdered after they were all kidnapped dreamed that her mother and brother showed themselves to be safe and then bid her goodbye. There was an obvious omission of her beloved father from the dream. The kidnapper had reassured her that her father was all right, despite the blood stain on the floor where she had last seen him tied and gagged. Before addressing these matters in treatment, she could not accept reassurance in her dreams that her father was unharmed.

Life Issues

Going through a traumatic experience may challenge a child's beliefs. Among these may be religious beliefs. One Kuwaiti child dreamed that someone did good deeds, prayed, and ate with family, all valued behaviors by the good Kuwaiti Muslim; even so, Saddam Hussein came and shot young children.

Another belief concerns the status of adults. Children younger than six or seven, in particular, commonly believe that "big people know best" (Stilwell, Galvin, and Kopta, 1991) and that adults will always protect them and keep them safe. Traumatic experiences prematurely challenge that belief. Issues of protection and safety become prominent especially for pre-school- and elementary-school-age children. A young woman who was molested from age two through age eight repeatedly dreamed that she was in danger, but she could not get the phone to work. This dream continued through her teenage years into her adult life. In reality it had not been possible to call for help to her mother, who had participated in the original molestation with her lover. A seven-year-old boy described how during a tornado he had a painful moment of indecision when a wall collapsed. He did not know whether to freeze or run. He froze, and the bricks landed on top of the area where he would have been if he had run. He was very angry with his parents for not preparing him for this moment. He dreamed that the tornado hit the house of a strange man while the dreamer was holding onto the doorknob of the house, deciding whether or not to go in. This dream replicated his near-miss experience and sense of indecision in the absence of family. As wished for, it removed the harm to a stranger. Children known to the boy were killed in the tragedy.

Dreams and "Working Through"

Dreams provide an opportunity to work through traumatic issues during sleep or in the treatment session. Either acutely after traumatic exposure or after a period of treatment, children may enact intervention fantasies, as discussed in the next section. Dreams point to issues for therapeutic focus and may portray the child's attempts to recover or repair. The superego can be relentless in condemning the trauma victim for lack of self-protection or other interventions (Grinker and Spiegel, 1943). Children may be relieved to discover through dreams, drawings, or play that they tried or wished to intervene or that they were courageous (Nader and Pynoos, 1991). After familial emotional and threatened physical violence led to divorce, a young girl repeatedly dreamed that she, her family, and neighbors had to evacuate because of war. In each dream she was compelled to go back into the war zone to get something (implements of warmth and nourishment, such as a warm sweater or food). She felt very relieved and stopped having this dream when someone said to her that it was quite courageous of her to go back into the war zone.

Wished For and Imagined Actions

Wished for and imagined actions may become incorporated into children's traumatic memory representations (Pynoos and Nader, 1989). Ongoing intervention fantasies are integral to children's reprocessing of traumatic events. They include the child's fantasies during and after the event of preventing or stopping harm, of challenging the assailant, of taking revenge, or of repairing damage (Nader, 1994). Kuwaiti children dreamed of trying to escape, for example, to Saudi Arabia, or of hiding from Iraqi soldiers when they came to search the house.

Children and adolescents given permission to express their fantasies of revenge without real harm to the object of revenge and without personal repercussions may readily express these fantasies, even acutely (Pynoos and Nader, 1993a). Children and adolescents from about age nine or ten may postpone focus on the intensity of their traumatic rage until they have made some amount of progress in treatment, after other issues have been mastered. An adolescent girl who was raped had dreams of endangerment through the first eight to ten months of her treatment. As her ego strength was restored, she began to focus on her rage toward the rapist. She dreamed that she took a spear and with purposeful intent penetrated and repenetrated his chest cavity, twisting her weapon. She woke up "feeling good." This revenge dream allowed her in-kind retaliation.

Children often express a feeling of relief after dreaming of successfully enacting a revenge fantasy. A preadolescent boy who witnessed the rape of his mother dreamed that he took a ten-foot samurai sword, used it against the rapist, and overcame him (Pynoos and Nader, 1988a). A Croatian boy dreamed repeatedly that he fought with the throat-slitting bearded Serbian soldiers and beat them up. One Kuwaiti child dreamed of shooting Saddam Hussein and his cohorts when Saddam pushed on the stomach of a pregnant woman; he then threw a grenade at him. In contrast, dreams of facing and overcoming the assailant or the enemy may not lead to relief if, even in the dream, the child or adolescent cannot escape the danger. A preadolescent girl was seized in her dream by two terrorists. She escaped and ran for home but was chased. She turned and confronted her chasers, finally beating them up. They ran away, but after a while they returned to chase her again and "the dream goes on without end" (Bilu, p. 386).

After a traumatic event some children draw a picture of a rainbow, perhaps wishing for the rainbow after the storm (Nader and Pynoos, 1991). The wish for a happy ending is also depicted in dreams. One Kuwaiti child dreamed that a prediction was made: Kuwait would go through three dark days and then there would be happiness.

Rescue fantasies appear in children's play and dreams. A girl who witnessed the suicide of a woman who had held her class hostage and then shot herself in front of them dreamed that she took the gun away from the woman before she could shoot. A five-year-old boy who witnessed the murder of his stepmother dreamed that he punched the assailant and ran for help; his play was filled with rescuing others from harm or sending others to the rescue. A Kuwaiti child dreamed that the Iraqis were trying to take someone away, but the child saved them. Croatian refugee children expressed a great deal of sadness and distress related to the destruction of their land and of their homes. One girl dreamed that her father was repairing their destroyed home. A Jewish boy exposed to the Arab-Israeli conflict (Bilu, 1989) dreamed that the police seized two Arab criminals and sought to transform them into law-abiding citizens. In his dream, the boy volunteered to tame them; he taught them Hebrew "until they became decent human beings."

Intense wishes during or in response to a traumatic experience may be expressed in action as well as in dreams. A teenage girl who was orally and otherwise molested at the age of eight had repetitive dreams of beating someone up. She began to assault other teenagers and, when drunk, beat up her best friend. During the molestation, she had wished she could kick the molester in the face.

Conclusion

Nightmares and night terrors have been reported for children after a variety of traumatic events. The prevalence of dreams may be affected by cultural factors, severity of exposure, and experience and severity of response. Loss of innocence, after traumatic experience, may occur for young children and may appear in dreams as well as in thoughts, verbalizations, and actions. Monster dreams following a traumatic experience may primarily depict a sense of fear and vulnerability for young children and may often represent some quality of the experience or the perpetrator for older children.

Aspects of the traumatic experience and specific traumatic imagery are replicated in post-trauma dreams for exposed children and adolescents. They may become more disguised over time or distorted acutely, in an attempt to disguise intolerable affects or to prevent undesired results. Children also dream of what they hear or worry about during an event.

Over the course of recovery, a focus on traumatic issues or a refocus on the deeper meaning of aspects of the event may be reflected in dreams. Dreams may serve as one of the guideposts to the need for therapeutic attention on some aspect of the traumatic experience. Moreover, the themes in repetitive dreams may become replicated in later actions (for example, enactment of revenge or rescue fantasies) or emotional experiences (such as a sense of being overwhelmed and/or of isolation).

Dreams and Nightmares of Burned Children

FREDERICK J. STODDARD, DAVID S. CHEDEKEL, AND
LAURA SHAKUN

Some of the most terrifying dreams occur to children during the initial weeks after suffering a burn injury. For example, a three-year-old girl in a bacterially isolated plastic tent is intermittently panicky and confused for hours, as she "sees" a "bee" flying around after her inside the tent. A five-year-old boy with a large burn, alone with no family nearby, stays awake night and day, fearful of falling asleep again because of "monsters." A hospitalized adolescent girl who burned herself sits upright, terrified and inconsolable, convinced that she is burning (again). This chapter addresses the subject of such dreams with an overview of children's sleep and dreams, an approach to clinical evaluation, a description of the pediatric burn unit setting, discussion of relevant studies, a developmental perspective with case examples, an enumeration of stressors experienced by burned children, and discussion of the implications for the psychology of trauma.

Overview of Children's Sleep, Dreams, and Nightmares

Dreams and nightmares in children provide a window on their stages of affective, cognitive, and neuropsychological development. Since infants average sixteen hours per day of sleep their total REM time is greater than at older ages, but total sleep duration decreases to twelve hours by age three, and nine hours by ages eight to twelve (Hanford, Mattison, and Kales, 1991, pp. 715–716). Rapid eye movement sleep decreases from about 50 percent at term birth to about 25 percent of total sleep time later in childhood. Nothing is known of the dreams of the preverbal child except by inference, but by the age of two to three some verbal children report their dreams and nightmares. Although children's dreams are often disguised, they provide valuable information on perception, memory, regulation of affects, cognitive integration, expression, and the effects of experiences, both within themselves and with their environments. Generally, children's dreams provide a very "real" sample of the world as they see it. As they grow older, their dreams increase in complexity and more children will be able to reflect on what their dreams might "be about." In our work, children's dreams and nightmares provide useful clues to their adaptive/internal coping related to their developmental phase and in response to the external realities and stressors associated with burn injuries.

Dreams play a role, perhaps a major one, in the lives of children. Freud highlighted dreams in the case of Little Hans, whom Freud treated indirectly with the help of Hans's father, but there has been little subsequent interest in children's dreams. Ablon and Mack (1980, p. 212) explain: "Through the child's dream we can study affective and cognitive development and learn about the growth of mental organization. The developing structures of language and their link to powerful drives and compelling emotional experiences can be approached through the exploration of the child's dream." How exciting to consider that language development might proceed through the experiences and telling of dreams. Hartmann (1984, p. 31) states that nightmares are common, especially for children before age four or five, and he adds that he "would not be surprised if a considerable part of non-specific 'waking up crying' of younger children were actually preverbal nightmares—or possibly preverbal night terrors."

Piaget applied his stepwise structural evolution of cognitive development to children's dreams. He describes three distinct stages in the child's understanding of dreams. "During the first (approximately age 5 to 6), the child believes the dream to come from the outside and to take place within the room and he thus dreams with his eyes. The memory of the dream is confused with other memories, such as of recent events in the child's life. Also the dream is highly emotional . . . During the second stage (age 7 to 8) the child supposes the source of the dream to be in his own head, in thought, and in the voice etc., but the dream is in the room in front of him. Dreaming is with the eyes; it is looking at a picture outside . . . it is unreal . . . Finally during the third stage (about 9–10), the dream is the product of thought, it takes place inside the head (or in the eyes)" (Piaget, 1975, pp. 90–91). Communications with children about dreams will optimally take these major cognitive differences into account, allowing for individual variation.

Sleep

Sleep research, which has existed for only about the last twenty-five years, helps to explain why the dreams associated with REM sleep can be valuable clinically. Hanford, Mattison, and Kales (1991, pp. 716, 721) note that "REM sleep, which is characterized by irregular respiration and heart rate, is considered an archi-sleep or primitive sleep" in contrast with the more controlled nonREM (NREM) sleep. They add that "two lower brainstem centers discharge together during REM sleep. The nucleus reticularis pontis caudalis stimulates an ascending activating system, producing EEG patterns of arousal, REM bursts, autonomic irregularity, myoclonic twitches, and pontogeniculoccipatal spikes. Conversely, the locus ceruleus triggers a descending inhibitory system, causing arreflexia and loss of muscle tone." According to Keener and Anders (1985, p. 381), "REM sleep is characterized by physiological activation and may be important for information processing and memory storage." A complex system such as this tends to react quickly to the physical and psychological trauma of a burn and burn treatment.

Sleep disorders are chronobiological interruptions of normal sleep patterns, often related to specific phases of development. Although dreams may not be associated with certain sleep disorders such as night terrors, with others such as nightmares or enuresis, they usually are. Sleep disorders are common in the general population, and for this reason their occurrence in burned children must be interpreted with caution, not necessarily as related to the burn or treatment. There is also a significant correlation with a history in other family members of sleep disorders such as night terrors, sleepwalking and sleep talking, and enuresis. In DSM-IV (APA, 1993, pp. Q:1–7), sleep disorders are divided into five major groups: Dyssomnias, which are disturbances in the duration, type, and pattern of sleep; the Parasomnias, which are experiences a child may have during sleep directly related to the sleep process and stages; Sleep Disorders Related to Another Mental Disorder, and two areas of considerable importance with acutely burned children, Sleep Disorder Due to a General Medical Condition and Substance-Induced Sleep Disorder, the latter including nightmares induced by a drug (for example, opiate) withdrawal.

Dreams

In taking a history from the child and parents, it is useful to learn whether or not the child reported dreams prior to the burn and whether or not they were frightening. Children who have been traumatized in other ways—for example, through loss, abuse, or illness— may report significant dreams or nightmares related to preburn trauma. A dramatic example was a boy who had been raped several months before his burn and who appeared to have hypnagogic hallucinations of the event during his early acute treatment and to be delusionally fearful that a male nurse was the perpetrator. His concerns were less with the pain or trauma of the burn than with the rekindled memories of his sexual abuse—feelings that were brought on both by his burn delirium and by painful dressing changes. As his wounds became less painful and his delirium decreased, his preoccupation with the sexual abuse disappeared. On the other hand, most verbal children will report dreams in the period immediately after their burns occur, but there appears to be a decrease in reporting of dreams over time. Most of the early postburn dreams will relate to fear or terror of the acute burn experience or treatment in the intensive care unit (ICU). As weeks, months, and years pass, those dreams related to the burn progressively shift to themes concerning body image, fears of loss of function or attractiveness, and stigmatization by family and peers.

Nightmares

Do all burned children have nightmares? In an early paper on developmental aspects of burns one of the authors (FJS, 1982, p. 739) stated that "night-mares . . . are common immediately after burns in childhood," but this matter remains an open question, not yet answered by retrospective studies. At the same time, many staff working on burn units continue to observe that most acutely burned children have nightmares, flashbacks, or night terrors. Only a prospective study of sequential admissions is likely to answer this question.

The Clinical Evaluation

The Pediatric Burn Unit Setting

The Shriners Burns Institute, Boston, is a clinical and research pediatric surgical hospital next to the Massachusetts General Hospital with a ten-bed acute unit and a twenty-bed plastic and reconstructive surgical unit. All care is free and supported by the Shriners Hospitals of North America. All medical staff have joint appointments at the Massachusetts General Hospital as well. Criteria for admission are that children be aged 0–18 for acute surgical care of burn injuries and 0–21 for plastic and reconstructive treat-ment of the scarring and functional losses due to burns. At this writing, there are both open wards and a few private rooms. Newly designed facili-ties are being built around and above the current hospital, more than tripling the total hospital size while keeping the number of patient beds the same. The staffing of the burn team is multidisciplinary, including trauma sur-geons, plastic surgeons, pediatricians, child psychiatrists and psychologists, anesthesiologists, respiratory therapists, nurses, social workers, physical and occupational therapists, special educators, recreation therapists, volunteers, various researchers, and administrative and support staff. The psychotherapeutic milieu at this hospital is an unheralded but important dimension of care of the children and their families. The staff is very experienced and highly skilled at acute physical and psychological triage and treatment of trauma. A process of meetings, both case-oriented and on general topics, and education and staff coordination occur continuously. Specialty and subspecialty consultation, as well as collaboration with outside public and private agencies, is extensive. Both relevant basic research and clinical surgical, pediatric, and child psychiatric research are ongoing.

Evaluation

In evaluating any traumatized or medically ill infant, child, or adolescent, a full developmental history is essential prior to planning clinical interventions. A careful prenatal, childhood, and family history prior to the trauma or illness is necessary. Particular care is taken to obtain the child's normal patterns of feeding, sleep, toilet training, and motor, cognitive, and interpersonal development in order to recognize any changes. With burned children, preburn risk factors include recent rapid motoric gains, poverty, previous accidents, possible child neglect or abuse, childhood mental disorders (for example, attention deficit with hyperactivity disorder, conduct disorder, depression, and mental retardation), and parental mental illness or substance abuse. This information will inform the evaluator of various meanings that may be attributed to particular dreams or nightmares. In order to evaluate a sleep disorder, the sleep history should include a description, time of onset, duration, frequency, severity, and—especially with trauma such as burns—the related circumstances including associated medical/surgical illness. Outside sources of information about the dreams of burned children include nursing and allied medical staff and the parents or guardians.

The children themselves are the most useful source of information, but they may be at first leery to speak of their nightmares or night terrors: nursing staff or parents are most likely to report them. How can so traumatized a child be encouraged to share a dream?

Often it is effective simply to ask directly, even with a young child. However, it is also useful to ask a young child in displacement, for example, utilizing in a play interview a pen or pencil (a "dream machine") that points toward the head of a "sleeping" doll or puppet. The evaluator then quizzically asks, "What is he/she dreaming about?" Most young children will report a dream of their own when this is asked, occasionally with some encouragement (a method derived from James Herzog, M.D., pers. comm.). In our setting, with those children who have largely recovered from their burns, this method is particularly effective in small groups of young burned children who then hear one another's dreams. Occasionally it is helpful to have a child draw a dream, if the child is not too verbal.

The assessment of nightmares and night terrors requires a thorough understanding of the circumstances of the trauma (the burn injury) and of any current stressors that might be compounding the earlier trauma. Risk factors that contribute acutely to anxiety dreams and sleep disorders include pain, fear, separation anxiety, sleep deprivation, grief, burn dressing changes, immobilization, burn delirium, medication effects, sepsis, fluid or electrolyte disturbance, and body image disturbances. In some instances, a single child may experience all of these factors at once.

Acute stress disorders (DSM-IV, pp. K:9–10), having many signs of Post-Traumatic Stress Disorder but being of only two to thirty days' duration, have some different manifestations related to developmental stage, but more similarities across stages. Sleep disorders, particularly nightmares, are sensitive indicators of these acute stress reactions. Those with acute burns have high circulating levels of catecholamines and corticosteroids—neurotransmitters and hormones that are also associated with the mechanisms of affective and anxiety disorders. It appears that the massive "fight-flight reaction" in response to the burn triggers central and adrenal release of these chemicals, which in turn contribute biologically to the development of the psychological aspects of the acute stress reaction.

In infants observers find behavioral signs of disturbed sleep, fretfulness, and crying early in the postburn period (most infant burns are due to scalds). These symptoms may be exacerbated when the burn was due to child abuse. Signs of separation anxiety also occur when the child separated from the mother, a circumstance that fortunately occurs less than when parents were restricted from the burn unit. Many nurses are skilled at providing warm nurturance to such infants, giving solace until the mother's return. Some burned infants, especially in the absence of the mother, manifest inconsolability, reduced or absent response to pain (another possible sign of child abuse), and later an affective withdrawal, actually a depressive state.

Preschool children will often experience and report dreams and nightmares. For the burned child of this age, this raises the question of what is normal and what is not. With dreams and nightmares, the content and quality of associated affect are usually clues to whether or not the dream is burn related.

School-age children, though capable of verbal reports with good reality testing, are usually more reticent to speak of dream experiences. Boys over about age eight, in particular, may even be experiencing recurrent nightmares and only speak of them when asked specifically, as in a research interview. One nine-year-old boy who had suffered 15 percent electrical burns to his head, suprapubic area including his penile foreskin, buttock, and leg told a school counselor he was having nightmares, but not his mother. He commented, "when you dream, doesn't it seem like it's real?" and "when you get hurt in your dreams it seems so real." The counselor also reported that at bedtime he was visualizing the accident.

Adolescents include those from early adolescence to early adulthood—a very wide span of development. Dreams in the early adolescent will usually reflect the dependency, body image, and peer conflicts typical of the pubertal child. The mid-adolescent, in the midst of changing identity, often has dreams reflecting the stress of this period. The older adolescent with acute burns, like an adult, may be adult sized and manifest agitated nightmares, flashbacks, florid deliria, and can be a potential danger to self and others. Diagnostic and therapeutic interventions regarding dream-related confusion and agitation can be lifesaving. For instance, a 180-pound seventeen-year-old adolescent athlete was admitted with a 50 percent burn and soon was distressed by severe insomnia and nightmares of the accident, becoming fearful that others (staff) were out to "get" him. Although his mental state was not always clearly delirious, he would awaken terrified, at times hallucinating, and he was judged to be potentially dangerous to himself since he was in the acute burn unit with IVs and other risks nearby. Two days of intravenous haloperidol was successfully used to ensure his safety and to correct his sleep deprivation.

Treatment

Can psychotherapy and/or medication improve long-term coping and outcome? Although no research has focused on the treatment of sleep disorders, studies of pain relief by opiates, behavioral interventions, and hypnosis point to improved outcomes by these methods. While none of these is primarily directed toward sleep disorders, all are important in relieving pain—a major cause of sleep disorders. Psychotherapy facilitates the child's verbalization and affective processing of the burn trauma. Crisis intervention or short-term therapy is the most common intervention for anxiety dreams or nightmares with burned children. More intensive therapy is neither feasible for most nor generally indicated, given that many are able to cope with the support of nursing staff and family. The nature of the psychotherapeutic interventions varies from reality testing, explanation, and reassurance in words that frightened young children can comprehend, to play and verbal psychotherapy by which the patients' anxiety is more fully understood and interpreted within the context of their developmental phase and stage of burn treatment.

Medication may also be used, but can be a contributor as well as a cure for sleep disturbance. Benzodiazepines and opiates, for example, may contribute to anxiety, disinhibition, confusion, and delirium as well as relieve them. Judicious brief use of short-acting benzodiazepines such as midazolam, lorazepam, diazepam, or clonazepam may relieve severe, persistent nightmares and other sleep disturbances that interfere with the child's much-needed sleep.

Outcome

A progressive pattern of postburn nightmares and dreams is commonly seen in burned children. The progression is from the more severe, at times organically related, sleep disturbances such as flashbacks and deliria to nightmares and then to dreams that may facilitate and reflect the psychological adaptation to changes in body image. Sleep disturbances, severe dissociative states, and intense PTSD symptoms immediately after a burn injury may represent predictors of future impaired adaptation to burn trauma (Black and Perry, 1984; Saxe, 1993).

Dreams, Nightmares, and Night Terrors in Burned Children

Dreams and nightmares occurring in burned children are readily distinguished from those normally seen in childhood by the anxiety associated not only with the original trauma, subsequent pain, surgical procedures, and the strange ICU setting but also with separation from parents or the security of home. These may occur nightly or when sleeping during the day, or under the influence of sedative or hypnotic medications.

Night Terrors

Night terrors (pavor nocturnus), which are associated with Stage 4 sleep and in which the content is largely not recalled, are especially notable in the early postburn phase, but they may also be seen much later, such as when returning to the hospital for subsequent surgical procedures. A few children will continue to have intermittent night terrors for many years. Night terrors must be differentiated from the more common nightmares or anxiety dreams. Night terrors are usually a transient disorder of preschool children that occur frequently but irregularly and are sometimes associated with maturational delays. During a night terror, the child suddenly sits upright in bed, screams, and is extremely aroused and frightened. The episode is associated with intense autonomic discharge: palpitations, sweating, and a "glassy-eyed," panic-stricken stare. The child is inconsolable and not responsive to surroundings. The child may get out of bed, pace about, talk in a very agitated manner, or seem to be responding to frightening "mental images." The child is difficult to awaken and, once awake, is confused and disoriented. Night terrors are usually not associated with recall. At most, a child may be able to describe some vague sensation or feelings, for example, "I remember feeling scared," but has no recollection of the experience in the morning. "The episode is brief, lasting 30 seconds to 5 minutes, rarely as long as 30 minutes, and is followed by a rapid return to sleep. Sometimes normal sleep resumes without an actual awakening. Because night terrors arise out of stage 3–4 NREM sleep, they are most likely to occur during the first 2 to 3 hours following sleep onset" (Keener and Anders, 1985, pp. 385–386). When burned children experience night terrors, they do at times speak of fear of or seeing "the fire"—thus some recall is not rare.

Patterns of Dreams

There has been no formal research to our knowledge, clinical or prospective, on dreams or sleep disorders in acutely burned children, although studies at a later stage, during recovery from burn injuries, are reported.

Kravitz and colleagues (1993) studied sleep disorders in eighty-two children one year or more after their burns (mean 7.3 years), forty-one boys and forty-one girls with mean burn size of 44 percent (range 2–91 percent total body surface area). Their nursing research study was very carefully done and, though not a random sample, has results consistent with our unpublished psychiatric study of ninety children. They found that 68 percent, or fifty-five of the children, reported dreams and that a subgroup of thirty children reported nightmares. Of the fifty-five reporting dreams, forty-five reported normal childhood topics, six burn injury–related topics, and five burn treatment–related topics. It appears possible that some of the "normal" childhood topics (for example, monsters, kidnapping, being killed, scary movies, dying, being locked up, parents dying, or a sibling harmed) may be burn related as well, whereas other topics (such as playing with friends, school activities, and being grown up) do not have an obvious connection. Topics clearly related to the burn injury were reliving of the event, smelling smoke, dreaming of others who died in the fire, and screaming "fire." Topics related to treatment included pain from burn dressing changes, anesthesia induction, fear of dying in the operating room, dreaming scars are gone, and fearing a burned hand will be amputated. In that study, nightmares involved clear disorders of arousal with screaming, thrashing, sweating, yelling, and so on. As in our earlier unpublished study, they found a history of enuresis in 24 percent of subjects(mean age = 9.5 years; range 3–20 years). They found sleepwalking in 7 percent of subjects. They do not refer to sleep terror disorder, but in our study this occurred in a few subjects.

Developmental Perspectives

Dreams play a role in the lives of children following burns. The process of dreaming takes on different meanings at various stages of development. Becker (1992, pp. 357, 359) has written, "Dreams may appear dramatized as part of a young child's play. Fantasies, dreams and events of the day merge into one another. A parent's report that his child awoke frightened during the night may be a clue to the occurrence of a dream. If the child told his parent he saw a monster or some other frightening apparition, we may be sensitized to this fear if it appears in the child's productions . . . 'Can you tell me about it?' will often elicit the dream. A young child will usually tell us dreams if we ask about the pictures he saw at night when he was asleep. He may be reluctant to describe anxiety dreams, because relating them may revive the dream anxiety. . . . A child suffering from night terrors will present them with eagerness in the hope of receiving help. However, if the underlying wish becomes evident while talking about dreams, or the fright is reexperienced, the child may reveal his dream with greater reluctance or they may cease."

Sarnoff (1987a) has considered the uses of dreams in child therapy from a developmental point of view. He states: "Anxiety dreams occurring before [24 months] contain direct reproductions of anxiety causing situations met with in daytime experience" (p. 272). As the examples we have cited demonstrate, post-traumatic dreams in burned children of all ages have this quality of being undisguised reproductions of the burn trauma. Sarnoff explains lucidly how play is more useful therapeutically than dreams, even in school-age children: "The latency-age child is capable of bringing to play therapy the kind of symbols found in dreams. Fantasy play contains such symbols. One might infer that fantasy play lives next door to the dream. In play, toys and actions take the place of visual dream imagery. Contained within the flow of fantasy play are reflections of latent contents as well as regressions in the face of stress. These regressions . . . are similar to those in the verbal free associations of adults. There is a direct relationship between the mental activity involved in the fantasy play activities of the latency child and the mental mechanisms involved in dreaming. The symbolic forms (ludic versus oeneric . . .) are almost identical" (p. 267). In another book (1987b, pp. 201–202), he states: "Spontaneous dream reporting is rare in the psychotherapy of latency-age children . . . Fantasy play serves a function so similar to dreaming that insights into one of these fantasy forms can help in understanding the functions of the other. The early adolescent, having lost the functional capacity of ludic symbols to communicate or to evoke inner moods, must turn to dreams and fantasies." He adds: "In early adolescence, it is possible to ask about day residues and to pursue the use of the session as an association to the dream as is done with adults. Because of the limitation on abstractions during early adolescence, free association to dream symbols is not particularly productive. On the other hand, the pursuit of secondary elaboration (themes that tie together content) can be very useful in giving clues to problem areas and defining goals for the therapy." These distinctions in the cognitive shifts involving play and later dream modalities for communication in psychotherapy are similarly seen in burned children, although children may need to communicate anxiety dreams at any age. As Sarnoff indicates, the young child is more likely to do this in the context of play than through direct verbal reporting.

The Progression of Sleep Disorders and Dreams in Burned Children

After acute burns, there is a progression in the types of sleep disorders and dreams usually seen in infants, children, and adolescents. These tend to follow the stages that accompany a burn injury, that is, the acute, intermediate, and rehabilitative stages of treatment and recovery.

As a result of the many physical stressors associated with acute burns, sleep disorders due to organic factors are often seen clinically; these include insomnia, flashbacks, and night terrors. Chronic insomnia commonly causes further problems. It results from pain, round-the-clock treatment interventions, the hypermetabolic response to burns, and drugs such as dopamine. Fear of intrusive imagery during sleep may contribute to the insomnia. Chronic insomnia can cause severe delirium, which is relieved by sleep. Parasomnias such as night terrors are common in the acutely burned, and periodically recur for many months. Enuresis, another disorder associated with sleep, is so common acutely that it is accepted as a part of the normal regression after burns. Persistent enuresis, however, is found in some children during later rehabilitation and plastic surgical readmissions.

During the intermediate and rehabilitative phases of burn treatment, the psychological adaptation of the body image to burn scarring is reflected in the images of dreams and nightmares that are sometimes reported but more often avoided. Examples of these are provided in the cases which follow.

Dissociation

There is a fluidity to the mental status during acute burns such that the definitional boundaries of delirium-hallucinosis-night terror-flashback-nightmare-dream may not be very distinct in many cases. Less intense dissociative states, often self-induced, appear to relieve pain or distress, even during normally painful procedures.

Drug Effects and Side Effects

Many of the commonly used drugs contribute to sleep disorders, dissociation, and delirium. Opiates lead to increased dissociation, may alter the sleep cycle, and can cause delirium. Benzodiazepines and other hypnotics lead to increased dissociation and also may alter sleep.

Paralytics, for example, curariform drugs, cause motor paralysis but leave the possibility of consciousness and pain sensation. They are occasionally used with severely burned children. They should always be accompanied by heavy dosages of opiates and/or hypnotics since the paralyzed patient cannot report feelings or thoughts, including pain or intrusive imagery.

Case Illustrations

A TODDLER

A three-year-old girl suffered 80 percent burns when a family member lit the house and himself on fire; her sister and her mother were also severely burned. She participated in a children's group on one occasion and was asked to draw a dream of hers. She drew a large circle and several smaller ones, which turned out to be her mother, herself, and siblings—heads only. She took great care with the large one, placing a disfigured face upon it, and a tiny circle attached to it. We later learned that her mother was pregnant—the girl appeared to have represented the expected sibling attached to the mother. She drew the picture with intensity, saying nothing, looking at no one, with a tone of sadness. She drew it despite badly scarred hands with several fingers amputated, a tribute to how important it was to her to make this drawing. On completing it her eyes twinkled proudly and a gentle smile showed on her badly scarred face. She nodded agreement when asked if the figures were her mother, the baby, herself, and her sibling.

A PRESCHOOL BOY IN A CHILDREN'S GROUP

Four young children were in a group of burned children talking of their experiences, mainly through play with puppets and three rubber dinosaurs (a tyrannosaurus rex, triceratops, and ptereopteryx). The child psychiatrist was holding the Curious George puppet, who went to sleep and snored loudly. The "dream machine" (a pen) was then pointed to his head, and the other puppets (children) were asked what they saw. Chris, aged four and a half, said that he was dreaming of a dinosaur eating him up as he held the tyrannosaurus rex in his hands. Later, after the children had spoken of some of their fears before surgery, the doctor announced that group would soon end. Chris took the tyrannosaurus rex and had it open its mouth very wide and begin to eat Curious George. He was quite adamant and would not stop.

Summary: At first Chris seemed to be expressing a possible derivative of one of his own dreams projected onto Curious George. At the end of the group his dream fantasy was acted out as he seemed disappointed, angry, and insecure at the idea of ending the group, which he had enjoyed very much.

A SCHOOL-AGE GIRL

A six-year-old girl with facial burns of less than 10 percent body surface area, both of whose parents died in the fire, developed a sleep disturbance. This tragically afflicted child experienced difficulty falling asleep on admission, apparently out of fear of reexperiencing both her burn and the loss of her parents. With the consistent surrogate presence of a grandmother and aunt, however, she was able to settle and gradually to indirectly acknowledge her devastating losses, mainly through her wishes and plans to live with her grandmother. Her sleep resumed, though without reports of dreams.

A SCHOOL-AGE BOY

An eight-year-old boy with 61 percent gasoline burns to his face, head, and upper body was burned after he poured gas on a sidewalk and his brother or another boy threw a match onto it. During the initial days after the burn, while the boy was sedated with morphine, his father, who was at the bedside, observed him to be agitated and restless in his sleep, and he was awakened from frightening dreams and nightmares.

A child psychiatric resident consulted, and the boy told him on the first visit that he had dreamt that his house had blown up and there was no one to help him. In the dream, he was surrounded by fire and looked for his parents and they weren't there. The resident inquired further, as the subject shifted from the dream to the accident itself. The boy said how scary and out of control it was for him without his parents. The resident resonated with his feelings, and the boy was able to talk more about the accident. He proceeded to speak in great detail about his memory of what had happened, including the ambulances and arrival at an emergency room, bringing the child psychiatrist along, step by step, to assuage his fear.

In addition to the nightmare just described, the boy had less scary dreams about what had happened to him as well as daytime flashbacks and intrusive memories. He had memories of the flames coming at his face—apparently triggered by red candy wrappers placed in the window of his hospital room. He was somewhat hypervigilant but, at that time, had no emotional numbing.

He responded well to planned nursing interventions reassuring him that the fire was not, in fact, recurring and that he was all right. Preoperatively, he was fearful of pain and of something happening to him in the operating room. Again, he responded well to reassurance that his pain would be relieved and that his surgery would help him to recover more quickly.

Summary: As this case illustrates, children commonly have terrifying nightmares of the accident causing their burns. Although they are initially almost inconsolable, many children are able to respond, as this boy did, to a focused intervention allowing them to tell, and often retell, their story until they feel less urgency and less threat. In this case the intensity of the fearful dreams waned gradually, aided by consistent reassurance, and the boy could tolerate the painful treatments more comfortably.

AN ADOLESCENT BOY

Louis was a fifteen-year-old admitted with an 85 percent flame burn and inhalation burn injury caused by a grease fire from a cookstove that occurred in a camp. One friend perished in the fire. Shortly after admission for burn treatment Louis reported trouble sleeping, bad dreams, and flashbacks of the events of being burned. He did not yet know that his friend had died, but he soon learned this news. He continued to have nightmares over the next six weeks. At that point he was moved to less intensive care, and his nightmares ceased. He reported then that if he thought about "positive things during the day that when he slept his dreams were positive" rather than nightmares. He recalled a dream of himself and his brother riding in the red sports car that was on a poster in his hospital room. He spoke of feelings of freedom, excitement, and the sense of being in control from this dream experience in contrast with earlier dreams. He continued to dream of activities he had done before his injuries with associated feelings of greater freedom and control.

A month later he described a different type of dream. This involved romantic fantasies about a female occupational therapist and the nurses caring for him. He and his therapist were able to talk about how such a dream is not unusual when a close relationship develops between a patient and caregiver. The dream also related to his being able to begin again to acknowledge age-appropriate emotions.

Near to discharge, Louis's nightmares recurred, and he commented that what he had gone through was the worst nightmare he could ever have. He also indicated, however, that he was having positive dreams related to returning home and resuming his life again.

Summary: This case illustrates a typical pattern in the evolution of dreaming experienced over time by many burned children. The nightmares are connected with the ICU experience and follow sleep deprivation, delirium, and numerous very severe bodily insults. As time passes and the children enter the rehabilitative phase of treatment, their outlook may become more positive and thus the content of their dreams may change, away from the post-traumatic nightmares and, through the relationships with caretakers, toward more developmentally normal dreams.

AN ADOLESCENT GIRL

Susan is a fifteen-year-old Indochinese girl admitted for reconstructive surgery for grafts to facilitate the restricted growth of one of her breasts due to burn scars. She was burned at age two when she accidentally knocked a pot of scalding water over onto her chest. According to Susan, she was supposed to be under her father's supervision but he was otherwise engaged. When she was very young, her father, she reported, was emotionally and physically abusive to both her and her mother. Her mother divorced him while Susan was in preschool. Currently Susan lives with her single mother and younger sister, and she is very attached to her mother's new partner, whom she calls "Dad." She rarely has contact with her biological father by his choice, leaving her feeling angry and rejected. She is in a special needs class in school, and her teacher reported that she is functioning at a third grade level in many academic areas.

After she had her chest skin grafting and her family had returned home, she disclosed to her primary nurse that she had been gang raped a few weeks earlier. Her mother was not aware of this until Susan was encouraged to tell her by telephone the next day. When her therapist (LS) first met her, she was trembling and suffering from flashbacks and nightmares related to the rape. She was eager talk about the incident. Although Susan had initially wanted skin grafts to facilitate the restricted growth of her breast, the separation from her family at such a vulnerable time was very stressful to her. During the next week Susan had considerable difficulty sleeping, frequently dreaming about the rape incident and waking up sweating with fear. She kept dreaming about boys "falling" on her. Susan said that the nightmares had increased significantly in frequency since the surgery. The painful and intrusive nature of surgery and postoperative care, coupled with the forced separation from her family, had propelled her into a full-blown PTSD reaction.

Treatment focused on empowering Susan as much as possible during her hospitalization and thereby differentiating it from the rape incident. Initially Susan said to her therapist that she was afraid to tell the nurses about her wants or needs, because she was afraid they might become angry with her. After some reality testing and collaboration with medical staff, she began to respond to encouragement to express her needs freely. For instance, she told her therapist that she did not like "men doctors"; thereafter, every attempt was made to have her examined by female physicians. As she became more empowered and formed attachments to other hospitalized peers and members of the staff, her dreams started to change in the second week after her operation. She informed her therapist that she was not having as many nightmares about the rape and that she had a "funny" dream that all the doctors had "eaten a lot and become fat." She seemed to enjoy the dream because the doctors were the ones with the distorted body image instead of herself. This dream may also have involved a projection of her pregnancy fear after her rape. The next night she had a dream that she had become Miss America, which was very pleasant for her. Susan had told her therapist that she often felt "ugly" because of the burn scars, but her dream reflected her hopes for improvement from the surgery and the reality of her improved physical condition. In general she was coping better with the hospitalization experience and was less preoccupied with the rape incident. She excitedly discussed her new friendships on the unit, for example, and some of her interactions with her "favorite" nurse. She also informed her therapist with pleasure that her new boyfriend had written her a letter and told her he loved her despite her scars.

Suddenly, to everyone's complete surprise, Susan became extremely ill and developed toxic shock syndrome. She was transferred to the acute care unit and the medical staff worked intensively to save her life for two to three days. They succeeded, and by the time her psychology intern met with her again, she had returned to the rehabilitation unit. For the rest of her stay, however, she remained in isolation because of her infection. This had been yet another severely traumatic experience for her, especially since it had required a pelvic examination. Psychotherapy again focused on helping her gain a sense of ego mastery through education about her recent medical progress and clarification of why the pelvic examination had been necessary. Susan reported a terrible nightmare in which someone "kept pounding on her back." After her therapist encouraged her to express how the dream felt, she vehemently pounded on a puppet, displaying the fear, pain, and helplessness of the experience. She also told her therapist how "sick" she was of all the needles, and that she was afraid of dying. Over the next several days she continued to recover from the toxic shock syndrome; the forced isolation from her peers caused her to want to leave the hospital even more. Toward the end of her stay, two family meetings were held to discuss her emotional needs with her mother and facilitate a referral to a psychotherapist in her home town.

A few days before discharge, Susan reported a mixed dream that had two parts. It started with her boyfriend telling her that she could kiss him, but he would not kiss her. She was very upset by this scenario, because she felt rejected by him. The dream seemed related to how anxious she was about how people would react to her when she returned home. In the second part of the dream, a girl appeared with a lighter and was trying to burn her. Susan ran to the doctor, and the doctor yelled at the girl and Susan grabbed the lighter away. She initially felt afraid of the girl, but with the doctor's support felt empowered in her ability to grab the lighter. Although this sequence may hold self-destructive elements, it primarily seemed to point to her increasing sense of self-worth in her decision to protect herself. Thus, at the end of her stay, Susan's dream life seemed to reflect both her concerns about her survival in the world but also a beginning sense of empowerment to cope with circumstances that might lurk ahead.

Summary: This case is complex owing to Susan's multiple traumas, cognitive limitations, and cultural influences, which all have an impact on her experience of the world. Although Susan is a burn victim and her dream process reflects some of the typical patterns in the healing process, the multiplicity of her traumas in a short time span make her case also somewhat unique. Initially the helplessness and intrusiveness of surgery and hospitalization triggered nightmares of an earlier trauma which, relatively speaking, was much more powerful than her burn scars. As she felt safer and more empowered in her current environment, her dream content shifted to more burn-related issues. The burn scars were less threatening than the rape incident and her dreams became more hopeful, even humorous, and reflected attempts at mastering the effects of her burn scars. With the occurrence of the life-threatening infection, her nightmares were naturally retriggered but with a greater focus on the intensive care experience and fear of survival. Toward the end, her dreams reflected fears about returning home yet, at the same time, a budding sense of her capacity to cope with the challenges ahead. Metaphorically, the last dream could express a growing awareness that she can cope with the burn of rejection and still feel her own worth.

Stressors Associated with Dreams

Children hospitalized for burns sometimes have been exposed many times over to stressful events outside the range of usual experience. This exposure has implications for the developmental study of dreams, nightmares, and PTSD in understanding of the effects of both physical and psychological traumas. Multiple stressors may need to be taken into account.

Preexisting traumas may be present. Prior to their burns, children may have been struggling with the effects of poverty, child neglect or abuse, parental mental illness, familial substance abuse, or childhood mental illness.

The more immediate trauma, fire, may frequently mean loss and grief.

Children may be forced to adjust to the death of a parent or sibling, the death of a pet, the loss of their home, or the loss of possessions--events which in some cases they may have witnessed.

Other stressors are found in the separations and the extreme helplessness and dependency that burned children experience. They may fear separation from or abandonment by their parents or guardians. The acute critical care unit itself is stressful, as is the child's loss of autonomy there. Children find themselves cared for by persons unknown to them, who may be associated with painful procedures. Depressive withdrawal is a not uncommon response.

Burns themselves and the treatment they require are stressful. Acute cutaneous injury, resuscitation, tracheal intubation and respirators, surgery, dressing changes, IVs, donor sites, and physical therapy are all sources of pain. Burn delirium may cause disorientation, confusion, agitation, and hallucinations. Children are also affected by others' trauma, as they become aware of other hospitalized patients' pain, procedures, or death.

The stages of recovery may be traumatic. Grief over body image alteration or loss is gradually experienced. At the same time, future surgery may be anticipated and feared. Discharge may ultimately mean social stigmatization (and narcissistic injury). Out of the hospital, children may mourn the loss of special treatment; at the same time, home and school are now sites where they may have to cope with rejection over disfigurement and functional impairment.

An array of traumatic stressors can thus affect the burned child and his or her dreams. In most cases, however, the burn experience itself stands out in memory as the primary unforgettable stressor.

Implications of Burned Children's Dreams for the Psychology of Trauma

In part, dreaming is a process that is an expression of unconscious wishes, drives, and needs; dreams serve as a way to make contact with fantasies that might never be expressed consciously. Many dreams of burned children are initially undisguised repetitions of the traumatic experience. Although some dreams can be very satisfying, these nightmares or flashbacks to the burn trauma are just the opposite: they frighten and produce added stress for the burned child. Optimally, dreams and even many nightmares can serve as a means of reexperiencing both pleasant and unpleasant life experiences and aid the dreamer in working through conflicts aroused by the trauma. Terr (1985) reminds us, however, that post-traumatic images, including dreams, may persist and become elaborated in many different forms—such as repetitive memories, memory elaborations and distortions, hallucinations, and intrusions and extrusions of memory—with the potential for enormous alterations and fixations in personality development.

Trauma as reflected in dreams or the lack of recall may signal the way in which the development of the child's personality will be affected. In discussing their twenty-year follow-up of children who survived the Buffalo Creek disaster, Honig and colleagues (1993, p. 351) write: "The particular way in which the individual's coping response to the trauma consolidates or does not consolidate appears to influence the ultimate resiliency or rigidity or the adult personality, the response to subsequent trauma, and the sense of meaning or purpose derived from life. The failure to elaborate stable, trauma-related, adaptive patterns would appear to leave the individual vulnerable to subsequent chronic PTSD. From another perspective, the absence of PTSD at long-term follow-up, far from indicating that the trauma did not have a significant lasting impact, may rather imply that highly significant and idiosyncratic effects need be sought, not in the review of symptoms, but through exploration of the enduring patterns of adaptation and their origins." As these researchers suggest, dreams are only one way of exploring patterns of adaptation to trauma—but, with burns, a particularly rich way. It may be that the structure of the post-traumatic dreams of burned children shapes the subsequent strength and development of defenses such as regression, denial, avoidance, and reaction formation. These efforts to defend against the feelings associated with the trauma may alter personality development.

We have interviewed children during both the acute and the reconstructive phases of their surgical treatment, and have learned of their dreams—a mutual learning process that may assist the child in recognition and eventual mastery of the traumatic experience. The quality and content of the dreaming process varies from one developmental stage to another, but a sufficiently devastating trauma appears to evoke nightmares in most children. Many children deny having any dreams or nightmares even though burned; others have vivid, frightening, detailed dreams reenacting the trauma. Burn dressing changes, surgery, and other surgical and nursing procedures compound the trauma of the initial event, and they too become incorporated into the manifest or latent dream content. For many, dreams also mirror, in an evolutionary way, their adaptive or maladaptive experiences following the trauma.

It is unusual to find a person burned as a child who, at some point, will not begin to acknowledge dreams. The burned child's dream often involves reliving or reexperiencing the event in which the burn occurred. The content of such dreams is often highly detailed, sometimes distorted, and may focus only on the most intense and stressful aspects of the event; other aspects may be defended against. Those who initially deny or continue to deny that they dream are usually repressing the emotional discomfort that they would feel if they told about the dream or nightmare. If they can tolerate the associated stress and anxiety, however, discussing dreams can be a means of helping them find words for many aspects of the traumatic events that led to their bodily injuries, which they often only slowly comprehend. Retelling a dream of the trauma or even reliving it in play with another, even though discomforting, often serves to allow affective expression and, eventually, integration by the ego of the experience that may have initially been so emotionally shattering.

When a dream is recurrent, the therapist seeks to help the child develop an understanding so that he or she may stop having the intrusive stressful recollections. It is also true that, long after the traumatic event, the dreams may again recur, often triggered by an event that in some form represents the original trauma. This "trigger" may not be a direct experience, but may even occur through reading or hearing of a similar situation, or seeing a television program or movie that serves as a reminder.

The child's understanding of dreams is based on his or her ability to recall and report the content of these dreams to another. Often this person will first be the child's primary nurse. Young children with limited language development may not be able to describe the dream experience, but they may be able to play it out with an injured puppet, in drawings (as did the three-year-old girl who drew fragmented body parts connecting her to her pregnant mother), or through stories read or told together. In these ways, the young child feels that the interviewer acknowledges the frightening experience, is helping him or her to make sense of it, and is a source of support and reassurance. With adolescent patients there tends to be a need to explore dream associations in greater detail, and they are usually able to benefit from an effort to understand the role of unconscious conflict or developmental issues in their dreams.

Dreams and nightmares in burned children have five major implications for the psychology of trauma:

1. Dreams and sleep disorders (nightmares, night terrors, etc.) seem to be one of the organism's common responses to severe emotional and physical trauma.

2. The dreams of these bodily traumatized children commonly evoke the dream-memory of reliving the damage to the body image.

3. Nightmares and night terrors are most prevalent acutely after the burn, and can be affected, even triggered, by pain and metabolic, infectious, or pharmacological factors.

4. The intensity of post-traumatic memory as reflected in dreams and sleep disorders decreases rapidly over time, as the child heals physically.

5. The psychological trauma of the burn experience may adversely affect the child's personality (for example, affective, cognitive) development rather than result in chronic PTSD; however, this subject requires longitudinal research.

Dreams may well represent a "royal road" to the understanding of the impact of trauma in children, particularly in young children where little is known. To establish this, however, will require increased focus on children's dreams and nightmares in therapy and clinical research.

Identifying Sexual Trauma Histories from Patterns of Sleep and Dreams

KATHRYN BELICKI AND MARION CUDDY

Despite the prevalence of sexual trauma, it is an unfortunate reality that this experience is underreported in therapy. Surveys of therapists indicate that they tend to underestimate both the prevalence of such trauma and the extent of the resulting psychological damage (LaBarbera, Martin, and Dozier, 1980; Attias and Goodwin, 1985; Eisenberg, Owens, and Dewey, 1987). We have found this lack of knowledge to be most eloquently demonstrated by the number of colleagues who have told us in one context or another that they have very little experience working with survivors of trauma. Briere and Runtz (1987), however, in a study of 152 consecutive female clients of a community health crisis clinic, found that 44 percent admitted to a history of childhood sexual abuse, although almost two-thirds did not mention this until asked. This finding is not surprising, given that surveys of nonpsychiatric populations have indicated that sexual trauma is a frequent event and given that a history of sexual trauma has been repeatedly demonstrated to be associated with increased psychopathology (see Herman, 1992). Therefore it is a reasonable assumption that all "general practice" therapists have considerable experience working with survivors of sexual trauma; unfortunately, they are unaware of this fact.

If it is reasonable to assume that survivors of sexual trauma are a routine part of a therapist's practice, why do clients so rarely discuss these experiences in therapy? Clients may have repressed or dissociated their memories of the trauma, particularly when this involves childhood experiences (for example, Maltz, 1991). In addition, again as a result of dissociative defenses, they may remember the occurrence of the trauma but may not have access to the emotions associated with the event and therefore may not recognize the relevance of the trauma to their current problems. Even when they do fully remember, talking about the trauma is often a terrifying experience and one that will be avoided unless a profoundly safe and supportive environment is provided. It is beyond the scope of this chapter to discuss all of the reasons why disclosure is so difficult (see Herman, 1992, among others, for an excellent discussion), but there are compelling pressures to maintain secrecy, beginning with those from the perpetrator of the trauma and supported in complex ways by societal forces. Furthermore, when the sexual trauma involved a violation of a caregiving relationship, the client will have learned under traumatic conditions to distrust anyone in a caregiving or authoritative role, and will therefore be hesitant to disclose to a therapist such "dangerous" information.

Therapists contribute in many ways to this "conspiracy of silence" (noted by, among others, Carmen, Rieker, and Mills, 1984; Ellenson, 1985; Greenson and Samuel, 1989; Herman, 1992). Many individuals are resistant to hearing about trauma histories, and many personal and societal factors inhibit therapists from pursuing these issues with their clients (Herman, 1992). Certainly it is the case that simply asking routinely about any prior history of trauma, as part of an intake interview, for example, dramatically increases disclosure. Sometimes this disclosure happens immediately, but more often it occurs after the establishment of a trusting relationship. The act of asking in a routine, "no nonsense" fashion signals to the client the therapists' readiness to deal with this material. Yet many therapists avoid asking that question even in assessments (Carmen, Rieker, and Mills, 1984; Ellenson, 1985; Herman, 1981, 1992; Summit, 1983).

It is worthwhile for therapists at least to entertain the hypothesis of a trauma history early in the therapeutic process. The most obvious reason for this is that the presenting symptoms of the client may be secondary to a history of abuse. Prince (1992), for example, has argued that chronic psychosis that is nonresponsive to traditional treatment may be associated with a traumatic history that has not been addressed in therapy. In addition, Gelinas (1983) and Siegal and Romig (1990) have argued that therapy that only treats presenting symptoms is not as effective as one that addresses the abuse history. We should not conclude from this that the therapist should forcibly direct the client's attention to the possibility of a trauma history: because reestablishing a sense of self-control is an important goal with trauma survivors, it is crucial that therapists allow clients to lead them to an examination of their history only as they are ready. But therapists are much more likely to be sensitive to the cues suggesting such a readiness (and can gently facilitate such a readiness) if they have first anticipated that there is a history to be considered.

In addition to this concern about the focus of therapy, certain treatment issues arise with people who have been sexually abused that can be mishandled if a therapist does not realize their source. Trust and intimacy, for example, are major problems for a person who has been abused; therefore, as the client begins to improve and draw closer to the therapist, this increased intimacy can cause tremendous anxiety, resulting in flight on the part of the client—which can take the form of abruptly terminating therapy, suddenly becoming dramatically regressed, or turning in anger on the therapist. Such a development can be very frustrating to the therapist and can lead to misconceptions on the therapist's part concerning client and/or therapy dynamics. Herman's (1992) more detailed account of the complexities that can arise in client-therapist relationships when there has been an abuse history is important reading. Some clients who have been abused have great difficulty in being touched, even with such simple gestures as a hand shake (Dunlop et al., 1987); we have had people tell us of terminating therapy simply because a therapist in a first session shook their hand or touched their shoulder.

Given that it is important to be aware of a possible history of sexual trauma, and given that routinely asking about such a history is helpful but not sufficient, there has been considerable research attention to identifying unique symptoms and signs suggestive of prior trauma (e.g., Belicki et al., Cuddy, Pariak and Weir, 1992; Briere and Runtz, 1987, 1988; Cuddy, 1990; Cuddy and Belicki, 1989, 1990, 1992; Ellenson, 1985). One such set of indicators are patterns of sleep and dream disturbance.

Before we turn to our findings regarding sleep and dreams, a comment on the issue of defining sexual trauma or abuse. The actual definition of what constitutes sexual abuse or trauma is debated. In our own practice we adopt a range of definitions. For our research we employ fairly conservative definitions consistent with other research literature, but in clinical practice we feel that anything a client has experienced as traumatic constitutes sexual abuse for that individual. It certainly has been both our clinical experience and the findings of our research (Cuddy, 1990) that those who have experienced what might be viewed as minor trauma (such as being forced to watch pornography) can show psychological damage similar to that of individuals who have experienced what would be more clearly accepted as serious sexual abuse (such as repeated rape or incest). Bloom (1990) offers a useful analogy here: if one's house is broken into, to some extent it does not matter if $50 is stolen or $50,000. In both cases there is a tremendous sense of personal invasion and loss of privacy and security.

We will use the terms abuse and trauma interchangeably, as both are widely used in the literature. In fact, we prefer the term "trauma," because the experiences of some individuals were not intentionally abusive but were nonetheless traumatic and were experienced as abuse. While the word trauma carries no implications as to the intentions of the person(s) who caused the event, the word abuse can be taken to imply some intent.

The Occurrence of Sleep and Dream Disturbance Following Sexual Trauma

As noted in the DSM III-R, nightmares and sleep disturbance are common symptoms following trauma (American Psychiatric Association, 1987). On this empirical basis alone it is not surprising that investigators would examine the occurrence of these symptoms in association with a history of childhood sexual trauma. Furthermore, because dreams can be conceptualized as particularly suited to the information processing of emotions and psychologically important events (Breger, 1969; Greenberg and Pearlman, 1975; Cartwright, 1986), nightmares would theoretically be a natural consequence of trauma.

There are also several theoretical grounds for anticipating increased sleep and dream disturbance in individuals who have experienced sexual trauma. Some people with a history of sexual abuse can clearly be diagnosed as experiencing Post-Traumatic Stress Disorder, while many others show dysfunctions not consistent with PTSD (Finkelhor, 1987); with both groups theoretical reasons lead one to expect disturbed dreams.

In considerations of PTSD, there has been some speculation about the alterations in information processing following trauma that would account for sleep disturbance and nightmares. One of the characteristics that make traumatic events traumatic is their unexpectedness. The individual is catastrophically confronted with the fact that unspeakably horrific events can occur unpredictably and without provocation (Roth and Newman, 1992). It has been argued (ibid.) that the frequent tendency for survivors of any form of trauma to blame themselves for somehow causing the event is a defense against the crippling helplessness one is otherwise left to feel. To believe one has provoked a sexual assault reestablishes, albeit at a tremendous cost, a sense of order and predictability to the universe. Another consequence of this shattering of assumptions of personal control and of the world's predictability is that the traumatized individual becomes hypervigilant and hyperaroused in an attempt to remain constantly ready for and prepared for the next catastrophe (Litz and Cain, 1989). Such hyperarousal and vigilance can directly disrupt sleep. They can also result in the easy triggering of associative responses, including memories of prior trauma, by ambiguous or mildly threatening stimuli, which may be experienced as flashbacks by day and nightmares by night. Nightmares (and flashbacks) may also reflect a struggle to make sense of the trauma and to integrate it with one's experiences and conceptions of self and the world (Horowitz, 1976).

But not all survivors of sexual trauma fit the diagnostic criteria of PTSD (Finkelhor, 1987), and Finkelhor and Browne (1985) have proposed what they call a Traumagenic Dynamics Model of Child Sexual Abuse to account for the varying dysfunctions that are seen in this group. They propose four dynamics (traumatic sexualization, betrayal, stigmatization, and powerlessness) that distort the individual's self-concept, world view, and emotional responses. If we develop the implications of this model for sleep and dream experience, we would not necessarily anticipate increased sleep disturbance (such as insomnia). Yet we would expect to see disturbing, unpleasant dreams, given that the elements of dreams are derived from self-concept, world view, and emotional response (a position that can be taken whatever one's theory of dream function—even if one endorses a theory such as Crick and Mitchison's, 1983, which attributes no cognitive value to dreaming).

Given the many theoretical reasons for expecting nightmares and/or disturbed sleep in survivors of sexual trauma, it is not surprising that several reports in the literature mention these as sequelae of abuse. There are several limitations to this literature, however. Most published reports give little detail about the nature of the nightmares, and many papers simply report case studies or the author(s)' impressions from clinical experience. The larger, better-designed studies often lack a nonabused comparison group (for example, Ellenson, 1985; Jehu, Gazan, and Klassen, 1985; Mannarino and Cohen, 1986; Briere and Runtz, 1987; Garfield, 1987), and even those that do have such a group lack a physical abuse comparison group. The inclusion of a physical abuse group is important to test whether the findings with a sexual trauma group are due to any physical abuse they may have experienced. Finally, researchers often lack expertise in categorizing and measuring sleep dysfunction. Nightmares may not be routinely differentiated from sleep terrors, also known as night terrors, for example. Despite these limitations, there is considerable consensus in the literature that adults who have experienced childhood sexual trauma frequently report impaired sleep and frequent nightmares. This consensus led to our current program of research.

In a preliminary study (Cuddy and Belicki, 1992), 1,043 undergraduate students completed a short inventory about their sleep experiences, the Beck Depression Inventory, and a questionnaire asking about any prior experiences of physical abuse or "unwanted sexual activity." In a subsequent study, for which participants were drawn from this larger study, found on follow-up inquiry that when women indicated they had experienced unwanted sexual activity, they meant by this (as we intended) traumatic incidents such as sexual assault; most of the men who had indicated they had experienced "unwanted sexual activity," however, had not experienced what most people would term sexual abuse or assault. Therefore, while asking about unwanted sexual activity is an effective technique for assessing trauma in women, it is not effective for men. As a result the men's data from the preliminary study were discarded, leaving 539 women, 124 reporting prior sexual trauma (including 63 reporting both physical and sexual abuse), 71 reporting physical abuse without sexual, and 344 reporting no abuse.

The sexual abuse group reported more nightmares, more repetitive nightmares, more sleep terrors, and greater difficulty falling asleep after a nightmare than did the no abuse group. The sexual abuse group also indicated sleeping fewer hours in a typical night, but this finding did not remain when depression was covaried out (while the other differences did remain). On all measures they showed greater disturbance than the physical abuse group, but on no single comparison was this difference significant. The findings were not only statistically significant but clinically substantive. For example, while the sexual abuse group reported a mean of 13 nightmares in the prior year, the no abuse group reported 6.8. Similarly the sexual abuse group reported a mean of 4.2 repetitive nightmares in the prior year and 4 sleep terrors, in contrast to 1.9 repetitive nightmares and 2.4 sleep terrors in the no abuse group. (The physical abuse group reported 9.7 nightmares, 3.3 repetitive nightmares, and 3.9 night terrors.) These figures should not be taken as accurate estimates of the actual occurrence of these events: it has been shown that retrospective estimates tend to greatly underestimate the actual frequency (Wood and Bootzin, 1990; Fernandez, 1992). It is clear, nevertheless, that there are relative differences in these distressing experiences.

In a follow-up study, we examined differences in the content of nightmares of people with trauma histories. Studies by Garfield (1987) and Ellenson (1985) had noted that there was more explicit violence in the nightmares of those who had been sexually abused. Some case reports (Burgess and Holmstrom, 1978; Kavaler, 1987) reported more sexual content. The presence of shadowlike figures had been noted (Robinson, 1982), as had snakes and worms (Weiss et al., 1955; Barry and Johnson, 1958; Dunlop et al., 1987).

In order to examine the possibility of content differences more systematically, we studied sixty women reporting sexual abuse (including fourteen reporting both sexual and physical), thirty-three reporting physical abuse, and seventy reporting no abuse (Cuddy, 1990; Cuddy and Belicki, 1989, 1990). These participants were all drawn from the prior study already described. They completed a detailed questionnaire concerning their abusive experiences, several inventories of psychological and physical well-being, and a sleep experiences questionnaire in which they recorded, if possible, the worst nightmare they could recall having and a typical nightmare. They also completed a detailed checklist on which they noted whether various themes, emotions, and objects had occurred in their nightmares. Embedded in these checklists were items culled from the literature, such as death of self or other dream characters, being chased, being attacked, positive sexual activity, negative sexual activity, and the presence of snakes, worms, or blood. The two nightmare reports (worst and typical) were blindly content analyzed for a subset of the Hall and Van de Castle (1966) categories of

Characters, Objects, Emotions, Social Interactions, and Regression, and for the presence of themes derived from the literature, including seven different categories of death, seven different categories of dying, six different categories of injury, twenty different unpleasant things that could happen to a dream character (choking, being trapped, being paralyzed, and so on). The worst nightmare report proved to be better than the typical nightmare report in distinguishing among the groups; in fact, many subjects had difficulty reporting a typical nightmare. In terms of the worst nightmare, a discriminant function analysis was able to sort subjects into sexual versus physical versus no abuse groups with 79 percent accuracy (in contrast to 33 percent accuracy if they had been sorted by chance). When separate discriminant function analyses were calculated for pairs of groups, the sexual versus physical abuse groups were sorted with 100 percent accuracy and the sexual abuse versus no abuse groups with 87 percent accuracy. This clearly indicates that the damage sustained from sexual abuse cannot be accounted for simply in terms of the effects of physical abuse.

In terms of the specific findings, the women who reported having been sexually abused tended to have more sexual themes in their nightmares, and sexual activity was more likely to be associated with such negative qualities as distrust, shame, guilt, jealousy, anger, or violence. Although sexuality was more frequent, however, most reports of nightmares had no sexual content. Only 15 percent reported a nightmare with a theme of explicit sexual abuse.

Another frequent theme was explicit violence. Although violence, or the threat of violence, was common in all women's nightmares, when explicit details were present, such as blood or dismemberment, the dreamer was likely to have been sexually abused. Sometimes the violence was a result of aggression on the part of humans, animals, or supernatural characters; other times it was caused by such events as car accidents and natural disasters. Women reporting physical abuse often dreamed of themselves dying (typically without explicit details of violence); women reporting sexual or no abuse were more likely to dream of others dying.

Several types of dream characters and objects were more common in the dreams of the sexually abused. They were more likely to have a male stranger as a pivotal character in the dream. These characters were often faceless (or the face was invisible), shadowy, or described as somehow evil. Sometimes a woman described dreaming of an evil "presence" that might enter her room or body. Snakes and worms were slightly more frequent in the dreams of the sexually abused, and references to parts of the body/anatomy (any part) were more frequent—as were, not surprisingly, references to sexual anatomy. In terms of this last point, the higher scores for anatomy usually occurred because sexual trauma survivors were more likely to describe the physical appearance of dream characters.

Overall, what is perhaps most interesting in these findings was that the nightmares typically did not replay the actual abusive event. This is consistent with Finkelhor's (1987) argument that many survivors of sexual abuse do not fit a typical PTSD profile. What these nightmares seemed to portray was the emotional reality of the event, for example, that for many women the trauma did not feel like a sexual event but an act of profound violence.

We next considered whether therapists, who are not going to score dreams with the detail and care that is used in research, could make use of a general description of these findings to identify people with a history of sexual abuse. As an initial attempt at addressing this question (Belicki et al., 1992), ten individuals, nine women and one man, were given 110 reports of worst nightmares (from Cuddy, 1990), coded and randomized so that the raters would not know from which of four groups each report came: women reporting sexual abuse (26 nightmares), both sexual and physical (28), physical only (27), and no abuse (28). The raters were informed that there were about equal numbers of nightmares in each group, and they were given a summary of the research findings.

Two of the raters were clinical psychologists (one woman, one man); the other eight were senior undergraduate university students. Four of the raters had a personal history of sexual abuse.

Despite the fact that the raters knew the four groups had a roughly equal number of reports, few of the raters made distributions that came even close to equal distribution. Although 48 percent of the reports had come from people who reported sexual abuse, the percentage of reports rated as involving sexual abuse (whether sexual alone or sexual and physical) ranged from 10 percent to 62.4 percent.

The raters were also not very accurate in identifying individuals with a history of sexual abuse: the percentage of individuals accurately identifying a history of sexual abuse when it was reported ranged from 9.3 percent to 66.7 percent. In this small sample of raters, at least, accuracy seemed not to be influenced by whether or not the rater had a personal history of sexual abuse; training, however, did appear to be of some importance, the psychologists being statistically significantly more accurate than the students. But even the psychologists only achieved 64.8 and 66.7 percent accuracy in identifying sexual abuse histories, a rate that is only somewhat more accurate than chance and falls considerably short of the 87 percent attained in the discriminant function analysis of the same reports.

In general it would appear that when we shift from careful content analyses to global judgments of nightmare content, there is a considerable loss of information. Although nightmare content yields clues to a history of abuse, at present no simple formula exists that will confidently point to such a history. Further research is needed in several directions to improve the diagnostic utility of content. First, dreams and nightmares are highly idiosyncratic to the individual dreamer and his or her circumstances. Therefore it is almost surprising that consistent themes can be identified at all when one is conducting such global comparisons as sexual versus physical abuse, lumping together in each category a broad diversity of traumatic experiences. A more detailed examination of content associated with more specific experiences may help to identify more readily discernible patterns. For example, the "developmental" differences in nightmare content that have been identified by King and Cuddy (see Chapter 4) corresponding to various phases of personal insight and therapeutic work may be useful here.

As another line of inquiry, because not all trauma is followed by nightmares, dream content in general needs further study in relation to trauma survivors. (It is an intriguing question why some individuals have nightmares following trauma and others do not.) Fernandez and colleagues (Fernandez et al., 1991; Fernandez, 1992) have conducted some initial work and have replicated much of our findings with nightmares, additionally noting a tendency for increased verbal aggression in the nightmares of women who have been sexually abused. They also looked at dream (non-nightmare) content and found only one significant difference: dreams of women reporting no abuse had more characters than those reporting either sexual or physical abuse. The larger number of characters seemed attributable to the tendency to dream more frequently about parties and social events. Although there was only one significant finding, Fernandez (1992) argued that dream content merits further attention, noting that she only scored the dreams for categories that had been identified in the literature (including our studies already described). Content differences may well exist that have not yet been identified in the rather sparse literature on dreams and sexual trauma.

One shortcoming of our own studies, and of some of the studies reported by others, is that they were conducted with university students, with the result that many of the trauma survivors studied were probably functioning relatively well. Studying individuals who have had less positive outcomes, such as those currently in the psychiatric or prison system, may reveal a clearer pattern of nightmare content. More important, findings from such studies would be more generalizable to the clientele of most therapists. Finally, there is a tremendous need for research on male survivors of childhood trauma.

In conclusion, although research in this area is in its infancy, it is clear that certain patterns of sleep and dream disturbance are associated with a history of sexual trauma. Individuals who have been sexually abused are more likely to report frequent nightmares and sleep terrors, and they will experience greater disruption of their sleep. Their nightmares will frequently involve explicit violence and are more likely to have sexual content. When sexuality appears it will usually be portrayed as involving guilt, shame, distrust, manipulation, or violence. Those who have been sexually abused are more likely to dream of a threatening or evil presence, which may take human, animal/insect, or supernatural form. Worms and snakes are slightly more frequent than in the dreams of nonabused, and there is a greater tendency to describe dream characters' physical appearance or in some other context to mention physical anatomy. At the same time, of course, it must be kept in mind that some survivors of sexual trauma show none of these patterns.

At present these patterns of sleep and dream disturbance are insufficient evidence to indicate a history of sexual abuse. It requires little time to inquire into the quality of a client's sleep, however, and most individuals are very comfortable talking about their sleep and dreams. There is virtually no cost attached to collecting such information, and to do so may assist a therapist in making an early identification of a client's history of trauma.

The Use of Dreams with Incest Survivors

JOHANNA KING AND JACQUELINE R. SHEEHAN

Witnessing the pain and distress experienced by clients who have survived incest has proved to be a powerful motivator for us to search for effective treatment modalities. We feel that we have found such a modality in the use of dreams, which has yielded some of our most profound and meaningful experiences as therapists.

Outside the psychoanalytic tradition, most therapists receive little or no training in the use of dreams in therapy. When training is received, it is usually theoretical rather than practical—therapists may read Freud's great *On the Interpretation of Dreams* ([1900] 1965) or Bonime's influential *The Clinical Use of Dreams* ([1962] 1988). Sometimes this theoretical information is intimidating; most therapists cannot imagine being so perceptive or learned.

Incest survivors, however, do not wait for therapists to feel ready. They are typically plagued by disturbed and disturbing dreams and generally are most anxious to talk about them. Therapists may be tempted to avoid the dreams for content-related countertransference reasons as well as fears about not knowing how to work with them; the dreams may tap into the therapist's own memories of abuse; the therapist may feel overwhelmed by the violence or disturbed sexuality in the dreams; or the therapist may feel unequal to the task of providing a safe container for dealing with the wound. These are fears and concerns routinely experienced by therapists dealing with trauma, but they may be magnified by the immediacy and drama of the graphic dream images of incest survivors.

Working directly with the dream material can nevertheless bring an increased sense of power, direction, and satisfaction into the therapy. Specific information is sometimes encoded in the dream images. Finding the therapist accepting and interested in the dreams, rather than frightened, indifferent, or rejecting, can increase the survivor's feelings of safety and hope. As work with the dreams progresses, the survivor may gain new respect for and faith in herself, as awareness of her own autonomous, creative, attentive inner life grows. Finally, as Cartwright notes (1992), working with dreams may speed up the process of therapy. "Working with people while . . . awake," she says, "[is] frequently slow going" (p. x).

Before proceeding, we note that almost all of our own work, like that in the literature, is based on the experience of women and girls. We have therefore elected to use the feminine pronouns. We cannot say if our comments would apply equally well to the experience of male survivors.

The Long-Term Consequences of Incest

Although "incest" has traditionally referred to sexual contact between a child and a blood relative, we use it to mean sexual involvement between a child or adolescent and any person in a position of power over the child or adolescent and from whom the child or adolescent would normally expect protection and affection. According to Anna Freud (1982), "where the chances of harming a child's normal developmental growth are concerned, it [incest] ranks higher than abandonment, neglect, physical maltreatment, or any other form of abuse" (p. 34). When the young, developing self is confronted by the betrayal of sexual abuse, the victim may be physically and psychologically dependent on her attacker and, as such, is faced with a dilemma of monstrous proportions. In the case of one-time abuse, the child may be plagued by intrusive, pervasive memories of the experience. In the case of long or repeated abuse, the child, in order to cope, may make use of the readily available defense mechanisms of denial, splitting, and dissociation (Terr, 1990). These latter survivors often report poor memory for parts of their childhood during which abuse occurred.

The negative psychological effects of this childhood trauma have been documented with increasing regularity since the early 1980s. Adult female survivors are particularly vulnerable to impaired self-esteem, depression, a deeply ingrained sense of shame, isolation, somatization, and anxiety (Courtois, 1988; Axelroth, 1991). They have higher levels of self-destructive and suicidal tendencies, sexual dysfunction, and difficulties with intimate relationships (Briere and Runtz, 1988; Blume, 1990). They are especially vulnerable to transference toward authority figures such as teachers, therapists, fathers-in-law, and employers. Some have suggested that a global syndrome, specific to incest survivors, be articulated to facilitate identification and treatment (Briere, 1992; Ratican, 1992). Judith Herman, in contrast, sees the symptom pattern as parallel to that of men who have suffered extreme combat stress (Herman, 1992).

The lack of ready verbal access to clear memories for the traumatic event can make the initial stage of therapy a slow and frustrating experience for both the survivor and the therapist. Survivors may wish to avoid direct discussion of the trauma and prefer to focus on alleviation of their painful current symptoms. And they want to talk about those dreams.

Marker Dreams

Two different dream patterns have been identified by researchers as being associated with childhood sexual abuse. One pattern is frequent and repetitive nightmares and difficulty returning to sleep after these nightmares. This careful research is presented in Chapter 3 (see also Cuddy and Belicki, 1992).

The other pattern, identified by Susan Brown (1988), is the confounding and confusion of sex and aggression in the same dream. Brown compared the dreams of two groups of women in therapy; one group reported sexual contact with an older male relative, and the other did not. The groups were equivalent on a measure of family dysfunction, but the incest group had been in therapy significantly longer. Although there was no difference on the number of dreams that contained themes of either sex or aggression, the confounding of sex and aggression in the same dream was unique to the incest group. She says that the sex/aggression dream "may be viewed as a clear indicator of an incest history" (p. 108), and that this kind of dream reflects the continuing struggle to resolve the conflict caused by the confusion of these two phenomena. One of Brown's examples follows:

> (. . . two friends [and I] are having fun with three men.) Then the next thing I knew—I was in bed naked. Some men were performing oral sex on me . . . Then it went from being something enjoyable to something violent. My girlfriends and I ended up getting raped by the three men. I remember screaming "stop, you're hurting me." Then we went to tell the police and they would not believe us. (Brown, p. 105)

Not all sexual abuse victims have these types of marker dreams, and not all those with these types of dreams are sexual abuse victims. For example, it is our experience that sex/aggression fusion dreams, in which sexuality is unpredictable and fear inducing, may result from more recent sexual assault experiences or from an emotional sense of being violated as well as from incest. We nonetheless consider them useful guideposts for further exploration.

Dream Stages of Healing

As a result of our work with survivors, and of reading and consulting with colleagues about their work, we have identified five categories of dreams that mark and illustrate stages of healing through which survivors of childhood sexual abuse may progress.

Clinicians will recognize that the stages are not necessarily linear. Nevertheless, we think they can be used to aid the survivor and the therapist in identifying therapeutic progress or the lack thereof. For example, we have seen long series of dreams in which the dreamer continually rehashes the abuse experience, like ghastly reruns of terrible movies. Mental repetition of the traumatic experience, while awake *and* asleep, is part of the normal process of striving to achieve psychic mastery; however, after a point, which may vary from person to person, continual repetition without alteration marks a failure of that normal process. Cartwright (1992) describes this in her comment that "dreams sometimes get stuck like a needle in the groove of a scratched record," revealing that recovery is not progressing, and "we need to find ways to lift the needle and move on" (p. 9).

Self-Protection

In the stage of self-protection the dreamer makes very clear that she does not want to know or to deal with what happened to her. This resistance to knowing is usually rooted in the normal self-protective childhood defenses of denial, repression, and dissociation and has typically served to shield the dreamer from overwhelming feelings for years. The dream images in this stage beautifully portray denial, pushing away, closing out. This type of dream most commonly occurs when the survivor has not yet openly acknowledged abuse, but may also occur as a reaction to devastating acknowledgment of abuse, as the survivor seeks to reestablish the relatively calmer waters of denial or avoidance. Looking back from a later, safer stage of healing, dreamers are often amused by their ingenious self-protective images.

The following two dreams occurred months apart, spanning the long period of time it took this survivor to work through her intense fears that acknowledgment of the incest would mean the total devastation of her family. (Unattributed dreams are from our own practice and teaching. Abridgment of dreams is indicated by ellipses.)

> There is a tape with information on it. I am reluctant to listen to it.—then it turns into a bag with bugs in it. I put it into the freezer.

> I am in the kitchen and I am cleaning up. But I see chicken legs sitting on the counter and I refuse to clean them up. They are too gross.

Gayle Delaney reports the following dream from a dreamer who, despite her anxiety that her therapy "work," was actually very guarded about her incest experience.

A good teacher wants me to attend a lecture on inbreeding. I say I can't bear to hear it. I leave and close the door behind me. (Delaney, 1992, p. 8–27)

Karen Signell reports the next dream, in which a part of the dreamer is not prepared for the painful "truth" of the physical abuse from her mother and sexual abuse from her father.

. . . I'm sitting near an open door, a closet, and I hasten to close and lock it. But there's a young woman named Verite sitting near me wanting me to open the door again. We argue about it and I have to fight her physically to keep the door locked for now . . . (Signell, 1990, p. 131)

Acknowledgment

In dreams of acknowledgment, often poignant and painful, the dreamer presents herself with images, thoughts, and feelings that replay the abuse, sometimes quite literally. Often the dreamer appears as a child, or another child is the victim of violence. Exploration of the following dream with Gayle Delaney brought into focus memories of early childhood molestation by the dreamer's father, and shed light on her adult attitudes toward men and sex.

[I] saw a little girl being raped by a man who looked like [my] father . . . the little girl was wearing one of [my] favorite childhood dresses . . . (Delaney, 1991, p. 385)

Two months after reporting the next dream, the dreamer told a memory of being molested by her father:

I am in the back of a truck with a two-year-old, my father, and two other people. I am crouched down and I feel a sharp barb pressing in my back. I think, "If we get in an accident, I'll be the only one killed." Everyone else is seated in chairs.

The next dreamer, a patient of Carol Brod, is a teenager who had been molested by her great-uncle by marriage when she was a young child.

. . . the man who was sitting next to her took a baby and smashed it through the driver's window. Then he took another baby and smashed it through the windshield. He just smashed them and he said, "Just another cabbage patch kid!" And the reporter announced to the world that he didn't kill them, he was just smashing them . . . (Brod, 1991)

The survivor saw through the next dream that her entire family colluded in the denial of family secrets.

My family is staying in an old yucky cabin. It was left dirty by a former tenant. There is filth everywhere. I am the only one who notices. Even my brother pours me a cup of coffee in a filthy mug.

The next dreamer, a twin whose sister appears sitting near her in the dream, found speaking about her incest experience so horrifying that she actually felt as though she were about to vomit when she did so.

I am on a train with a scary man who tells me we are going to get married. Another little girl sits near us and I hope that she will get help, but she doesn't . . . I'm so terrified I can't speak . . .

Effects

The manifestations of childhood sexual abuse as they present themselves in the current life of the dreamer are generally what bring the survivor to therapy, and dreams that identify and illustrate these effects are often the first ones presented to the therapist. The dreamer may or may not initially report incest, or connect current problems with that incest if she does report it.

The following dream was reported to Delaney. The dreamer described her constant sense of being rigidly encased in a stiff body, and connected this to her father's sexual abuse. Even as an adult she felt stiff, rigid, and unable to enjoy her own body.

[A] woman dreamt that her father was pouring concrete all over her body. (Delaney, 1991, p. 271)

The next dreamer's grandfather molested her from before she could remember until she was twelve years old. The dream is one of her most dreadful childhood memories, almost worse, she said, than the actual act of being molested. "I *still* have much older men make passes at me," she says. "It bothers me so much that I get physically ill just thinking about it . . . I find myself paralyzed."

> The nights that I would stay with my grandparents, I would dream that this big, mean black cat would come into the room where my sister and I slept. Then the cat would go back outside and bring in thousands of its big, mean friends. They would all pile into our room and they would all turn into huge eels . . . I would wake up screaming and crying, still seeing the eels . . .

Even after months of therapy, the next survivor of multiple sexual abuse experiences dating from young childhood into adolescence still could not trust the therapist (Johanna) enough to reveal her feelings. Instead, she saw the therapist's efforts as another assault.

> . . . A lady . . . took me into her office and started talking to me as if she was a counselor. The expression was of great concern for me. She would ask me certain questions about how I was truly feeling on the inside right now. I would lie and tell her I'm fine. She grabbed my arm and stuck a needle in it and told me that I looked sick and pale. She really wanted me to be honest with her and open up . . .

The next dream was presented early in therapy, when the dreamer did not trust that the therapist would do anything but expose, lecture, and wound her.

> I am swimming in a deep river, very deep, with my lover. On the shore is a seven-year-old girl who has been pulled from the river. She has been raped. A woman who is a combination Jackie and my professor points to the child and says (in an accusing, lecturing way), "See, there is no hymen." I feel the pain of the child . . .

Growth and Understanding

Dreams of growth and understanding excite both the survivor and the therapist. In them, the dreamer behaves or feels differently, sees things from a different point of view, attends to some element of the situation that she has ignored in the past, sees new possibilities emerging. The affective tone of the dreams becomes more positive. The dreamer may come to realize for the first time that she did the best she could at the time of the incest, or that she had no viable options. She may see more clearly the role of significant others, then and now.

One such dream is reported by Patricia Garfield, who sees the motif of connectedness and purpose in this report of a teenage survivor as indicative of the girl's growing ability to cope with the trauma.

Ann dreamt of being knifed in the armpit, and saw herself being rushed to a hospital. She says, "I almost died, but I hung on for my boyfriend and my sister." (Garfield, 1987, p. 96)

The following dream is reported by Delaney:

Francesca dreamt of being in Los Angeles. To her surprise, she saw that LA now has two rapid transit systems in place, but that it still has the problem of the homeless. (Delaney, 1991, p. 125)

The dreamer connected the smog and pollution of Los Angeles with the unhealthy family environment she grew up in, which was polluted by her father's sexual abuse. The rapid transit system led her to say, "At last, they're getting on the ball and dealing with their problems." This reminded her of her own progress in therapy, but she knew there was still more to do.

The next dreamer, the one who could not initially trust her therapist, months later could see herself in a trusting relationship with an authority figure, even if she was not the one doing the trusting.

I'm standing in the hall and my English teacher comes out to tell me something. I can't remember what it is but it's very personal. She is treating me like a friend, and wants me to listen to her problem. I feel really glad, and listen carefully. People are going back and forth past us in the hall.

Renegotiation

In the stage of renegotiation the survivor finally comes to terms with what she has experienced, puts in it perspective and in context, and allows her new growth and understanding to inform her thoughts, feelings, decisions, and behavior. We specifically call this stage "renegotiation" rather than "resolution"; we do not encourage survivors to imagine that the incest is no longer an issue in their lives, or is resolved. We like the more open construct "renegotiation," because it allows room for continuing growth and occasional continuing problems, and encourages new solutions depending on circumstances.

In the following example, the teenager molested by her great-uncle by marriage demonstrates powerful mastery over the traumatic experience.

. . . So when they both got started lifting up my skirt high this time, I got so mad I turned around and I punched them both . . . Like six times. Wham, wham, like that . . . I just turned around and did it and then I felt satisfied . . . Like everyone said sing, sing for us. So I got up and I said okay but the piano player was gone. So that's okay, I can sing with no music. My third cousin was there and he gave me a corsage . . . (Brod, 1991)

Brod says that upon hearing the dream *she* felt like giving the dreamer a corsage.

Sue Blume reports the next dream.

I was parked in a remote area. Desolate. A guy came over to the car. He said he wanted drugs but I had a feeling he wanted sex, you know? He said, "You're right, I want sex." And then I knew he wanted to rape me. I said, "You know what I like?"—in a very seductive voice. He said. "No, what?" "I like to sit on a hot—." (I said it in the dream, but I can't say it to you.) He broke into a grin. And I opened my jacket, and pulled out my lighter, and held it under his penis until it glowed!! (Blume, 1990, pp. 190–191)

Blume notes that while revenge is not a necessary part of healing, this dream nevertheless illustrates very clearly that the dreamer no longer felt like a victim.

In the following dream, reported by Delaney, the survivor is able to be assertive and to set firm and clear boundaries, and her resulting mood is very positive.

. . . I make it clear that I will not stay on the hotel's ground floor for security reasons. I ask that they give me a room higher up, and to my surprise they cooperate and give me a lovely room with a view and a good lock on the door. I feel safe and happy. (Delaney, 1992, p. 8–29)

The next dreamer had identified three childhood "selves" who had been damaged by her childhood sexual experience, and in this dream she has the medicine necessary to heal them and the strength to protect them.

There is some vagina medicine in the dresser drawer for three little girls. I am standing by a well also. One little girl jumps in and I save her.

THE CASE OF KAREN

We recount here the highlights of the growth and healing of Karen, an incest survivor who worked with Jacqueline for about two years. When she came to our college counseling center, Karen, thirty years old, was completing her undergraduate degree. Prior to coming, she had worked with a counselor on issues related to growing up in a family with alcohol and physical abuse problems. She felt that she had made great strides as a result of this work; most important, the door on family secrets and on her own strong tendency to repress had been cracked open. Long ignored painful memories had begun to flood in. Just before entering therapy with Jacqueline, she dreamed of being sexually abused by her Uncle James when she was four years old. She immediately phoned her mother to ask about it, and her worst fears were confirmed. Her mother said, "We were hoping that you would never remember."

She was haunted for months by another dream, the first she presented. It poignantly illustrates the effects of the abuse, highlighting damaged childhood innocence, and the confusion of sex and aggression identified by Brown as characteristic of the dreams of sexually abused women.

The first dream segment:

It is my four-year-old self and I am playing a flute in a field. There are swirls of colored light in which there are holes. The holes become mouths, the flute becomes a razor blade and I am unable to hold it. I am terrified.

The second segment:

I am eighteen years old. I am sweeping in a movie theater lobby. I look up and see a romantic movie poster. The swirls of light return again. The broom turns into a razor blade and I am unable to hold onto to it. I am terrified.

The third segment:

I am my present self. I see a popular actor. I cannot think of his name but I know him at a very deep level. He takes me to his bedroom. He quickly undresses. I see the same movie poster from the movie theater lobby. It is now over the bed. The swirls of colored lights appear. The actor becomes demonic. He grabs me by the wrists and pulls me to the bed. I am terrified.

Karen worked very hard in therapy. She encouraged her family to stop denying the incest, alcoholism, and violence that had characterized their home. She talked twice a week on the phone with her mother, asking many questions, and her mother was responsive. Her Uncle James had lived with her family for six months when she was four years old, and her mother now believes that the molestation occurred for the full six months. Karen remembered his smell of tobacco and alcohol. She remembered her pleas for help.

One distress call was perfectly clear: she walked into her parent's bedroom and said, "Uncle James is hurting me." This plea was not acknowledged, but a later, more dramatic one was. Her mother awoke late one evening to a noise outside the house, and when she went to investigate, she discovered four-year-old Karen in her nightgown, crouched down in the dirt, digging a small hole with a tablespoon. Bewildered, her mother asked Karen what she was doing, and Karen replied, "I'm digging a hole to bury myself so that Uncle James can't hurt me anymore." Karen's mother understood at once, and put an immediate end to the abuse. Soon Karen's father discovered what James had done and exploded in a violent rage, beating James. A neighbor, fearing that James would be killed, called the police and the father was taken into custody. Karen's mother frantically called friends to get bail money, and hauled her three small children off into the night to retrieve her husband from jail.

Quickly a shroud of silence fell over these dramatic events, and no one in the family spoke of them until Karen was twenty. She was visiting relatives in another state, and someone commented to her, "You seduced your uncle when you were four years old." She was confused and alarmed by the comment, but quickly blocked it from focused memory. By that time her uncle had died in an alcohol-related accident.

There were moments in this painful and difficult process of reconstructing her past when Karen felt overwhelmed by the enormity of the issues confronting her, and she yearned for her old defense mechanisms of repression and denial. This yearning can be seen in this "self-protection" dream:

> I am in an open house. I feel very uncomfortable. The breeze is blowing through the house and fluttering the lace curtains. I run around the house and try to close all the curtains, windows, and doors.

Despite her efforts to "close up the house" again, intrusive memories continued, and Karen was able to reconstruct much of her past, exposing more painful family secrets along the way. One involved a shocking experience she had about the same time she heard about "seducing her uncle." She had became pregnant with her first serious boyfriend, an alcoholic. When she was five months pregnant, he rammed her abdomen into an open car door, and she miscarried. Karen was living at home; nevertheless, neither she nor her parents said a word to acknowledge her pregnancy, the violent act, or her miscarriage.

A few years later, Karen was living on her own and fell in love with a young man she described as nurturing and caring. The relationship lasted about two years, and then he was killed in a motorcycle accident.

Karen retreated. She cut her long hair, gained seventy-five pounds, moved back in with her parents, no longer dated, and no longer cared. She finally entered therapy in an act of desperation, and then came back to college.

As therapy progressed, Karen worked to established healthy boundaries with her family, but also to confront and talk about family relationships. Her weight continued to trouble her, but she was afraid that being thin would entail sexual risks for which she was not ready. She continued to work on relating her current life to her previous traumas, and to banish secrecy. She was very successful academically, and accepted leadership roles in campus activities. She got a roommate. She made friends and developed a fuller social life. Her progress and courage, so beautifully illustrated in this "growth/understanding" dream, were a joy to watch.

> I am standing on a bridge between winter and fall. Ron [her boyfriend who had been killed in an accident] is on the winter side. He is telling me to return to the fall side and that I am okay. I awake sobbing.

Finally, she and her mother talked about her pregnancy, the assault by her boyfriend, and her miscarriage. Her mother admitted that she knew Karen was pregnant. Then Karen began to give men a small space in her life. Two days before graduation, Karen came to say goodbye, and said, "By the way, have I told you this dream?"

> I am in a remote jungle-like region. I am holding the hand of a four-year-old girl. I know that a volcano is going to erupt but no one will believe me. I hold the hand of the four-year-old child. I continue to warn people of the impending danger yet no one will believe me. I have to get to the top of the mountain, to the very edge of the volcano. It is very difficult to climb, the trail is steep and slippery. It is too hard for the little girl, so I have to put her on my back. There is a feeling of doom if I don't get to the top. It is so steep and difficult that I now have to crawl on my hands and knees, still carrying the child. At the top of the mountain, the volcano starts to blow, and at the last moment, a man in a helicopter swoops down (he is an actor and although I cannot think of his name, I know him at a very deep level). He rescues me and the child. I say to him, "I always knew you would come." Inside the safety of the helicopter, the little girl sits in my lap. She turns and looks in my eyes. It is me. We embrace.

Using dreams has brought a dimension of deep-felt richness and joy to our work with incest survivors. Through them, we have watched the empowerment of the survivor as discoverer, renegotiator, and healer, and we have treasured our own role as guide, witness, and validator.

Dreams in Multiple Personality Disorder

DEIRDRE BARRETT

Dreaming is often described as a dissociated state of consciousness (Prince, 1910; Gabel, 1989, 1990; Barrett, 1994b). This assertion is based on dreams' lack of continuity with waking experience, projection of aspects of the self onto other characters, and propensity for amnesia. Waking dissociative symptoms have often been referred to as "dreams" (Breuer and Freud [1883–85] 1955. p. 45; Janet, 1929, p. 64). Multiple Personality Disorder (MPD) is the most extreme of the dissociative phenomena. MPD has recently been rechristened Dissociative Identity Disorder in the DSM-IV nomenclature; I will use the older, better-known term here, for consistency with earlier literature that I will be citing. Despite controversy, the consensus is that MPD is usually, if not always, related to early trauma; therefore, much of the earlier chapters' discussions of post-traumatic dreams apply. However, the symptoms of MPD have an additional relationship to dreams by virtue of their dissociative nature.

References to dreams in the multiple personality literature are rare and tend to be brief. When dreams are mentioned, nevertheless, it is usually to state that they are invaluable tools in the therapy of dissociation. Putnam (1989) writes:

Although nightmares, night terrors, hypnogogic and hypnopompic phenomena, and other evidence of sleep disturbances are common in multiples and other victims of trauma, little has been written about the role of dreams in the dissociative disorders . . . My experience with dream material from MPD patients suggests that it can provide access to deeply hidden trauma . . . MPD patients seem more willing to share and work with dream material than with other forms of memory for trauma. (pp. 201–202)

Kluft states that "dreams often monitor integration" and may represent "some sort of healing process in which the mind may or may not be assuming a new configuration" but he warns the published accounts of dreams in MPD have been too few so far to justify clear conclusions about them (Sizemore, 1989, p. 123).

Several authors do present dream material in their discussions of MPD. Thigpen and Cleckley's (157) *The Three Faces of Eve* and their patient's three autobiographical books (Lancaster [pseud.], 1958; Sizemore, 1989; Sizemore and Pittillo, 1977) all contain accounts of her dreams. Jeans (1976) describes using dream work to help a "host personality" (the one in control the majority of the time) become aware of her "alters" (auxiliary personalities which are "out" less frequently). Gruenwald (1971) and Salley (1988) note that there are sometimes alters who communicate with the host personality mainly in dreams, and they utilize this for therapeutic purposes. Marmer (1980) presents fifteen dreams representing perspectives of various alters. Paley (1991) described a series of dreams from an MPD patient that reflect the host's gaining control over the behavior of a persecuting alter. Schreiber (1974) describes therapeutic work with several of Sybil's dreams and makes the following observation:

In her dreams Sybil was more nearly one than at any other time. "Sleep and forget" did not apply. To be awake was to forget; to be asleep was to remember. Her dreams reverted to the original events that had caused her to become multiple and that in waking life were reproduced in her other selves. (p. 345)

Prince ([1905] 1978), in the first detailed account in Western literature of a case of MPD, gives perhaps the most interesting account of dreaming. He describes one alter as remaining awake all night while the patient sleeps. The alter's description of sleep mentation predates by half a century science's discovery of REM sleep cycles and the fact that recall of many dreams a night is available if one is awakened after every REM episode. However this is very much what the alter seems to be observing:

"I don't exactly understand what you mean by dreams," said Sally. "Miss Beauchamp's mind is going off and on, all night long. She imagines then all sorts of things. some of the things that she thinks [that is, dreams] she remembers when she wakes up, and some she doesn't. If she remembers them, you call them dreams, and the others you don't. I don't see why all the other things she thinks are not just as much dreams as what she remembers." (pp. 326–327)

Survey

I conducted a survey of therapists who treat dissociative disorders, asking about characteristics of their patients' dreams. The remainder of this chapter will present the findings on types of dreams found in patients with Multiple Personality Disorder, and will illustrate these types with examples from the survey, the literature, and my clinical practice. These dream categories will first be described in terms of characteristics and frequencies among MPD patients; then the discussion will consider whether these dream characteristics and/or patients' associations to them distinguish these from the dreams of non-MPDs. The dreams' usefulness in the treatment of MPD will also be explored.

The twenty-three patients with MPD in the survey had a mean age of twenty-eight years and averaged seventeen known alters. Eight types of dream phenomena that had been noted in the literature or observed in my practice were included in survey questions, and two more were described by survey respondents in an "other" category. The frequencies of these ten types of dreams are presented in Table 5.1.

Table 5.1   Types of dream phenomena reported in MPD patients

Dream phenomena	Number of patients reporting ($N = 23$)	Percentage
1. Switch during dream	3	13
2. Alter's experience as dream	4	17
3. Multiplicity metaphors	19	83
4. Alters as dream characters	13	57
5. Different perspectives on the same dream	6	26
6. Host is alter[a]	4	17
7. Dream maker	6	26
8. Retrieving memories	15	65
9. Different dreams[a]	8	35
10. Integration in dream	2	9

a. Not asked about specifically; compiled from "other" category.

Categories of MPD Dreams

Switch during Dream

Three patients, or 13 percent of the sample, were reported to have dreams, usually nightmares, which triggered a "switch" between personalities, much as a waking stressor might. One patient experienced the majority of switches this way; for the other two it was an occasional phenomena.

The patient who experienced most of her switches this way had a history of "losing time" a few times a year ever since her teens, before which she had few memories. She had memories of being violently sexually abused by her much older brother, and there was strong evidence that she had a more extensive history of multiple abuses by him and her parents dating back to early childhood. At a time when her brother had, within a two-week period, both moved to the city in which the patient lived and become the father of an infant girl, the patient began to have vivid nightmares of sexual violence for a period of about a month.

After several weeks of nightmares and insomnia, the patient began a pattern of sleeping for three to four hours, then whimpering in distress as she had in her nightmares and waking up in a state in which she manifested several different personalities, called herself by other names, wrote poetry with a different handwriting, and interacted in an uncharacteristically hostile manner with her roommate. After several hours of this she would go back to sleep and wake up amnestic for these episodes. A sleep lab evaluation was negative for delta parasomnia or any other physiologic anomaly to explain these episodes as sleep-related. Hypnotic exploration in therapy led to contact with several aspects of the patient which corresponded to the alters who continued to emerge predominantly from the sleep state.

Alter's Experience as Dream

> If you could pass through Paradise in a dream, and have a
> flower presented to you as a pledge that your soul had really
> been there, and if you found that flower in your hand when
> you awoke . . . What then?
>
> COLERIDGE, 1816

It is hardly Paradise that MPD patients are visiting in their dreams, but four in the sample, or 17 percent, reported what later turned out to be actual waking experiences of their alters as "dreams," which they at first believed had occurred only in their sleeping psyche. They most often found out the "dream" event had really happened by some equivalent of Coleridge's flower.

One woman who had recurring "nightmares" of catching evil cats by the throat and stuffing them in garbage cans awoke from one of these dreams to find the velour jogging suit in which she slept covered in cat hair. She did not own a cat and was so disturbed by the implication that she both brought in the top of the jogging suit to make sure that her therapist also saw it covered with the hair and searched trash cans in her neighborhood.

Some patients were not so quickly aware of the nature of these experiences. One had "dreams" of sitting on the bank of a river at night feeling very soothed as she stared at it; many months later an alter owned up to these being real nocturnal jaunts.

Sizemore and Pittillo (1977, pp. 64–65) describe "Eve" as having a Coleridge-type experience as a child when she lay down for a nap and "dreamed" of watching a redheaded girl steal and smash her cousin's coveted new watch, "only to awaken to find the ruined treasure in her own hand."

Multiplicity Metaphors

Multiple personality was symbolically depicted in dreams of nineteen patients, or 83 percent, according to their therapists. This was often reported at a stage in therapy when the patient was not fully aware of the diagnosis. Multiplicity may be the most frequent dream phenomena for those with MPD because it is an issue of concern to all of them. However, it may also be that as the most subjective of the ten categories, multiplicity metaphor estimates are inflated while types that are harder to spot may be underestimated.

One patient, not yet in therapy, was aware that she "lost time" and was hearing what later proved to be her alters as voices. She was not aware of the nature of the voices or the blackouts when she recorded:

> I had a dream. I was sitting in a photo booth trying to get it to take a picture of me, but all the pictures that came out showed other people—or at least faint outlines of other people. In the mirror, where you see what will come out, the face kept changing, like ghosts.

Stoller (1973) described dreams from his MPD patient early in therapy that included: "I dreamed I was lying down, and a spirit got up and left my body" (p. 368) and "I dreamed I was at home with my mother and my brother and sisters, and I was twins" (p. 394).

Sybil reported a dream of this type early in analysis. She sees a starving kitten and, examining where it has come from, finds the body of a dismembered mother cat covering three more kittens, even closer to starvation. She throws the parts of the mother cat into a river but worries that they may float back to shore. She picks the kittens up, and discovers yet more kittens under them. She finds a blanket identical to the one on her own bed, gathers the kittens into it, and sets out for home with them, hoping she can find someone who will know how to make everything all right and that they can all become a family. This dream was eventually interpreted as representing Sybil's fragile alters that she was going to nurture and bring together with the help of her therapist as she began to distance herself from her deceased abusive mother (Schreiber, 1974, pp. 345–346).

Salley (1988) describes one of his patients having this type of dream at a stage where the host is aware of only one other personality, a "helper" named Self:

> Frank reported a dream of standing outside a crowd. The people in the crowd were shouting for Frank to do things for them. One person stood between Frank and the crowd throwing the crowd members aside and shouting, "Leave Frank alone! You'll take everything he's got and I won't let you!" Frank's defender is attacked and bleeding: together they run from the crowd.

Interpretation of this dream led Frank to view Self as the dream defender. Self then revealed for the first time that Frank had multiple personalities. The crowd in the dream represented the angry personalities. Self described the nature of many of the personalities and said that they were enraged at Self for exposing their cover (seen in the dream as Self fighting the crowd). Therapy then focused on getting to know the personalities one at a time through trance.

Obviously people without dissociative disorders can have similar dreams about various aspects of themselves that might be represented this way. Carl Jung ([1916–45] 1974) and Fritz Perls (1969) have developed entire dream theories based predominantly on this premise, but the associations of other dreamers do not lead to anything like those quoted above.

Alters as Dream Characters

In the dreams of thirteen patients (57 percent), their alters appeared as dream characters. One dreamed of a blond little girl begging her repetitively, "Don't let them hurt me; take me home with you." The patient was not yet in touch with this child alter but the therapist recognized the description as an alter that had come out in moments for which the host was amnestic to implore the therapist with exactly those words. Two patients who had made suicidal gestures which they attributed to accidents or intoxication had dreams which later played a great role of explaining them. One had dreamed of a woman determined to commit suicide, the other of one vowing to kill the dreamer. These turned out to be alters responsible for much cutting and one overdose.

At one stage in Sybil's therapy she had been told she had MPD (because one alter had been popping out in therapy sessions), but she was still resistant to learning who the alters were and unsure of their numbers. Sybil then reported a dream in which she had taken her parents to another house in which they could all go to live to escape doom:

> . . . she had been standing in the large living room of the house in another town, face to face with the children of these people she had known—seven sets of twins and one singleton lined up in a row. Four sets of twins had dark brown hair; the other three sets, blond hair. The one singleton standing apart from the others had hair identical to Sybil's.
>
> "How about introducing your brothers and sisters to me?" Sybil had asked one of the older children.
>
> Suddenly, however, the parents and their fifteen children had started to move out, and Sybil and her parents had begun to move in. As Sybil realized that the introduction to these children, who all but one, were standing in a row in twosomes, had not taken place, she had awakened. (Schreiber, 1974, p. 335)

Sybil ultimately turned out to have fifteen alternate personalities, all but one of them "paired" by age, gender, and temperament.

Paley (1991) describes a persecutory alter appearing as a recurring character, first triumphing, then detected as an "imposter" of the dream ego.

Gruenwald (1971) reports intentionally inducing a dream of an alter for therapeutic purposes in a host "A." who has been unaware of an alter "B." Gruenwald tells B. that she could speak to A. in a dream and tell her about wanting to integrate.

> The strategy was successful in that A. did report the "dream." It was set in the context of her repetitive anxiety dreams of a dark, threatening cave or a corridor with many doors, the last door always having been especially dangerous; entering it meant that she might never return . . . This time, however, the corridor was wide, well lit and had windows through which she could see trees, grass, and flowers. Everything smelled "fresh and nice" . . . In this corridor she had a visitor, "a nice girl who looked exactly like me." She repeated in detail what the visitor told her, a verbatim repetition of what I had said to her [as B.] the previous day. (p. 44)

Different Perspectives on the Same Dream

Six patients (26 percent) had had personalities experience the same dream from different perspectives. This can be seen as a variation on category 4, alters as dream characters, but has one distinctive difference. In category 4, the alter appearing to the host as a dream character sometimes has no experience of this, or in other instances experiences the host as dreaming but the alter as awake. In many cases, the therapist asks only the host about dreams and it is unclear what the alter might be experiencing. However, for these 26 percent of patients with dreams in category 5, two or more personalities reported dreaming at the same time and experiencing each other as characters. Sometimes one personality also watched and was not observed as a character by the others. When this happens early in treatment, the host and sometimes the alter do not recognize each other until the dream experiences are discussed awake, as in the example below. Further into the therapy process they are likely to recognize each other as soon as they appear.

> The host personality, Sarah, remembered only that her dream from the previous night involved hearing a girl screaming for help. Alter Annie, age four, remembered a nightmare of being tied down naked and unable to cry out as a man began to cut her vagina. Ann, age nine, dreamed of watching this scene and screaming desperately for help (apparently the voice in the host's dream). Teenage Jo dreamed of coming upon this scene and clubbing the little girl's attacker over the head; in her dream he fell to the ground dead and she left. In the dreams of Ann and Annie, the teenager with the club appeared, struck the man to the ground but he arose and renewed his attack again. Four-year-old Sally dreamed of playing with her dolls happily and nothing else. Both Annie and Ann reported a little girl playing obliviously in the corner of the room in their dreams. Although there was no definite abuser-identified alter manifesting at this time, the presence at times of a hallucinated voice similar to Sarah's uncle suggested there might be yet another alter experiencing the dream from the attacker's vantage.

Host Is Alter

Four (17 percent) of the patients' host personalities had experienced a dream in which they were one or, rarely, two of their alters, as in the following example:

> I dreamed there was a corporation that my father ran that sold meat at some kind of carnival, like an amusement park with rides. He sold these big slabs of meat. They were gross and bloody and he was trying to fry them up and giving them to people to eat. I'm a vegetarian anyway, but I discovered that it was human meat and I had to stop him. There was a big knife that he used for cutting up the meat. I took it and stabbed him and

he fell down dead. Then I knew that I had to kill myself. The scene changed and I walked out of a building with my brother leading the way. I was a martyr dressed in a long black robe. We walked through a beautiful garden and down to a room. There were little boats about six feet long and my brother indicated I get in one. I lay down in it and folded my hands over my heart and began to float downstream. That was death, this was how it was done.

This dreamer had a child alter who had hallucinatory images of her father, sometimes with a knife, sometimes cooking meat. Another alter was a would-be "martyr" who, in her internal variation on Catholicism, intended to achieve martyrdom by suicide. She could communicate with these alters but awake she perceived them as "other." In the dream she experienced being first one and then, with the scene shift, the other.

Marmer (1980a, b) reports series of fifteen and seven dreams respectively from the same patient that illustrate her identifying with many of her alters in dreams. This case has the unusual detail that the alters have color-linked names and predominant colors also serve to identify their dreams. The author's discussion of this material is alarming, however, in interpreting apparent childhood trauma associations as Oedipal wishes and memory of a gang rape at age fifteen as a fantasy.

"Eve" described a dream late in her progress toward integration which involved moving in and out of a merger with her "Attic Child":

I painted my first installment in the "Attic Child" series because I had such a dream. And that dream was the first time I was ever *inside* the overall picture. It was bizarre. I momentarily became the girl in my dream. But looking through her eyes, I could not see all around every object. Everything suddenly seemed flat and the lines stark. But just as quickly, I was no longer the girl. No longer looking through her eyes. And it was such a relief to be dreaming normally again. (Sizemore, 1989, p. 203)

Prince ([1905] 1978) describes that his MPD patient as having two personalities (he did not use the distinction of "host" versus "alter") who were always merged for dreams:

As a result of the inquiry into dreams, it transpired that however distinct and separate was the ideation of BI and BIV during the waking state, during sleep these personalities reverted to a common consciousness and became one and the same. That is to say, the dreams were common to both . . . each remembered them afterward as her own. (p. 342)

Dream Maker

Six (26 percent) of the patients had at least one personality able to design dreams to be experienced by other personalities. The most elaborate account of this type is one from Frank, the same patient described above who has a helper alter named Self and also suffered from psychogenic seizures, a common symptom in MPD:

> Self, in somnambulistic trance, explained that the seizures resulted from a struggle between Frank and Self at those times when Frank would resist regaining consciousness after a blackout and Self would attempt to force him to be conscious. Self stated that his only line of communication with Frank was through dreams and that he would create a dream that would explain to Frank the functions of the seizures. Out of trance, Frank, as was typical, had no memory of what had occurred in hypnosis.
>
> That night Frank dreamt that he was standing on a pedestal and two voices were shouting at him; one voice shouting "Yes!" and the other "No!" The vibrations from the shouting were so intense that the pedestal began to shake and split open, where upon he fell to the ground shaking. Free association to the elements of the dream led Frank to relate the shaking to his seizures and the screaming to internal conflict and his resistance to regaining consciousness after as blackout. In the two years since he had this dream, he has experienced no recurrence of the hysterical seizures. (Salley, 1988)

One patient in the present sample had an alter who stated of the host: "I show her images a lot, even while she's awake, of memories and things I feel and want to do. But she sees them best if I show them to her while she's dreaming." Salley (1991) reports this ability is also used negatively by malevolent alters:

> Helpful alters are not the only organized units of the personality structure that can directly influence dreaming. In another multiple personality patient, Bryant, a dissociated personality claimed responsibility for recurring nightmares.
>
> In this nightmare, Bryant saw himself holding a gun sitting in a chair. Sun was pouring through a window in front of him. Behind him was fog. He felt that someone in the fog wanted him to shoot himself. The dream would end suddenly with him shooting himself in the head. While this dream was recurring, Bryant was experiencing much anxiety and sudden impulses to kill himself by leaping in front of cars.
>
> Bryant had no awareness of this dream's meaning until he became aware of a personality, the Poet, whom he had not differentiated earlier. The Poet had as a child received much of the abuse from his father. He spoke poetically with a morbidly depressed, existential flavor . . . The Poet admitted that these dreams were his weapons to depress Bryant and force him into suicide. (p. 153)

Retrieving Memories

Fifteen (65 percent) of the patients had experienced one personality, usually the host, gaining memories from a dream that have previously belonged only to another personality. In many ways this phenomenon is just like the dreams that any other trauma survivor may have except that these memories have been held by the alter rather than being completely repressed. This category can sometimes overlap category 7, dream maker, when the alter presents these memories intentionally. More often it seems to happen naturally as the patient approaches integration.

All but one of the reports of this category involved an alter's memories being regained by the host; one example was from one alter to another alter with whom he had been in conflict, resolving the conflict. "Eve" describes this phenomena happening to her final personality: "But memories did start coming back to me . . . and the earliest were in the form of dreams. During the first two weeks after the unification, these dreams intermingled imagination with what I would subsequently recognize as re-creations of actual scenes from my alters' lives" (Sizemore, 1989, p. 34).

Salley (1991, p. 153) describes the same alter, the Poet, feeding Bryant horrifying memories as well as manufactured images. One such nightmare was of being buried up to his neck while his father threatened to run over his head with a lawn mower, a fairly literal enactment of a memory which the Poet had experienced and Bryant had been previously amnestic for. The Poet succeeded in making Bryant feel suicidal following these dreams but not in actually making him kill himself. Instead the traumatic memories were eventually worked through and the Poet gradually became more cooperative and less suicidal.

Different Dreams

Eight (35 percent) of the patients had different personalities who simply experienced different dreams. This is of course quite analogous to their waking experience.

One patient had three alters who recalled dreams from the same night. The host had a mild anxiety dream about arriving at school unprepared for an exam. A male alter who had experienced much physical abuse had a fairly realistic post-traumatic nightmare about that abuse. A female child alter, who was usually the happy one who could respond as if the trauma had not occurred, had a dream with a castle and cute baby animals—content fairly typical of children's dreams. Another female child alter who had suffered much of the sexual abuse reported she had not slept in weeks because of terrible nightmares.

Integration in Dream

Very rarely, lasting integration of two personalities seems to take place in a dream. This was reported to have occurred for two patients (9 percent) only one and two times respectively. One dream was of a wedding in which only one person stood at the altar at the end of the ceremony. Another involved a fairly literal conversation saying goodbye, after which the alter moved forward toward the host and "faded into me like mist." The third involved seeing someone whom the host knew to be the alter but who looked exactly like the host, which the alter had definitely not, previously. With both patients, there had been much recent therapeutic work toward dismantling amnestic boundaries between these personalities. It is hard to say whether the integration truly occurred in the dream or was merely reflected by it. "Eve" reported a final integration with *all* her alters in an example far more elaborate than any in the present survey:

> This final stage of MPD integration was related to a series of recurrent dreams . . . In each sequence, I saw all of my former alters, ranging in ages from a toddler to Andrea, my last adult alter. And they were always in a templelike structure made of marble and tall columns . . . Each sequence began with my alters appearing ominously, one by one in the order in which they had existed, only to turn on me and attack as a group. Dr. Thigpen, laughing at me, encouraged the alters. But before they could do harm, Dr. Tsitos would intervene and stop the attacks by calling me into another templelike room with a view of lush trees and flowers and a green lawn juxtaposed against the somberness of a childsize casket on a dais in the center of the room. Each time, Dr. Tsitos would encourage me to give up my vigil beside the casket and enter the beauty outside . . . This moment invariably made me weep, disavowing any responsibility for the death of whoever was in the casket.

After one such repetition of this nightmare, her husband asks Eve, "Who have you not killed?" and she says, "Auntie Meme's baby." She did much work about her feelings of guilt surrounding her nephew's death before her final version of this dream:

> My mind's stage was set, therefore, for the night I said goodbye to all my former alters. It was early in 1977 and two-thirty in the morning when I awakened knowing that I had just had the most important dream of my life.
> At first I thought it was another of the dream sequences. But I quickly realized that this one was different. Dr. Thigpen and Dr. Tsitos were not in it, and more peculiarly, neither was I. The only people in the dream were my alters. And the templelike room that they entered was more beautiful than in the earlier dreams. This time it was in perfect balance . . . And these sisters of mine were beautiful, too. Each entered from the same door and proceeded in a curving line down a few steps to the center of the room. When they stopped, the line

they formed was also concentric to the walls and columns and steps, and my alters were in the exact order in which they had lived.

Then they turned, joined hands, and smiled serenely, as if all were aware that I was watching. But no one spoke. Their communication seemed spiritual. In a moment, Eve Black moved. She had been in line between the children and adults, but she left the line and went into a small niche amid the columns behind them. When she returned, she was bearing a small white casket. It was tiny, the size of a matchbox, and it fit easily in her cupped hands.

But Eve Black did not return to her place in line. Instead, still carefully bearing the tiny casket, she stopped in front of the youngest alter. They all joined hands once again, and Eve Black led them out through the exit. Their disappearance was orderly, ritual-like, and final. The beautiful circular room fell silent, and my vision of it clouded, as if a veil had fallen between the dream and me, the dreamer. That's when I awakened.

After that night, I have never felt or seen my alters again . . . That dream was MPD's last drama in my life. (Sizemore, 1989, pp. 123–128)

Conclusion

For most people, the state of dreaming is characterized by a degree of hallucination, amnesia, discontinuity with normal experience, and projection of aspects of themselves onto others that they experience at no other time. One of the most striking observations of this survey is that dissociative disordered persons experience much more of this dreamlike state in their waking life. These similarities of normal dreaming and dissociative disorders and the implications they may have for the etiology of MPD have been discussed in detail elsewhere (Barrett, 1994b). As category 2 (alter's experience as dream) results suggest, these subjects may be reporting some phenomena from a physiologically awake state as well as REM content as "dreams." For the psychotherapist as well as the dreamer, however, the questions of most interest concern the characteristics and the possible usefulness of the subjectively remembered dreams.

No characteristic of the dreams of these MPD patients is so distinctive as to never be found in those of other dreamers, but several features are mentioned unusually often. Most objectively identifiable are the high number of recurring nightmares and the frequency with which overtly sexual content appears in nightmares.

An admittedly more subjective category that nevertheless appears to be higher in MPD than in the general population is the rate for dreams about other parts of the self. As already mentioned, clearly people without dissociative disorders can have similar dreams but at lower frequencies, and the associations of other dreamers do not lead to anything like the ones described by MPD patients. These associations to other selves, forgotten recent experiences, and early traumas are much more distinctive than the actual dream content, which is unusual only in terms of frequencies.

Nothing in this survey suggests that dreams can be definitive in establishing the diagnosis of MPD, although the associations that arise in discussing them might. The situation in which dreams appear be most helpful is when one knows a patient has some dissociative disorder and one is trying to discover whether there are alters or similar ego states holding amnestic material. Once the diagnosis of MPD is established, dream content and associations can continue to be extremely helpful in identifying alters and facilitating communication among them. In someone with this diagnosis, any dramatic dream character—especially a recurring one—should be explored for its possible representation of one of the personalities. With patients who have identified alters but do not yet have easy communication with them, it is often desirable to suggest that they reflect on, and perhaps lucidly enhance, these communications with dream character/alters. Specifically asking if alters have "dream-maker" capacities may open even more direct communication channels, and this can also be enormously helpful in controlling the post-traumatic nightmares which the majority of them suffer.

The extremely different dreams that various alters can report emphasize that for dream work to be most effective with these patients, alters should be included in the questioning rather than focusing only on the host personality, as has often been the procedure in the past. Finally, although the spontaneous rate for integration within a dream was low, this phenomenon has great potential for intentional cultivation. In situations in which the patient is very close to integration, such dream work might serve much the same catalytic function as the more commonly used hypnotic rituals described by Kluft (1992).

Adult Trauma in Wars and Natural Disasters

The Healing Nightmare:
War Dreams of Vietnam Veterans

HARRY A. WILMER

War nightmares are a unique form of dreams. There are no other dreams like them. Freud did not treat any war neuroses; he despaired of explaining them because they were exceptions to his theory of libido and wish fulfillment. Jung, too, was pessimistic about treating them, saying that one had to wait and let the dreams more or less play out and stop of their own accord. However, when I asked Marie-Louise von Franz, Jung's collaborator, why Jung didn't work with these combat veterans, she told me that in fact he did and related this unpublished case:

A British officer came to Jung because of a war nightmare that had tormented him for several years after World War II. In the dream, the man is in his home and suddenly becomes terrified. It is night. He goes to the front door and locks it. Then the back door. He locks all the windows on the first floor. But the sense of terror and panic continues to build, and he goes upstairs and locks all the windows, but just as he begins to close the last window a grenade explodes outside the window. This dream recurs again and again during three months of analysis, until suddenly one night, when he goes to close the last window, a roaring lion appears and the dreamer wakes in terror.

Jung thought, "Ah, that's good. The instrument of danger has become an instinctual animal." And so it continues until finally one night, as the dreamer closes the last window, he sees the face of a man. Jung said to himself, "Now he will not have the dreams anymore." And that was the case. The danger had been faced and was his own reflection, and that could be analyzed (Von Franz, pers. comm., 1983).

Vietnam veterans' war nightmares are symbolic of our national nightmare, a hideous reminder of what transpired in that country. As one veteran told me, "We want to let them know what actually happened and what caused the Vietnam veterans to be as they are. It's going to be hard for them to understand how Americans could behave like savages when, of course, they would have behaved exactly the same way if they were over there. Yeah, that's the way they'd have behaved." The American people want to forget Vietnam, but we run a high risk of repeating it in another war, in another international police action, unless we face that nightmare horror— hear it, see it, know it. Having remembered it, perhaps we can then begin to forget it when we realize that what we are facing is the personal and collective shadow, and that this is part of each one of us.

No one who has not experienced war first hand can imagine exactly what it is like. I submit that the next most available way is to experience the war dream world, not as a clinical phenomenon to be reduced to psychoanalytic interpretation, but as human experience. I am not particularly drawn to the horrors of war, but neither have I turned away from them. Empathic acceptance of these horrors in another person may impart hope. Listening without contempt, depreciation, or condescension means accepting the dreamer and his dreadful images and memories. That, I regret to say, is a rare healing experience.

The Study and the Subjects

In 1980, I had the opportunity to devote one full sabbatical year entirely to interviewing and doing therapy with Vietnam combat veterans at the San Antonio Veterans' Hospital. A second year was devoted to studying the transcripts of these sessions and writing observations. The average interview lasted three hours over two or three days. For men in whom the interview stirred up symptoms and who did not otherwise have access to a psychotherapist, I offered therapy, which lasted from a few sessions to over two years.

Three hundred and sixteen men were interviewed. Three hundred and four of them described a combat nightmare and these were the subjects included in the present study. Two thirds of the veterans interviewed had volunteered for military service. They had spent an average of fourteen months in Vietnam with a range of two to thirty-two months. They were 54 percent Caucasian, 33 percent Hispanic, 7 percent black, and 6 percent other. Distribution among branches of the service was Army, 67 percent; Marines, 20 percent; Navy, 11 percent; and Air Force, 2 percent. Their mean age was thirty-four years old at the time of the study. At the time of the study, the diagnosis of Post-Traumatic Stress Disorder (PTSD) was not officially recognized by the Veterans Administration, so there is no reliable evidence of diagnosed incidence of PTSD in this group.

This is not a random sample, but consists of men who saw themselves as psychologically troubled and in need of help. It also should be noted that the interviews were conducted seven to sixteen years after the veterans had returned to the United States from Vietnam. Twelve of the men did not recall any dreams about Vietnam. It is unlikely that they had not dreamed of Vietnam, but only the remembered dreams were noted and the veterans were not pressed for dreams.

No VA hospital record of these men contained any information on their nightmares. Even more astonishingly, none contained any report of their Vietnam military experience. My research assistant reviewed all of the records with the same finding. Almost all of these veterans confirmed that their doctors had not asked them about their war dreams or war experiences, and they had not volunteered this information. The present study was often the first time they were recounting these dreams to anyone.

The Dreams

Although the combat dreams constituted only a part of the long interview, the veterans knew of my particular interest in this area. After the patient told his dream and elaborated on it, he was invited to give his interpretation and impression of the dream's meaning. There was an explicit assumption that dreams have meaning that should be ultimately helpful, and that combat dreams in particular might illuminate the veteran's understanding of his war trauma. Although I held a basically Jungian attitude toward dream meaning, I kept as unbiased an attitude as possible by adhering to the method of multiple working hypotheses (Chamberlain, 1965). We were dealing with vivid images, powerful narratives, and tremendous affect, so I relied heavily on the veteran's ideas about his dream and his metaphors and rarely indulged in deep interpretations.

Three hundred and fifty-nine dreams were collected which, because of their recurring nature, represent literally thousands of occurrences of dreams. Although the veterans were exposed to multiple war traumata, usually one event was so deeply ingrained in their memory that it alone constituted the basis of their characteristic dream, expressing how it had actually happened with attendant feelings. There is no conceivable way of checking exactly to what extent the dream images followed the event. In rare instances when it seemed obvious that the dream was embellished or partially fabricated, such dreams and "war stories" were not included in the study. With patients who were psychotic, there was little difficulty in distinguishing a natural dream from a dream flowing over into the unconscious psychotic process, its content mixed with delusions and hallucinations.

Classification of Dream Format

The manifest content was divided into three structural formats (see Table 6.1).

Category I is the characteristic terrifying nightmare of the actual event as if it were recorded by cinema verité. The dream portrays a single event in recurrent replays. It is the hallmark of PTSD and "war neurosis." Many veterans spoke of these not as dreams but as facts and reality. No such dream was remembered as having occurred in combat. In fact, when asked if he had dreamed in Vietnam, the usual response of a veteran was incredulous, "Dream in Vietnam! in combat?" Even if they had dreamed such a nightmare, it is probable that on their waking to the reality-nightmare the dream paled and was forgotten. Category I constituted 53 percent of the total dream sample. They are the only human dreams that define themselves in a completely predictable manner. They do not relate to the day's residue, the here and now, or pretraumatic life experiences. They bear no relationship to transference, which may partially explain psychoanalysts' general disinterest in them.

Category II or the "variable" nightmares contain plausible war sequences that conceivably could have happened but did not actually occur. In general these dreams are limited to catastrophic events of violence but may contain images of the here and now or the dreamer's life experience intruding onto the war sequence. Category II accounted for 21 percent of the total dreams.

Category III dreams are like ordinary nightmares, but their identification with the specific trauma or place of the trauma, that is, the Vietnam war, is always present. Their metaphorical or symbolic quality is mostly self-evident. They frequently have images of the here and now and follow stimuli from the preceding day which can be clearly identified or inferred. But such dreams are obviously nightmares, and the story, or the set of images, could not have occurred in outer reality. An illusionary and fantastic quality readily separates them from the other two categories.

Table 6.1   Three categories of catastrophic dreams

Category	Absolute numbers	Percentage of dreams
I Actual	189	53
II Variable	76	21
III Hallucinatory	94	26
Total	359	100

It is hypothesized that in psychotherapy, or in spontaneous healing, Category I dreams are transformed into Category II dreams and then into Category III dreams, although in clinical practice one might encounter the change from I to III and not any intermediary stage. If this theory is correct, the emergence of an ordinary nightmare after prolonged recurrent reliving of the exact trauma in dreams is a healing process, and therefore I call this process the Healing Nightmare. It is the psyche's attempt at healing. In therapy, transference enters into the Category III dreams.

Classification of Dream Motifs

Regardless of the format, it is possible to subdivide the manifest content of traumatic nightmares into broad but specific motifs. In therapy of other forms of violence, different narrative sequences might be inferred that are broadly anticipatory, experiential, and reflective. In the case of the Vietnam nightmares, there was an evolving story of war: anticipation, entry into zones of combat, approaching combat, engagement, alternate violent scenarios, return home, longing to return to Vietnam.

Dream motif was used as the term to designate the dominant thematic quality of the dream. Although there were images in dreams that related to other motifs, it was possible to determine a principal motif in 319 dreams (see Table 6.2). To simplify classification, where there were multiple motifs, only the two primary ones were scored. This occurred in forty instances.

The five ranking motifs were of war phenomenon in general, and the next four were principally dreams of killing. Attack, war, and firefights were mainly Category I, while dreams dominated by the theme of the dead were equally divided between Categories I and III. When death is the overriding motif, the dead (body count, corpses) are static in contrast with killing and dying motifs as images of action. Killing dreams are predominantly Category I. Metaphorical expressions of killing are by definition Category II or III. It is of interest that the dreaded experiences of being captured and tortured, which was a reality for only one of these veterans, was predominantly Category II—showing a strong reality hook and little resemblance to metaphoric nightmares. Being wounded is represented in all categories evenly. Nightmares of the dreamer's being killed or decapitated, by definition, must be Category III dreams. Dreams in which others are decapitated are listed under atrocity dreams which were limited to Categories I and II.

Dreams of killing others were more frequent and more disturbing than dreams of being wounded or killed oneself. Atrocity and mutilation dreams ranked low, suggesting that such events and images create less disturbance in the unconscious and more in haunting consciousness. The dark and archaic side of human nature presents affect-images of archetypes such as

Table 6.2 Dream motifs ranked according to number of dreams, showing also the number of dreams with each motif and the three format categories

Motif classification	Dreams (N)	Dreamers (N)	Categories of Dreams (N)		
			I	II	III
1. Under attack	47	34	25	15	7
2. "War"	41	27	30	10	1
3. The dead	28	24	14	1	13
4. Firefights	27	22	17	10	0
5. Killing women and children	24	19	18	4	2
6. Metaphorical	23	16	0	4	19
7. Killing enemy	22	20	14	6	2
8. Killing buddies	22	18	20	1	1
9. Captured	19	11	1	14	4
10. Somewhere in Vietnam	17	13	11	4	2
11. Being wounded	16	12	7	5	4
12. Chase and running	16	12	4	11	1
13. Home	16	11	2	10	4
14. Being killed	13	11	0	0	13
15. Animals	13	10	3	7	3
16. Decapitation	13	9	0	2	11
17. Looming danger	12	10	10	0	2
18. Shot down	11	9	6	5	0
19. Atrocities	10	8	7	3	0
20. Return to Nam	9	8	0	4	5
Totals	399[a]	304[b]	189	116	94

a. Forty dreams classified in two categories.
b. Approximately three dream motifs per subject.

the shadow and even evil (Stevens, 1982). In war, the archetypes of the hero and his battle with evil are dramatically experienced and exploited. Category I dreams may be the archetypal dream of war par excellence.

Examples of Dreams and Therapy

Examples of Category I Dreams

> I dream about my buddies. I can see blood pouring out of nowhere, and I see faces of friends of mine. Dead. I see battles going on and RPGs {rocket-propelled grenades] and tracers, and I hear explosions and see flames of napalm. Usually it is a lot of gory stuff. Dead. Mutilated bodies. Things like that. In the dreams I get terrified. They are in living color. I hear explosions and screams. Crying in pain. I don't feel it, but I sense the guys are feeling it. Once in a while I see guys I had contact with being hurt or killed. And dreams of getting even with the Viet Cong.

A specific event of violence appears in a recurrent unchanging dream:

> This happened at Meli Peak, Hill 101, where about fifty men were killed shortly after I arrived in Vietnam. I come in by helicopter. My buddy and I are about two feet apart in a foxhole on top of the hill. We get to know each other pretty good over three or four days. We have to stay in the same foxhole. We can't even get out to stretch our legs because of the sniper fire. I am talking with my buddy. It is dark. He lights a cigarette and all of a sudden his head blows off. His brains come out all over me. I wake up screaming.

Vietnam veterans were often labeled as baby killers. One veteran was haunted by this dream:

> I am on a patrol through a village, and this little kid five or six years old starts running toward us hollering, "GI! GI!," and holding up his hands. He has a grenade with the pin pulled in his hand. I shoot him before he gets us. I had to. He has more than one grenade strapped to his chest. He just blows up. There's nothing left of him.

Example of Dream Transformation in Therapy

Jim is a thirty-six-year-old Mexican-American combat veteran who had a recurrent nightmare almost every night for twelve years before I saw him. At first I saw him every week for two or three one-hour sessions, and then once a week for six months, and less frequently for two years. His nightmare was always about the same ambush:

> We are getting our gear together, and our briefing about the VC. I am point man for the platoon, and we go into a ravine. Suddenly there is shooting and yelling, and everyone is falling down and shouting or screaming in pain. There are seventeen men, another sergeant, and myself. The other sergeant and I get out of the ravine and blow away a VC in a foxhole and drag the guy down a jungle trail. I say, "I've gotta go back to the ravine." He says, "I ain't going back." I say, "I am." I jump into the foxhole and look down into the ravine. I don't do nothing because a VC officer is holding their heads by the hair and executing them one by one, and then he has shot them all and it's quiet and there is no more moaning. I throw a grenade and run back.

Jim had led seventeen newly arrived soldiers to their death. Nothing seemed to stop the dream. To cope with his agitation, insomnia, and nightmares, he had been in and out of VA hospitals and had resorted to drugs, alcohol, heroin, and large doses of psychotropic drugs. After two months the dream suddenly changed and, to his surprise and mine, he dreamed that he was the VC officer executing his buddies. Then his dreams became more hallucinatory:

> The whole platoon is after me. I can see the faces of the kids that got killed. They get me and tie my hands behind me and make me kneel on the ground. They put my head forward, and the sergeant cuts my head off with a sword. It rolls down the hill toward the ocean. After he cut off my head they let me go and I keep running and running, but I can't reach my head. I wake up in a cold sweat.

After the actual ambush, Jim made his way back to the base camp, and the next day they went to the ravine to get the bodies. There they found that all the men had been beheaded and their heads put on punji sticks and smeared with excrement. Some were mutilated.

After a series of dreams where I [Dr. Wilmer] appeared, the original ambush dream began to recur less frequently, and finally he said, "I still have the nightmare but I don't pay no attention to that bullshit."

Example of Transference Dreams

> Everybody is getting killed. Harry, they got you in the center of the ravine bleeding from gunshot wounds. You are leaning against a tree and crying for help. I freeze and wake up drenched in sweat. I change pajamas and

go back to sleep because I want to finish the dream. Now I am standing on top of the ravine, and a nurse is with me. She and I slip into the ravine. I hit the Viet Cong over the head with the butt of my rifle, and she dresses your wounds. I carry you out on my back. Sometimes in the dream your hands are tied. When I pull you out I wake up in tears. When it's you I cry. Before when I woke up it was always in a cold sweat but never crying.

Jim's dreams had changed abruptly from Category I to III. Jim was the hero rescuing the wounded healer. I appear in other roles in the dreams: "You were the commander of the battalion. The bodies were lying in the water, and you were screaming at me, 'Get out! Get out! This isn't for you! They're dead. Forget them.' " A far cry from the nightly ambush.

Examples of Category II Dreams

A veteran dreams that he pushes a Viet Cong out of a helicopter, something he had never done but had seen done. The obvious shift in the dream from the real event to what might have happened shows his unmistakable sense of guilt. He recalled:

Just out of Chu Lai in a helicopter, a Vietnamese interpreter was trying to get the NVA [North Vietnam Army] prisoners to talk. And he told them in Vietnamese to talk or we would throw him out. This was done by us. Still all in all it was something that was inhuman. He wouldn't talk. I don't know how high we were, but they kicked him out of the helicopter. He hit the ground. We were high enough to where I didn't even look back to see, but when we went down I saw he was literally split into four pieces.

One Vietnam veteran who had been involved in mutilation of prisoners' bodies and decapitation dreamed:

I see heads hanging on a clothesline. There are five to ten heads. I am taking them off and holding them by their ears, reversing the way in which they are hanging. They are always oriental heads hanging by their left ear. When I'd hang them by their right ear and move to the next head. What dawns on me in the dream was that there were teeth missing and that I am looking to see if there are any gold teeth left.

Examples of Category III Dreams

There is the stink of dead bodies. I am burying the dead—just the heads with big holes in them.

A medic tells me this dream:

It is very hot. I am lying on my stomach in this field of grass. I can smell the pollen. I hear a guy crying, "Doc! Doc! Doc!," and I crawl through the grass until I come to the edge of the road. I have to get up and get him. I'm afraid. I get enough guts to go across the road to get him. As I do I get shot. It seems about fifty times, but I don't feel any pain. I just feel the thudding of whatever is hitting me. There's blood all over, but I still don't feel any pain. When I get over to where the guy is, I see that it's a buddy of mine called Cobb who was one of the first wounded guys I worked on in Nam. Actually he's been dead for a long time. In the dream though he is just looking up at me, and his face is all bloody. He says, "Welcome home!" I wake up drenched in sweat.

The dreamer comments, "I can't sleep. I'm afraid I'm going to have this dream which I've had over and over again. It never really happened. It's not even a realistic dream. The only thing that ever changes is their faces. Everything else is always exactly the same. One of the worst fears I had in Nam was that I would be afraid to go and get those guys who were wounded. But that was something that never happened. I always did my job. I never punked out going to get anybody. They gave me a Bronze Star for doing that. So I did my duty but in the dream I'm afraid. When I got shot in the leg up here [points to his left groin], when I came to I knew where I had been hit, but I couldn't feel any pain, and I was afraid to put my hand down to see if my leg was still there. Then I began to feel some pain. The next thing I felt was my crotch to see if it was still there. It seemed like hours because I was afraid to put my hand down there."

A Special Forces Vietnam veteran began to develop nightmares twelve years after the Vietnam War was over:

I am in a goddamn firefight. People are getting hit and firing back. Explosions are going off. Commands are being given. People are crying. We are tangling with the NVA in some small valley. We could see them coming over, and we seemed to be moving toward them. My damn weapon jams. I pull the damn cartridge out, whip it back in and start firing again. I pull it out, put in a new clip, but the automatic gun won't fire. By this time they are all over us. I look to the right and see a monk in a brown habit on the side of the mountain looking down. His hood slips down, and there's a skull, and it seems like it is laughing. I am scared shitless.

Example of Dream Therapy with Nightmare
Identification with the aggressor is a well-known defense mechanism. Identification with the enemy, not as aggressor, but in a human role is a common

dream experience. In a sense it is befriending the shadow. This often involves a return to Vietnam. Dream example:

> I am living in Vietnam and putting myself in the place of the Vietnamese people. I am a leader in the village. I see the Americans coming to attack; we had nothing to defend ourselves with, and I felt that they aren't going to injure us, but I get my people and lead them to escape from the village. We had attacked villages like this one, and I know how it was.

I asked him, "Did the dream help?"

"No," he replied, "it would put me on one side I saw. I've been on his side now. I know how the guy felt when he saw us coming because I took his side. I've been on both sides. It didn't help when I put myself in the place of the man who was leading these people out. I wanted to get out. I knew that if we stayed there we'd go back to the refugee camp at Saigon or Da Nang, or something. Because I'm a Marine I know that we don't do those kinds of things, you know. In other words, murder people and stuff like that. They were civilians. I gathered the people, children, women and old men."

It didn't help him to realize the fear and terror he had inflicted, but rather made him feel more helpless; he did not understand how I meant help as in providing insight. The dream disturbed him. And yet because he denied atrocities in the name of being a United States Marine, it was his unconscious that made him question his role. How then to help him see deeper into the dream?

"Do you suppose," I inquired, "that there was any danger of their being hurt by the Marines?" He tightened visibly and replied adamantly, "No. I don't think so. That's the way I felt."

"You could see both sides," I continued, "and learn to anticipate danger and get out. You could identify with the enemy, not as enemy but as other people, and see yourself as an invader and leader of the people. Of course, there were times when they were shot or killed."

He bristled. I had touched on the shadow and taken a chance in contradicting his feelings. It didn't work. He retorted angrily, "Well, this is my dream! This is the way I felt. This is what I experienced. This is me."

I had intruded. I was an invader. I had challenged his truth. But since I was neither angry nor hostile, and I understood his feeling, I went on, "Yeah, but you saw the others too, didn't you?"

"What?"

"Well, in other companies. I'm not saying that there's anything wrong with your dreaming. I think it's very good and very right."

He seemed relieved and sat back in the chair. Yes, maybe others. And he responded, "Right. Right. That's true. Because I saw a lot of the . . . [long pause] . . . I feel like the way you're saying it, because it is true."

Now I touched on his own heroism and courage. Changing the subject to help gain insight, I asked him, "How was it when you stepped on the mine?"

"Like a Marine! Once a Marine, always a Marine!"

Once a man, then always a warrior, with the persona and shadow of the heroic ego. While his collective projection on the Marines was positive, so was his collective projection on the Vietnamese. By befriending the enemy, taboo to a Marine, he was assimilating his shadow, and it was helping him to integrate his war experience. In this understanding he needed another human being. Neither the war experience nor his military identification was a block to me since I had been a Navy captain during the Korean War, a positive experience, but we did not talk of these things.

The Wish to Return to Vietnam

Sometimes a patient will awaken from a nightmare and want to go back to sleep to finish it, as in the case of Jim when he had left me bleeding and wounded, leaning against a tree in a Vietnam ravine. He wanted to go back to finish the action. In the case of Category III dreams, the return to the dream world allows the spinning out of the dream metaphors. The return to the Category I nightmare, in contrast, allows only more of a predictable horror. Sometimes veterans want to do this because of pleasure in the killing and a sense of power, but also they had a conscious wish to go back and finish the job right, to win the war, to beat the enemy, which of course never happened. Return to the war experience by vivid dreaming reinforced in some men a fierce sense of pride and masculinity, confrontation with death, and an illusion of invulnerability. One veteran expressed this desire in these words, "I've had a real urge, a bad urge again of wanting to go back to something that is over and done with and gone. Quite a few guys in units like mine still want to go back, especially ones that were wounded, because they figure they got a score to settle or they never got an opportunity to finish their job over there."

A veteran who spent two years as a door gunner on a helicopter reported this conversation, "My brother said, 'What's wrong with you? You just got back from Vietnam and you want to go back there.' 'I don't know. I just feel bored here. Over there you kept on going.' "

Segment from an Analysis

A veteran whom I will call Sam sought my help but didn't want to be a part of the VA, so he saw me in my university office. He had a service-connected disability following extensive wounding when he stepped on a land mine. He was shy and spoke quietly and hesitantly. He tried to avoid being identified as a Vietnam veteran and had difficulty in trusting anyone, but over a period of eight months of weekly or twice-weekly sessions he was able to trust me. His placid, controlled persona covered a volcano of affect and smoldering rage. He became particularly bitter when, during his work with me, a friend suggested that he apply for compensation for Post-Traumatic Stress Disorder, which had just been recognized by the VA. To his humiliation, he was hospitalized for evaluation at another VA hospital, was diagnosed as malingering, and a hostile report was put into his VA record. This was the only time during my study that I allowed my work to enter into the VA records, not on behalf of his compensation, but to contradict the accusation of malingering for this brave and depressed man. His usual dream was about the time of his wounding, but the night before his first session with me he dreamed:

I am carrying a baby in my arms. I think it is my little boy. I don't remember seeing his face. I am inside this building trying to get shelter. WE are under attack. I can hear the bombing, Poom! Poom! Poom! I am scared and running and running, carrying the baby. I don't recognize the other people. I don't know who is trying to drop bombs on us and kill us.

All of a sudden I am running scared when I get hit. One of those things lands right next to me. I can feel the pain that the baby and I are going through. It is really real. I have this weird feeling like dying, man and the baby, and I say, "Oh my god, this is it." It seems like the real thing until I find myself shaking in bed. That is when I realize it is a dream.

The dream reminded Sam of the time when he was searching a hooch (native hut), and the instant he opened the door he heard a strange noise and jumped back thinking it was a booby trap. He said, "I didn't see it until it happened. A baby was lying on the cot." He began to cry. "I saw the baby. It still hurts. It was so burned. I knew the baby was inside the hooch. It wasn't my fault, was it?" Sam worried constantly that something might happen to his ten-month-old baby, who was jut beginning to crawl. He thought, "What is going to happen to him if I die? I'm still living the same nightmare [about the mine]. I told the physician when I was evacuated in Japan and he said, 'Don't worry. It'll go away.' Okay. Then it never went away and they told me to see a psychiatrist. It doesn't happen every night. Every now and then it happens. When I go through this [Sam hits the table with his clenched fist] like when I got hit, I hate the booby trap. It scares me when it happens. When I don't have these dreams I'm okay. You know what I mean? They seem like the real thing. And I think when I dream like that, when they seem like they are the real thing, sometimes in the dream I say to myself, 'Is this a dream I am dreaming?' "

"In the dream itself?" I ask.

"Yeah. Getting worse. I just . . ."

"Well, that's not a bad sign at all. That means that even in the dream you can question whether it is a dream, because in the most total dreams that question never comes up in the dream."

"I see."

"So that's a good sign."

"I used to think like that."

"It suggests that maybe you are half-asleep and you are kind of half-conscious, half-dreaming. Is that right?"

"Sometimes like that, right."

Sam's therapy took a positive turn around the time of a series of particularly violent episodes: the shooting of President Reagan; an incident in which a berserk Vietnam veteran opened fire from an RV (recreational vehicle) at a parade in San Antonio, carried live on television; and a series of gruesome murders in San Antonio. Dealing with this overt violence seemed to diminish the nightmare of the mine, which subsided into relative obscurity. Sam remained moderately depressed but was able to handle his war trauma with more control, strength, and understanding.

The question "Am I dreaming?" means the dreamer is becoming more conscious. And his initial dream anticipating his first visit to me was already a transformation of the Category I dream (the mine) to a Category II dream (the baby), symbolically the one (also) booby-trapped, as well as his actual child and himself. That major shifts can occur just prior to a significant consultation has been observed many times: I have reported an instance of a patient whose disabling symptom disappeared right after mailing his letter to me for an appointment. The spontaneous healing of symptoms and such symbolic transformations in dreams suggest the psyche's processing mechanism vis-à-vis medicatrix naturae, the healing power of nature.

Commentary

"Merlyn," said the king, "It makes no difference whether you are a dream or not, so long as you are here. Sit down and be patient for a little while, if you can. Tell me the reason for your visit. Talk. Say you have come to save us from this war" (White, 1977).

There is something intrinsically shattering in hearing and being with a survivor of a catastrophe as he tells his story. The shattering factors appear to be that the listener is unconsciously involved in the horror, which evokes the therapist's own shadow and awakens feelings of his own violence, murderous impulses, primitive thoughts and feelings. Of course, it is possible for the listener to deny or avoid listening to the pathos, and thereby be neither disturbed nor involved—not even there, really. Although evil is a part of war, so are great acts of heroism, altruism, bravery, and sacrifice. War also brings out the archaic savage that still lives within us all. Listening arouses in the therapist a moral agony of good and evil, black and white, healer and destroyer, right and wrong, with conflicted feelings such as attraction and revulsion, and hence intense countertransference. The therapy of violence needs bonds such as dreams provide.

C. G. Jung wrote:

> We could say without too much exaggeration, that a good half of every treatment that probes at all deeply consists in the doctor's examining himself, for only what he can put right in himself can he hope to put right in the patient. It is no loss either if he feels the patient is hitting him, or scoring off him: it is his own hurt that gives the measure of his power to heal. This, and nothing else is the meaning of the Greek myth of the wounded physician. (Jung, 1966, p. 239)

Hence the admonition, Physician, heal thyself.

In psychotherapeutic interviews with survivors it seems wise to be also reminded of Novalis's aphorism, "Every word is an exorcism. Whatever the spirit that calls, a kindred spirit will answer." No matter how we look at catastrophic violence, we are of two minds about it. When the listener hears the story of the trauma, it is literally in the mind of both the teller and the listener; and while in the latter it resembles the former, in each it is perceived according to his or her training, experience, and nature.

The collective feelings and symbolic legacy of the war are entombed in the Vietnam war memorial in Washington, D.C. There, over 58,000 names of Vietnam veterans killed or missing are engraved in four hundred feet of polished black granite. When you look closely, you see your own dark face reflected back at you, coming from behind the names of the dead.

Who Develops PTSD Nightmares and Who Doesn't

ERNEST HARTMANN

From the point of view of understanding and treating trauma, the presence of nightmares may appear relatively unimportant, as just one of the many symptoms of Post-Traumatic Stress Disorder (Herman, 1992; Everstine and Everstine, 1993). But for the understanding of nightmares and dreams in general, traumatic nightmares may be extremely important just because they are so different from ordinary dreams.

Here I will first describe post-traumatic nightmares and ordinary nightmares and summarize our studies of several groups of Vietnam veterans with and without Post-Traumatic Stress Disorder (PTSD). I will relate the nightmares from these groups to those found in our studies of civilians with lifelong nightmares.

On the basis of these studies, other sleep laboratory studies, and clinical experience I will propose that the post-traumatic nightmares of PTSD are not truly nightmares but a memory intrusion into dreams as well as into waking life. I will discuss the factors—both situational and personal—that determine the presence of long-lasting post-traumatic nightmares. Along the way I will examine briefly what these nightmares can tell us about the role and functions of dreaming.

The Post-Traumatic Nightmare

Some nightmares incorporating the trauma are experienced by almost every traumatized individual, especially in young persons—children or adolescents. After a severe accident, a fire, or the death of someone close, dreams dealing with the trauma in various ways occur and continue for a few days or a few weeks. Then in a few of these individuals the traumatic scene, or a variant of it, recurs in nightmares over and over—often for many years; these repetitive post-traumatic nightmares are a hallmark of Post-Traumatic Stress Disorder.

These long-lasting nightmares are most often characterized as a replay of the traumatic scene. Among the Vietnam veterans studied by our group (van der Kolk et al., 1984) the most common description was something like:

> I was right back there. Just the way it was. Shells were bursting all over the place. My buddy was hit by a shell right next to me. There was blood and screaming. It was just the way it was. Please don't ask me any more details.

The same scenes appeared over and over again in the dreams of these veterans studied many years after their Vietnam experiences. Strikingly, however, we found that although the soldier often describes the nightmare as being "just the way it was," there was often at least one significant alteration. For instance:

> They tell us to wait. They are in the middle of doing their job on the guy. They cut down his clothes with a razor blade, hose him down with a garden hose, and poke into the wounds with a stick and count the holes. They write it down on a piece of paper and they tag the body and put the body into a clear plastic bag which is tagged and once again it is put into another green plastic bag which is tagged again. It is all very professional. They stack them up three deep and four high. You go in; they unzip the bag and they ask, "Do you know who this is?" and one after the other I recognize guys. Then they had trucks outside. It was a very busy day. They were dairy trucks with the refrigeration units, with the same set-up as inside the morgue: the overflow. (So far it's exactly the way it really was.) When we went out to the trucks, I identified a couple of guys and in my nightmare then—I identify myself! At that point I start to run and can't stop running until I wake up. Sometimes I wake up by myself or sometimes my wife will wake me up.

This soldier relates that he had indeed had exactly that experience, identifying his buddies and so on, except of course for the last part of the nightmare where he identifies himself.

Similar examples have been reported by Wilmer in Chapter 6. In these dreams, what is being repeated over and over again is not simply the traumatic scene but the scene with an added element involving "me or him?" or "survivor guilt." What has burned itself into memory is the actual scene plus this terrible realization of "I'm alive; he's dead." The nightmare with this addition then may repeat unchanged for years.

"You've had this same nightmare a number of times?"

"Yes, it's exactly the same. I must have had it hundreds of times. Sometimes I have it when I am not even asleep, just sitting there daydreaming or relaxed; or when I think of Vietnam, picture it, see a movie about it."

The Ordinary Nightmare

Ordinary nightmares which my colleagues and I have examined in several research studies (Hartmann et al., 1981, 1987; Hartmann 1984) are quite different. The content can be almost anything. It almost always involves the dreamer being chased, threatened, or wounded by some form of a chaser or attacker.

> I was out in the street. I had just come out of a party. This gang of men started chasing me. I didn't know quite who they were. They got closer and closer. I felt someone put his hand on me and then I woke up terrified. I've had dreams something like this for many years. In my childhood it was usually monsters chasing me. There was almost always something after me. I couldn't get away. I usually woke up just before I was hurt or killed.

There is almost always danger of some kind to the dreamer:

> I was at my parents' house. There was a lot of glass all over. I was outside or something. I saw someone in the yard that seemed threatening. I tried to fight with him. Several people appeared at that point who were all hostile. I ran inside the house, locked myself in. They broke down the door—I could hear the crashing sounds. I had a gun and shot one of them, but I was outnumbered. They started to shoot at me and at that point I woke up.

The content is usually described as vivid and with many different sensations:

> I was swimming in cool water. It was all in brilliant color and I could feel everything. I felt the cool water and then the hot pain of a knife slashing into my arm; I saw my blood spreading out in the water and I could see slices of my flesh drifting off away from me. It was very real. I could definitely feel the knife and feel the pain in this dream.

"Have you had this nightmare before?"

"No. But all my nightmares are a bit like this. I'm being chased or hurt.

It's always very vivid. I can see, hear, and usually feel everything that happens."

This sort of "ordinary nightmare" can of course occur in Vietnam veterans as well as others, and may even involve scenes from Vietnam.

> The theme is almost always that I am being chased. Like I had one dream in which I was in the jungle and this whole mob of Viet Cong came out of the bush waving machetes and knives and something. I tried to get away, but I couldn't really move. They were just about to kill me when I woke up.

"Did anything like that actually happen to you?"

"No."

"Were you actually in combat in Vietnam?"

"No. I had an office job in Saigon. But I knew some guys who had been in combat and they'd tell stories."

In this man the "chase nightmares" with Vietnam scenes were simply a continuation of "chase nightmares" that he had had since childhood except that the Viet Cong take the place of the monsters that used to chase him. The theme was always being chased or being in danger, but there was a great deal of variation in content. The nightmare did not have the repetitive quality of the true post-traumatic nightmares.

A Comparison of Three Groups of Vietnam Veterans

Starting with detailed questionnaires filled out by 1,572 veterans at a VA outpatient clinic (van der Kolk et al., 1980), we studied three groups intensively by interviews and psychological tests (van der Kolk et al., 1984). All groups consisted of male veterans and were roughly matched for age. The first group included fifteen veterans with frequent nightmares (more than one per month; usually many more) that began during or after their Vietnam combat experience, who had a definite diagnosis of Post-Traumatic Stress Disorder and who had no other DSM-III Axis I psychiatric disorder (with the exception of Alcohol Abuse, which was fairly frequent in this veteran population). The second group consisted of ten Vietnam veterans who had no actual combat experience but were lifelong nightmare sufferers—who described nightmares beginning in childhood and continuing at least sporadically throughout their lives. Third was a "combat control" group consisting of eleven men who had severe combat experience—similar to the experiences of the first group—but had had no complaints of nightmares in the past eight years. All subjects went through three to five hours of psychiatric interviews and interviews about sleep characteristics and took the Rorschach, MMPI, and other psychological tests (van der Kolk et al., 1984; Hartmann, 1984).

There were a number of interesting results. First of all we compared the nightmares in groups 1 and 2 (see Table 7.1): group 1 (the PTSD group) had nightmares earlier in the night; the nightmares replicated an actual event more frequently; the nightmares were more repetitive; and the nightmares were associated with more movement, thrashing in bed, and occasionally physical attacks on bed partners. The content of the nightmares differed as described earlier.

Much of the study involved attempts to assess the current functioning and

Table 7.1   Nightmares in veterans: Differences in nightmare characteristics—
Post-Traumatic Stress Disorder group compared with lifelong
nightmare group

		Group 1[a] PTSD (N = 15)	Group 2[b] LL (N = 10)	p
When nightmare occurs in sleep cycle				
Beginning (11:00 A.M. to 2:00 A.M.)		4	1	
Middle (2:00 A.M. to 4:30 A.M.)		11	3	
End (4:30 A.M. to 8:00 A.M.)		0	4	<.05
Nightmare replicates	Yes	11	0	
an actual event	No	4	10	.0003
Nightmare is repetitive, almost	Yes	15	3	
exactly same content	No	0	6	.0006
Body movements concurrent	Yes	15	0	.0001
with nightmare	No	0	8	
Positive effect of medication on	Yes	8	2	n.s.
nightmares	No	4	7	
Positive effect of psychotherapy	Yes	6	2	n.s.
on nightmares	No	2	5	

Source: B. van der Kolk, R. Blitz, W. Burr, S. Sherry, and E. Hartmann, "Nightmares and trauma: A comparison of nightmares after combat with lifelong nightmares in veterans," *American Journal of Psychiatry,* 141: 188, 1984. Copyright 1984, the American Psychiatric Association. Reprinted with modification by permission.

Note: Where numbers do not add up to the total *N* in a group, information was not available. N.s. = not significant.

a. Group 1 (PTSD): Frequent nightmares began during or after combat experience; diagnosed as suffering from Post-Traumatic Stress Disorder.

b. Group 2 (LL): Lifelong history of nightmares; no combat experience.

the pre-Vietnam characteristics of the groups. Both the PTSD group and the lifelong nightmare group had current difficulties, but difficulties of differing types (see Table 7.2). The lifelong group had multiple problems in social adjustment and even some psychotic features. The PTSD veterans were less disturbed in those senses but showed some affective disorder (both depression and "flat" or absent effect), an extreme evidence of expression of aggression, and a sense of little control over their destinies, compared with the combat control group.

In addition, the lifelong nightmares group already had many problems in childhood or adolescence, while the PTSD group was very similar to the combat control group (see Table 7.3). This will be discussed further below.

Repetitive Post-Traumatic Nightmares Are Not Nightmares

From our studies of Vietnam veterans and other similar studies (Wilmer, 1982; Kramer, Schoen, and Kinney, 1984; Hefetz, Metz, and Lavie, 1987), the characteristics of post-traumatic nightmares and their differences from ordinary nightmares have gradually been clarified.

I believe that the repetitive post-traumatic nightmares we have discussed are not nightmares at all and should be considered a different class of phenomena and perhaps given a different name such as "memory intrusions." I will argue that they differ completely from nightmares in their content, their repetitive quality, their time of occurrence, and their underlying biology insofar as we know it. They do not participate in the "connecting" functions of dreaming, furthermore, and they tend to occur in different sorts of people.

The differences in content have already been discussed. The exact replay, over and over, of an actual scene or an actual scene with one important change, is unique to the post-traumatic nightmare. Ordinary nightmares are frightening dreams and, like all dreams, show great variation in content. I have interviewed many adolescents and adults without PTSD who report that they have repetitive nightmares, but it turns out that they mean the same themes or characters or the same settings ("it was that sharklike monster again, only this time it . . ."). They do not mean an exact repetition of an experienced event.

There also appear to be clear biological differences. An ordinary nightmare is usually defined as a frightening dream that awakens the dreamer. Laboratory studies have shown that these almost always occur during long stretches of REM sleep (Hartmann, 1970; Fisher et al., 1974).

It is recognized that a very different nightmarelike phenomenon called night terrors occurs during deep non-REM sleep early in the night (Broughton, 1988; Fisher et al., 1974). These episodes are associated with

Table 7.2   Nightmares in veterans: personality variables

	Group 1[a] PTSD (N = 15)	Group 2[b] LL (N = 10)	Group 3[c] CC (N = 11)	PTSD vs. LL (p level)	PTSD vs. CC (p level)
Typical current relationship					
Longterm relationship	14	2	11	.0003	n.s.
No relationship, changeable, or mainly fantasy	1	8	0		
Still lives with members of family or origin					
Yes	0	4	0	.017	n.s.
No	15	6	11		
Affective disorder (depression)					
None or slight	3	1	7	n.s.	.032
Moderate or high	12	9	4		
Tangential speech or running on					
None	10	1	8	.007	n.s.
Slight to high	5	9	3		
Unusual openness					
None or slight	12	5	10	n.s.	n.s.
Moderate or high	3	5	1		
Denial					
None or slight	10	2	10	.028	n.s.
Moderate or high	5	8	1		
Projection					
None or slight	15	4	9	.001	n.s.
Moderate or high	0	6	2		
Obsessive compulsive defenses					
None or slight	9	8	2	n.s.	n.s.
Moderate or high	6	2	9		
Hysterical defenses					
None or slight	6	5	10	n.s.	.011
Moderate or high	9	4	1		
Psychotic symptoms					
None	15	1	10	.0001	n.s.
Slight to high	0	9	1		
Extreme avoidance of expression of aggression					
None or slight	4	8	11	.013	.0002
Moderate or high	11	2	0		

Table 7.2   (continued)

	Group 1[a] PTSD (N = 15)	Group 2[b] LL (N = 10)	Group 3[c] CC (N = 11)	PTSD vs. LL (*p* level)	PTSD vs. CC (*p* level)
Flat affect					
None or slight	8	5	11	n.s.	.01
Moderate or high	7	5	0		
Passivity					
None or slight	12	0	11	.0001	n.s.
Moderate or high	3	10	0		
Preoccupation with mystical, philosophical, or religious ideas					
None	10	0	5	.001	n.s.
Slight to high	5	10	6		
Sense of control over destiny					
None or slight	13	10	1	n.s.	.0001
Moderate or high	2	0	10		

Source: Reprinted with permission from Hartmann (1984).

Note: N.s. = not significant.

a. Group 1 (PTSD): Frequent nightmares began during or after combat experience; diagnosed as suffering from Post-Traumatic Stress Disorder.

b. Group 2 (LL): Lifelong history of nightmares; no combat experience.

c. Group 3 (CC): No nightmares in past eight years; heavy combat experience.

considerable movement: they occur during an arousal, and they are associated with no dream content or a single image rather than a real dream. Recently it has become accepted that night terrors (though occasionally called stage 4 nightmares in the past) are not actually nightmares.

In terms of sleep laboratory recordings the post-traumatic nightmares of Post-Traumatic Stress Disorders are different from either night terrors or nightmares. On the one hand, they resemble night terrors in that they often entail muscular activity and partial arousal. On the other hand, they definitely have a great deal of dream content or at least story content, unlike night terrors. And they can occur both during non-REM sleep when night terrors occur and during REM sleep when most ordinary nightmares occur (Hefetz, Metz, and Lavie, 1987; Kramer and Kinney, 1988). Kramer and colleagues (1984) have reported that post-traumatic nightmares are associated with unusual irritability or excitability by various physiological criteria. And in fact they have noted in veterans with PTSD that the typical post-traumatic nightmare could be induced by a slight "nudge" or mini-arousal.

Table 7.3 Nightmares in veterans: Childhood and adolescent adjustment

	Group 1[a] PTSD (N = 15)	Group 2[b] LL (N = 10)	Group 3[c] CC (N = 11)	PTSD vs. LL (p level)	PTSD vs. CC (p level)
Appropriate relationships with girlfriends prior to Vietnam					
None or slight	3	10	3	.0001	n.s.
Moderate or high	11	0	8		
Close friends in adolescence					
None or slight	5	7	4	.045	n.s.
Moderate or high	10	2	6		
Enjoyed academics					
No or slightly	6	9	5	.016	n.s.
Moderately or highly	9	1	5		
Member of organization or group					
None or slight	4	9	3	.003	n.s.
Moderate or high	11	1	6		
Participation in athletics					
None or slight	4	6	3	.02	n.s.
Moderate or high	10	1	6		

Source: Reprinted with permission from Hartmann (1984).

Note: Where numbers do not add up to the total *N* in a group, information was not available. N.s. = not significant.

a. Group 1 (PTSD): Frequent nightmares began during or after combat experience; diagnosed as suffering from Post-Traumatic Stress Disorder.

b. Group 2 (LL): Lifelong history of nightmares; no combat experience.

c. Group 3 (CC): No nightmares in past eight years; heavy combat experience.

It is important to remember that the same post-traumatic nightmare sequence involving the same content can occur not only during various stages of sleep but during waking; at such times it is called a flashback rather than a nightmare. Thus I would say that the repetitive nightmare of Post-Traumatic Stress Disorder is an encapsulated memory that can intrude suddenly into the consciousness either during sleep (non-REM as well as REM) or during waking. It is not a REM sleep dream, although it may intrude upon a dream.

The chemistry of the nightmares, suggested by response to medication, also appears to be different, although these differences have not been studied in a systematic manner. Post-traumatic nightmares in PTSD are sometimes reduced by various medications such as fluoxetine, monoamineoxydase inhibitors, or other antidepressants. Ordinary nightmares are not helped by these medications, but can be helped (when necessary, in severe cases) by dopamine blockers (Hartmann, 1984).

There are also differences in who experiences the nightmares. First of all, it is noteworthy that people who report a great many ordinary nightmares do not report the repetitive PTSD nightmares. I have carefully examined notes from 50 research subjects studied in my previous detailed nightmare studies, another 50 subjects studied less formally, and over 50 patients with nightmares whom I have treated. All reported having frequent long nightmares (at least one per week) for many years—usually since childhood. It is striking that not a single one of these 150 reported the true repetitive nightmares seen in PTSD. (Who does develop PTSD will be discussed in the next section.)

This is not because these people had experienced no trauma, or because the trauma failed to influence their dreams. I have a number of sequences in which these research subjects and patients experienced trauma—a death in the family, muggings, attempted rapes—and reported how their dreams changed after the traumatic episode. These were people who reported that they generally had at least one nightmare a week, usually with changing content, being chased, and so on; they noted that immediately after a traumatic or disturbing event the number of nightmares increased, and the event would definitely show up in their nightmares. Some stated that early on they had one or two nightmares that repeated the trauma almost exactly the way it happened; but within days or weeks, the content changed—other elements appeared—and fairly soon their dream content returned approximately to normal. This sequence is similar to that reported by Stoddard (1982; Chapter 2 above). What seems to occur is a gradual combination or connection of the traumatic events with other themes in the person's life.

I have suggested before that a function of dreaming is to make connections—to connect recent material with older material or older memory paths (Hartmann, 1973, 1991b). This process can be seen most clearly in the nightmares that occur after a traumatic event—in which the trauma is "connected" and "absorbed" in the manner just detailed. In these cases the dreams return to their usual themes after a while, and do not develop into the repetitive nightmares seen in PTSD. The PTSD nightmare appears to involve an absence or failure of this "connecting" or "absorbing" process. The traumatic material (or the traumatic material with an addition of "Why me?" or survivor guilt) does not become absorbed. It is branded or etched into memory. It is "encapsulated" somewhat like an abscess, separated from the body by a wall and yet tender to the touch.

Data from our Vietnam studies also suggests that quite different people develop the two phenomena. Table 7.2 shows marked differences in the social functioning and defensive/cognitive styles of the two groups with nightmares; but, of course, it must be remembered that this refers to their adult states, after the trauma in those with PTSD. Table 7.3 suggests great differences in childhood and adolescent functioning as well, at a time before the group members' Vietnam experiences.

Therefore in many senses a post-traumatic nightmare is quite different from an ordinary nightmare. It may also be worth examining further who develops post-traumatic nightmares and under what conditions, as opposed to who develops ordinary nightmares.

Determinants of Repetitive Post-Traumatic versus Ordinary Nightmares

Looking over the data on post-traumatic nightmares in our studies and those of other researchers, some points are fairly obvious. First of all, it clearly requires a severe traumatic event to produce the sequelae of Post-Traumatic Stress Disorder, including the repetitive post-traumatic nightmares. Most of the veterans with PTSD experienced truly horrifying events, including almost being killed themselves and participating in the killing of others. In our cases, however, the most traumatic event or at least the one that became the basis for the repetitive nightmare involved a close friend or buddy—usually the subject's closest buddy—being killed right next to them. The soldier was usually right there, in a situation that posed the question, "How come he's dead and I'm alive?" Others as well as our group have commented that the situation usually involved a very close "narcissistic" or "merging" or "self-object" relationship with the buddy—a relationship that involved a temporary blurring of personal boundaries (Fox, 1974; Blitz, 1983; van der Kolk et al., 1984).

Thus severe trauma in this sort of situation seems to be a prerequisite for the later development of PTSD with repetitive nightmares. It is noteworthy that in our group of veterans with lifelong nightmares who served in Vietnam but had not experienced trauma directly (group 2), no one developed repetitive post-traumatic nightmares, even though this was a group one would have to consider vulnerable to having nightmares.

Another point not often appreciated is that the soldiers who developed Post-Traumatic Stress Disorder were very young when the serious traumatic event occurred. In our sample, we calculated as closely as possible the age of the soldiers at the time when their buddy had been killed; the results showed a mean age of 17.4 years. In other words, these were adolescents; these were not mature seasoned soldiers who had been fighting for their country for many years, but rather adolescents (legally, children) at the time the trauma occurred. This is consistent with the work of others showing that trauma has a greater effect on younger persons.

And finally we must ask the difficult question of possible predisposition. Are there some soldiers in severe combat who develop Post-Traumatic Stress Disorder with post-traumatic nightmares and others who do not (for instance our "combat control" group), and if so, how do the groups differ? In our studies the differences could in large part be related to the factors already mentioned (age and death of a close buddy). It turned out that the "combat control" group had been a few years older when they were in Vietnam. In this group we could not date a single traumatic event replayed in post-traumatic nightmares, since the group did not have such nightmares. However, we determined how old they were when they served in Vietnam and we asked at what age they experienced their most severe traumatic combat experience. In this group the average age for such an experience turned out to be over 21. Further, when we asked the combat control group about close buddies, these soldiers frequently answered, "I avoided having close buddies" or "I didn't want to have someone I was really close to get himself killed." These individuals were not only older but consciously avoided the specific situations that most often led to post-traumatic nightmares.

Thus it may be the case that anyone who has a severe enough trauma at a young enough age and a trauma involving a very close buddy may develop post-traumatic stress disorder with repetitive nightmares. Perhaps no other predisposing factors are required; nonetheless it may be interesting to ask whether the soldiers who developed Post-Traumatic Stress Disorder and repetitive nightmares might be prone to having nightmares in any case. If one assumes, as most people do, that post-traumatic stress nightmares are nightmares—simply nightmares which deal with a particular traumatic event—then we would expect persons who already have nightmares to be more likely to develop traumatic nightmares. As mentioned above, however, this is not the case, at least in our studies.

As I have discussed in detail elsewhere (Hartmann, 1984; Hartmann et al., 1987), ordinary nightmare sufferers tend to be characterized by certain personality features that I have called "thin boundaries." They are open, sensitive in many senses, easily hurt, self-disclosing, vulnerable. They often merge thoughts and feelings and sometimes have vivid fantasies that are difficult to tell from reality. Most of us have a mixture of thick and thin boundaries. But the lifelong nightmare sufferers seem to score "thin" in all senses. Everything "gets through." The origins of such "thin" boundaries are at this point obscure, but it is clear from many of our case histories that the condition is already present in childhood, perhaps even in early childhood. We have hints that there may be genetic factors; but early environment probably also plays a role in producing thin boundaries.

In any case our question now is whether veterans with Post-Traumatic Stress Disorder and post-traumatic nightmares fit this pattern. In addition to having experienced severe trauma, were they vulnerable to nightmares in the sense of having thin boundaries? Based at least on our sample my answer would be no. At the time we studied the Vietnam veterans we did not have the Boundary Questionnaire. But we did obtain quite detailed childhood and adolescent histories. We found no evidence of "thin boundaries" such as unusual sensitivity, vulnerability, painful adjustment, and artistic talents in the childhoods of these veterans; we did find these characteristics in the veterans with lifelong nightmares (van der Kolk et al., 1984).

On a global rating we rated 47 percent of the post-traumatic group as having a "good" premorbid adjustment, 40 percent as "average," and 13 as percent "poor." By contrast, in the group with lifelong nightmares, 10 percent were rated "average" and 90 percent "poor" in terms of childhood and adolescent adjustment.

Aside from these studies, I have also recently seen clinically four male patients with a diagnosis of Post-Traumatic Stress Disorder, who had suffered a severe trauma in late adolescence or early adulthood. Three were veterans with traumatic wartime experiences; one had serious civilian trauma. None of the four had thin boundary characteristics before the trauma. Two of them took a Boundary Questionnaire and actually scored thicker than average.

My tentative conclusion based on our study group and these patients with PTSD is that they definitely did not have the very thin boundaries found in those with lifelong nightmares. They had average or thicker-then-average boundaries. Perhaps those who tend to form thick boundaries—character armor, solid defenses, and so on—in a variety of situations might also be those who following severe trauma would "encapsulate" their experience—attempt to keep it walled off, separate from the rest of life. Of course, the symptoms—disturbing nightmares and flashbacks—indicate that the attempt is not really successful. The material is walled off in the sense of being kept separate from other memories, not integrated, yet under certain conditions it is suddenly and involuntarily "replayed."

It needs to be kept in mind that the research subjects and patients mentioned here have all been men. I have seen many women who have been victims of trauma—either prolonged trauma in childhood and adolescence, or an assault or rape in adulthood—but I have very rarely seen any who developed the specific Post-Traumatic Stress Disorder with repetitive nightmares seen in the veterans discussed.

In the last years the frequency of severe sexual and physical abuse in childhood and adolescence has begun to be appreciated. There is no question that such trauma can lead to severe pathology. The victims are frequently given the DSM-IIIR diagnoses of borderline personality disorder, various dissociative disorders, or somatization disorder. It has been suggested that a new diagnosis, Complex Post-Traumatic Stress Disorder, should be introduced to cover these many sequelae of prolonged early trauma (Herman 1992).

This is too large a topic to be discussed here. But concerning nightmares, it is worth noting that these victims of childhood and adolescent abuse often report nightmares among their many symptoms, and at times the nightmares include content relating directly or indirectly to abuse. These patients seldom, however, develop the kind of Post-Traumatic Stress Disorder (sometimes called Simple Post-Traumatic Stress Disorder to differentiate it from the complex form) involving the long-term repetitive post-traumatic nightmares that I have discussed. The differences may be due to the length of time the trauma or abuse was experienced, or the age at which it occurred. But there may be a gender difference as well, which perhaps relates to the fact that women have somewhat thinner boundaries than men in many senses, and indeed score thinner on the Boundary Questionnaire (Hartmann, 1991a). In practical clinical terms this means that women may be less likely to use the "thick" defenses involved in walling off or "encapsulating" a part of their experience; they are also less likely to avoid emotion and to avoid emotional contact with others—which is exactly what is done by the male veterans with Simple Post-Traumatic Stress Disorder.

Conclusion

Starting with our studies of Vietnam veterans, I have discussed in detail the repetitive post-traumatic nightmare and contrasted it with the ordinary nightmare. My conclusion is that the post-traumatic nightmare is a different phenomenon, a kind of memory intrusion—not truly a nightmare at all. It differs from the ordinary nightmare in content, repetitiveness, biology, and function. It occurs after an especially severe trauma, such as the death of a buddy occurring at an early age (adolescence), and involves a "walling off" or "encapsulation" of the traumatic memories. It is possible that young men (who tend to develop thicker boundaries than women) are especially susceptible to this particular series of events or type of nightmare. Patients with repetitive post-traumatic nightmares have different personality characteristics from those who develop ordinary nightmares.

Sleep, Dreaming, and Coping Style in Holocaust Survivors

PERETZ LAVIE AND HANNA KAMINER

Much effort has been invested in recent years in trying to understand the long-term effects of traumatic events on victims' everyday lives (Chodoff, 1963; Klonoff et al., 1976; Figley, 1978; Eaton, Sigal, and Weinfield, 1982; van Dyke, Zilberg, and McKinnon, 1985; Kluznik, Speed, and von Valkenburg, 1986; Goldstein et al., 1987; Hefez, Metz, and Lavie, 1987). But the literature on the "Survivor Syndrome" and Post-Traumatic Stress Disorder presents a lack of consensus regarding the prominent etiological factors in the development of the late sequela of traumatic events. Even less is known about the coping mechanisms that differentiate between successful and unsuccessful recoveries.

We have reported that well-adjusted Holocaust survivors who adapted to postwar life without any noticeable scars differed from less-adjusted survivors and from normal control volunteers by having a dramatically low rate of dream recall after planned awakenings from REM sleep (Kaminer and Lavie, 1991; Lavie and Kaminer, 1991). Moreover, the few dreams reported by well-adjusted survivors differed qualitatively from those of normal volunteers by being less complex and less salient. They also evoked less emotion than the dreams of both other groups after awakening. Otherwise, there were no differences in any of the sleep measures between the well-adjusted and the control group. Since it has been suggested that disturbed dreaming is at the core of Post-Traumatic Stress Disorder (Ross et al., 1989), we interpreted these findings to mean that a decrease in dream recall serves as a defensive adaptive function in these survivors. If this interpretation is correct, then significant relationships between the rate of dream recall and dream characteristics, on the one hand, and coping style and clinical characteristics, on the other hand, should be expected.

Design

The design of the study has been described in detail in Kaminer and Lavie (1991) and Lavie and Kaminer (1991) and therefore will be only briefly summarized here. Thirty-three subjects (twenty-three Holocaust survivors and ten control volunteers) participated. Of the Holocaust survivors, eleven were survivors of Nazi concentration camps, and twelve had spent most of their time during the war in hideouts or constantly on the move. All the survivors were free from major physical or mental illnesses, and were able to abstain from taking medication or other drugs for the duration of the study beginning at least ten days before its start.

Division of the survivors into those who had successfully adjusted to postwar life and those who had less successfully adjusted was based on clinical interviews regarding six areas of life: problems at work, marital and familial problems, social relations, somatic complaints, mental problems, and dissatisfaction with life in general. It should be emphasized, however, that none of those classified as less successfully adjusted had ever been in a psychotic state or hospitalized owing to mental illness.

All the survivors were interviewed by an experienced clinical psychologist: those with complaints in at least three of the six areas were included in the less-adjusted group. This group comprised eleven survivors (five male, six female) with a mean age of 57.5 ± 5.7 years. They had a mean number of 3.8 ± 0.98 complaints. The well-adjusted group contained twelve survivors (five male, seven female) with a mean age of 62.7 ± 4.4 years. They had a mean of 0.9 ± 1 complaints. This division, based on the clinical interview, was further validated by the Structured and Scaled Interview to Assess Maladjustment (SSIAM) by Gurland and colleagues (1974) and by the SCL-90 (Derogatis, 1977). Significant differences between the well-adjusted and less-adjusted groups were obtained for each one of the nine SCL-90 scales, and for eight of the nine SSIAM subscales (see Lavie and Kaminer, 1991, for details). In both groups, survivors had immigrated to Israel soon after the war; nineteen immigrated between 1947 and 1959. All were from the same socioeconomic middle-class group.

The control group included ten (five male, five female) Israeli-born age-matched normals (mean age 61.1 ± 5.4 years). None suffered from any form of trauma, and they were free from medical or mental illnesses. Their mean number of complaints was 1.1 ± 0.8.

A battery of psychiatric and psychological tests was used to characterize the clinical condition and coping style of the two survivor groups and, whenever appropriate, also that of the controls. This included a modified version of the PTSD questionnaire (PTSDQ) based on the DSM-IIIR, the Horowitz Impact of Events Scale (IES) (Horowitz, Wilner, and Alvarez,

1979), the MMPI (Butcher and Gur, 1976), the Byrne Repression-Sensitization Scale (Byrne, 1961), the Taylor MAS anxiety scale (Taylor, 1953), and the Ego-Strength questionnaire (Barron, 1977). The PTSD questionnaire was adapted to the present study by replacing the word "war" wherever it appeared by the word "Holocaust."

The sleep study included four whole-night polysomnographic recordings during which EEG, EOG, EMG, EKG, respiration and leg movements were continuously monitored. During the first, third, and fourth nights subjects were awakened for dream recall from all REM periods, starting from the second REM period. Dreams were analyzed with respect to dream structure and content.

Results

Details of the differences between groups regarding sleep structure, dream recall rate, dream structure, and dream content have been previously published (Lavie and Kaminer, 1991; Kaminer and Lavie, 1991). Therefore, only the highlights of these findings are presented here.

Sleep data showed significant differences among groups in the direction of more disturbed sleep in the less-adjusted group. They had significantly longer sleep latency than either of the other groups ($p < .0001$), and lower sleep efficiency index than the controls ($p < .01$). There were no significant differences among the groups with respect to REM percent, REM latency, and percentages of sleep stages 3/4 and 2. It should be also stated that none of the subjects was found to suffer from a primary sleep disorder such as sleep apnea or periodic leg movements in sleep.

All REM periods were also scored for eye movement density, heart rate and respiratory rate. There were no significant differences among the groups for any of these variables.

Dreaming

Rate of dream recall, calculated as the percentage of positive dream reports per total number of REM awakenings for each subject, differed significantly among the three groups. The well-adjusted had the lowest rate—33.7 percent; the less-adjusted and controls had 50.5 percent and 80 percent, respectively ($X^2 = 38.1$, df = 2, $p < .00001$).

There were statistically significant differences between elements of dream structure of the three groups. These were found with respect to dream complexity ($p < .004$) and dream salience ($p < .01$). Post-hoc Duncan tests revealed that the control group had significantly more complex and more salient dreams than the well-adjusted, while the less-adjusted held an intermediate position that was not significantly different from either group. The well-adjusted also had significantly higher scores than the other two groups for denial of emotions toward the dream ($p < .002$). For all anxiety scores the control group had lower scores than the two survivor groups, but no differences were perceived between adjusted and less-adjusted survivors. Significant differences were found for general anxiety ($p < .02$), and for three subscales: death anxiety ($p < .06$), guilt anxiety ($P < .002$), and diffuse anxiety ($p < .04$).

IES Questionnaire

The IES questionnaire assesses two characteristic post-traumatic coping styles: intrusion and avoidance. It was presented only to the two survivor groups. They were requested to complete the questionnaire twice, first with respect to their behavior at the time of the study, and then to attempt to assess their behavior during the first year after the end of the war. Table 8.1 summarizes the results for intrusion, avoidance, and denial and gives the total IES score. There were significant between-group differences for intrusion and avoidance measures, for both the past and the present scores. The less-adjusted survivors had significantly more intrusion of Holocaust-related

Table 8.1 Mean IES scores for the two groups of survivors at present and for the first year after the war

	Well-adjusted		Less-adjusted			
	Mean	SD	Mean	SD	F	p
Present						
Intrusion	2.20	0.63	3.43	1.25	8.6	.001
Avoidance	1.85	1.12	3.34	1.34	5.4	.01
Denial	1.88	0.62	1.96	0.50	0.3	n.s.
Total IES	1.98	0.43	2.91	0.66	7.9	.001
First year after war						
Intrusion	3.35	1.13	4.12	1.03	6.8	.01
Avoidance	1.97	1.20	3.50	1.29	6.2	.01
Denial	1.84	0.64	1.75	0.96	0.1	n.s.
Total IES	2.39	0.57	3.13	0.60	8.8	.007

thoughts, memories, and emotions. They also made significantly more effort to avoid Holocaust-related stimuli than the well-adjusted. It is important to note that differences in the coping styles of the two groups had already developed one year after the end of the war. The past and present scores were significantly correlated, both for avoidance (0.84, $p < .001$) and for intrusion (0.63, $p < .01$). This indicates great stability in individual coping style across the years.

PTSD Questionnaire

The PTSD questionnaire included thirteen statements describing typical symptoms of PTSD. The subjects were asked if they had experienced these symptoms immediately after the war, five to ten years after the war, twenty to thirty years after the war, or during the year before the study. Table 8.2 presents the mean number of positive symptoms in each group for the four time periods. The less-adjusted survivors showed more symptoms for all periods, but multiple analysis of variance (MANOVA) revealed significant differences only for the last year ($p < .016$) and for twenty to thirty years after the war ($p < .025$). The differences for the two earliest periods only bordered on statistical significance (immediately after the war, $p < .1$; five to ten years after the war, $p < .08$). A significant interaction between group and period ($F = 5.94$, df $= 3.19$, $p < .01$) indicated that the differences in PTSD symptomatology between the well-adjusted and less-adjusted grew wider over the years.

MMPI

MANOVA revealed significant differences between the three groups for the following MMPI scales: D ($p < .03$), PT ($p < .0001$), Sc ($p < .004$), SI ($p < .04$), and MF ($p < .03$). Post-hoc Duncan tests revealed that for all significant

Table 8.2　Mean number of positive symptoms in the PTSD questionnaire for the two survivor groups for four different time periods after the war

Time	Well-adjusted		Less-adjusted		*F*	*p*
	Mean	SD	Mean	SD		
Last year	3.75	2.42	6.73	3.07	6.7	.016
20–30 years after the war	3.0	2.22	5.55	2.84	5.8	.025
5–10 years after the war	2.83	1.90	4.55	2.66	3.2	.08
Immediately after the war	3.25	2.01	4.91	2.84	2.6	.11

scales, the less-adjusted had higher scores than both the well-adjusted and the controls. There were no significant differences between the groups with respect to the four validation scales.

Three additional scales were derived from the MMPI which assess coping style: the Manifest Anxiety scale (MAS), Repression-Sensitization scale (R-S), and the Ego Strength scale (ES). MANOVA followed by Duncan tests revealed that the less-adjusted were significantly different from the other two groups with respect to the R-S scale. They had significantly higher scores ($p < .0009$), indicating more sensitization, while the well-adjusted and the controls showed the opposite trend of being more repressors (Table 8.3). The less-adjusted also had significantly higher anxiety scores ($p < .0009$) and significantly lower scores of ego strength ($p < .02$) than the well-adjusted and the controls. There were no significant differences between the well-adjusted and the controls with respect to any of these scales.

Interrelationships between Clinical Parameters and Coping Style Scores

Table 8.4 summarizes the correlation matrix for the clinical and coping style scores. This revealed that except for the IES score for avoidance, there were significant correlations among the different clinical scales, and between the clinical scales and the coping scores. All scales measuring stress and maladjustment were significantly positively correlated with each other (number of PTSD symptoms, MAS, sensitization, SCL-90, SSIAM, and the intrusion score of the IES scale), and significantly negatively correlated with ES.

Interrelations among Clinical Parameters, Coping Style, Dream Recall, and Sleep Structure

Table 8.5 summarizes the correlation coefficients between the clinical measurements (SSIAM–total score, SCL-90–total score, IES–intrusion for the last

Table 8.3 Mean scores of coping style scales for the two survivor groups

Scale	Well-adjusted		Less-adjusted		Controls		F	p
	Mean	SD	Mean	SD	Mean	SD		
R-S	31.0	11.3	63.4	19.5	38	21.0	9.4	.0009
MAS	12.7	5.6	25.4	8.5	16.3	7.3	9.4	.0009
ES	45.2	5.8	36.7	8.2	45.0	6.9	4.6	.02

Note: R-S: Repression-Sensitization; MAS: Manifest Anxiety; ES: Ego Strength.

Table 8.4 Correlation coefficients between clinical scales and coping style scores

	R-S	ES	MAS	DSM-IIIA	INT	AVO	SCL-90	SSIAM
R-S		−.87#	.94#	.73#	.48**	.11	.85#	.62#
ES			−.82#	−.76#	−.35	−.04	−.81#	−.67#
MAS				.76#	.54***	.14	.80#	.53***
DSM-IIIA					.73#	.35	.67#	.66#
INT						.39*	.48**	.45**
AVO							.27	.37*
SCL-90								.72#

*p < .05.   **p < .01.   ***p < .005.   #p < .001.

Note: R-S: Repression-Sensitization; ES: Ego Strength; MAS: Manifest Anxiety; INT: Intrusion; AVO: Avoidance.

year, PTSD–number of positive symptoms for the last year) and the coping style measurements (MAS, ES, and R-S scores), on the one hand, and sleep measures (sleep efficiency [SE], sleep latency [SL], REM latency [RL], percentage REM, eye movement density during REM sleep, and dream recall data [percentage dream recall, mean scores for dreams' anxiety and dreams' aggression]), on the other hand. These correlations were calculated for the two groups of survivors only (combined).

Measures of sleep quality, SE and SL, were correlated with the clinical parameters and with the coping style parameters in a consistent way. Sleep latency tended to be longer and SE to be lower in survivors with more severe clinical pictures, although only two of the correlations were significant. Sleep latency was significantly positively correlated with the number of PTSD symptoms ($r = .50$; $p < .01$), and with the R-S score ($r = .44$; $p < .025$). Borderline correlations were obtained between SL and ES ($r = −.38$; $p < .05$) and between SL and MAS ($r = .34$; $p < .1$).

Neither REM latency nor percentage of REM sleep were correlated with any of the clinical or coping style parameters. Density of eye movements during REM sleep (EM), however, was significantly positively correlated with R-S ($r = 0.43$; $p < .025$), with MAS ($r = 0.45$; $p < .025$), and with the PTSD score ($r = 0.49$; $p < .01$). Eye movement density also had a borderline negative correlation with ES ($r = −.39$; $p < .05$). The largest number of significant correlations was obtained for the rate of dream recall and for the scores of dreams' anxiety and dreams' aggression. The pattern for all three variables was similar to the pattern of correlations obtained for eye movements density. Dream variables were significantly positively correlated with

Table 8.5 Correlation coefficients between psychological variables and sleep laboratory findings

	R-S	ES	MAS	DSM-III	INT	AVO	SCL-90	SSIAM
SE	−.30	.34	−.23	−.30	−.34	−.22	−.18	−.20
SL	.44**	−.38*	.38*	.50***	.35*	.23	.30	.35*
RL	.07	−.04	.02	.08	−.13	.12	−.09	.12
R%	.03	−.06	.05	.12	.04	−.12	.09	.00
EM	.43**	−.39*	.45**	.49***	.15	.33	.29	.36*
D%	.43**	−.54***	.40*	.45**	.35*	.40*	.39*	.42**
DX	.55***	−.53***	.57***	.49***	.48**	.01	.37*	.32
DG	.47**	−.34	.56***	.54***	.62#	.08*	.55***	.39*

*$p < .05$.   **$p < .025$.   ***$p < .01$.   ****$p < .005$.   #$p < .001$.

Note: R-S: Repression-Sensitization; ES: Ego Strength; MAS: Manifest Anxiety; INT: Intrusion; AVO: Avoidance.

SE: Sleep Efficiency; SL: Sleep Latency; RL: REM Latency; R%: Percentage of REM Sleep; EM: Eye Movement Density in REM; D%: Percentage of Dream Recall; DX: Dream Anxiety; DG: Dream Aggression.

sensitization, MAS, number of symptoms in the PTSDQ, IES intrusion score, total SCL-90 score, and with the total SSIAM score. Dream variables were negatively correlated with ES.

Discussion

These results, which demonstrate significant and consistent relationships between the rate of dream recall and dream characteristics and coping style, placed the dramatic decrease in dream recall in well-adjusted Holocaust survivors within the broader context of long-term adjustment to traumatic life events. Lack of recall was significantly related to a stronger ego, a repressive coping style, lower levels of anxiety, less intrusions of thoughts and memories related to the Holocaust, and fewer symptoms suggestive of PTSD. In contrast, frequent dream recallers and survivors whose dreams scored high on the anxiety and aggression scales had lower ego strength, higher anxiety, scored higher as sensitizers, and had more symptomatology suggestive of PTSD. They also tended to have higher eye movement density. In an earlier study, Hersen (1963) also reported weak ego strength and high levels of anxiety in patients suffering from frequent nightmares and disturbing dreaming.

The results of the clinical evaluation indicate that the less-adjusted fit the description of the "concentration camp syndrome" or "survivors' syndrome" (Chodoff, 1963). Since many of the symptoms of this syndrome are also characteristic of PTSD, a great overlap between the two is probable.

The persistence of symptom characteristics of the survivors' syndrome more than forty years after the trauma is congruent with reports concerning other groups of survivors, including World War II prisoners (Van Dyke, Zilberg, McKinnon, 1985) and prisoners of war of the Korean War (Goldstein et al., 1987; Kluznik, Speed, and van Valkenburg, 1986). Disturbed dreaming, sleep disturbances, flashbacks, and hypervigilance were these subjects' most preponderant symptoms. Similar to the present findings, MMPI scales of prisoners of war also revealed elevated scales for depression, hypochondriasis, and hysteria, a combination indicating a state of anxiety with depressive shades (Burke and Mayer, 1985).

More recently, Rosen and colleagues (1991) reported on a group of Holocaust survivors living in the Pittsburgh area who were found to have significantly greater sleep impairment than normal healthy controls. The survivors particularly complained of frequent awakenings caused by bad dreams. Of those contacted, however, only 25.3 percent responded to the sleep questionnaire, and therefore a sampling bias could have affected these results.

Most post-traumatic literature has focused on the phenomenology and diagnostic criteria of the syndrome or on its epidemiology and natural history, and very little has been written concerning coping styles and their efficacy. The results presented here show that the well-adjusted group of survivors was characterized by an absence of survivors' syndrome, by strong ego forces, and by a repressive coping style. During wakefulness, this style expressed itself in low penetration by, avoidance of, and distancing from threatening stimuli, and repressed emotions. In sleep, high sleep efficiency was revealed, characterized by nonrecall of dream content and a relative absence of nightmares. In fact, the well-adjusted group was very similar to the control group, with the exception that the latter had a coping style more balanced between repression and sensitization and a much higher percentage of dream recall.

In contrast, the less-adjusted group showed characteristic post-traumatic symptoms during both wakefulness and sleep. These were expressed in wakefulness by a high penetration of thoughts, memories, and emotions related to the trauma, adjustment difficulties, distress, and higher psychopathology. In sleep, they were expressed in increased sleep latency and in a high rate of anxiety dreams.

From the dramatically low level of dream recall, we raise the hypothesis that the dream repression mechanism plays a significant role in survivors' adjustment. During the sleep process, this mechanism acts as a filter that prevents the penetration of traumatic contents into consciousness, enabling effective sleep. Thus in contrast to Freud's argument about dreams as the safeguard of sleep (1900), on the basis of the present findings it can be argued that it is dream repression that guards sleep. This position is reinforced by the observed differences between the groups in dream content. The few dreams recalled by the well-adjusted were modified in a way that reduced their chances of being recalled. They were less complex and less salient.

As already noted, the well-adjusted survivors also displayed a repressive tendency in their daily lives. Throughout the many years since the Holocaust, most of them had never discussed the subject. In some cases, avoidance had been so dominant that even their close relatives were almost ignorant of their war experiences, and in many cases these relations were completely unaware of the fact that some of their own family members had personally experienced the Holocaust. According to the survivors, this did not mean that they had forgotten their Holocaust experiences, but that during wakefulness and in sleep, they consciously avoided recurrent penetration of the negative sensations experienced during that period.

The process of repression is common to a list of defense mechanisms, including denial, reaction formation, rationalization, and projection: its primary aim is to protect the ego. In fact, denial was the first mechanism described by Freud ([1915] 1957) as an unconscious defense mechanism against external painful stimuli. He referred to denial as a refusal to recognize painful reality. Similarly, Freud saw repression as an unconscious defense mechanism that excludes unpleasant and painful emotions from conscious awareness. The literature is ambivalent regarding the fate of repressed emotions, memories, or conflicts. Is the outcome of denial or repression always negative, and does it lead inevitably to neuroses or psychosomatic disease? Or, perhaps under some specific conditions, can denial and repression be considered as adaptive coping mechanisms? Psychoanalytical thinking has been very explicit regarding the negativity of repression. Denial and repression have been considered pathological, maladaptive, and primitive, and ranked at the bottom of the hierarchy of the defense mechanisms. This view has been responsible for the dominant approach in psychiatry and clinical psychology, which holds that mental health is dependent on an accurate and correct perception of reality. This approach has greatly influenced the development of therapeutic methods striving to force the patient to face reality, however painful it may be (Marmar and Horowitz, 1988; Danieli, 1988; Hackett, Cassem, and Wishnie, 1968).

Recent research has cast some doubt on the claim that repression always reflects a primitive, regressed, and disorganized mechanism. Coronary heart patients who used denial have been reported to have a better chance of survival and, during extremely stressful conditions, denial contributed to the reduction of stress level as well as some of its physiological symptoms (Stern, Pascale, and Mcloone, 1976; Breznitz, 1983). According to Bresnitz, denial and repression used as coping mechanisms are flexible, and are specific to certain aspects of reality which they minimally distort. Lazarus (1966) has also pointed to conditions in which denial could be a useful coping mechanism. Rofe and Lewin (1979) reported that repressors were better adapted than sensitizers to the stress of living in a border town in Israel that frequently came under terrorist attack.

Do the differences in coping style and dream repression between the two survivor groups reflect differences in personality style and mechanism that existed before the Holocaust, or differences in the post-trauma adaptation of coping styles? Although there is no immediate answer to this important question, several considerations lead to the conclusion that the differences between the groups do not reflect premorbid personality differences. First, the personality dimension of repression-sensitization per se was generally reported to be unrelated to dream recall frequency (Cohen, 1974). This may suggest that the repressive style of well-adjusted survivors is not a trait but a state-like characteristic representing a specific adaptive mechanism. Second, the fact that on the basis of their responses to the PTSDQ, the differences between the survivors' groups immediately after the war were not significant might suggest that the two groups had initially the same level of symptomatology. But while the well-adjusted gradually improved, the symptoms were either aggravated or remained static in the less-adjusted.

The finding that repression is an effective coping mechanism after severe traumatic events sheds light on the unresolved issue of treatment approaches to traumatized patients. Abreaction and catharsis, which are used to relieve the emotional distress of traumatic events, are traditional treatment methods (Nichols and Zax, 1977). Also popular are attempts to cognitively desensitize traumatized patients to past events by repeated and controlled exposures to elements related to the original trauma (see Shapiro and Surwit, 1979, for review). Our findings may suggest a different therapeutic approach that is diametrically opposite to these methods. They indicate that assisting patients to seal off or consciously attempt to disregard past terrors may have a highly adaptive value for the long-term adjustment of some severely affected survivors. We do not know if such an approach would be effective with all traumatized patients, or should only be initiated in chronic sufferers. In order to determine the techniques by which voluntary erasure of dream recollection could be achieved, further research is essential.

Dreaming Well: On Death and History

ROBERT JAY LIFTON

If we do not dream, then the day is not very good.
ZINACANTEC INDIAN SAYING

I am dreaming and I would act well, for good deeds are not
lost, even in dreams.
PEDRO CALDERON

Some years ago, when embarking on a study of Nazi doctors, I had a talk
with a friend who was both an authority on the Holocaust and himself an
Auschwitz survivor. I complained to him about the horrors of the material
I was uncovering, that it was affecting me a great deal, especially in my
dreams—that I was having horrible dreams about concentration camps,
dreams that involved not only me but also my wife and children. My friend
looked at me with a combination of sympathy and toughness. "Good!" he
said. "Now you can do the study." We smiled at each other in recognition.
He was telling me that my dreaming about this terrible subject meant that
it was entering my mind in some important way, that I was not remaining
distant from it but permitting it, however involuntarily, to connect with my
own internal images. He could confirm and approve, as a survivor, my
coming from the outside, so to speak, and experiencing a survivor's dreams.
And still further, he was implying that dreaming about these events was also
necessary to my intellectual—broadly speaking, creative—function in the
work.

Those dreams have by no means disappeared. But the dreaming function
is never simple. In doing the work and getting even closer to the material
(through interviews with both Nazi perpetrators and Auschwitz survivors),

I not only have dreamed of camp and other expressions of Nazi cruelty but have also had much more pleasant dreams, as if to counteract the fearful ones, some of them highly erotic.

The principle revealed here may be expressed in an anthropologist's comment on the dream patterns of the Zinacantec Indians of southern Mexico: "Dogs dream and cats dream. Horses dream, and even pigs, say the Zinacantecs. No one knows why; but there is no question in the mind of a Zinacantec why men dream. They dream to lead full lives. They dream to save their lives" (Laughlin, 1976, p. 3).

Or to put the matter another way: dreams have a more central role in the human imagination than we have realized. They are formative events and ingenious renditions of "the state of the mind"—its conflicts and prospects. In many ways an advanced psychic domain, they are notably prospective: that is, in their symbolizations, they can bring qualities of ingenuity that suggest, more than other forms of waking thought, directions in which the self is seeking to move and often will move.

Applying the paradigm of symbolization of life and death to dreams makes especially clear that it is not a thanatology but a psychology of life. Within this paradigm, there is a continuous struggle to evoke and preserve the sense of the self as alive, and to avoid the sense of the self as dead. In this way, motivation revolves around life and death imagery, often experienced, respectively, as form and formlessness. There is great stress upon the image as the link between nervous system and environment, but also as anticipatory in nature—that is, the image as what Eric Olson calls "schema for enactment"—an important concept in relationship to dreams. Combined or elaborated images become "forms" (or constellations)—and the term "form" takes on the philosophical meaning of "the essence of something as opposed to its matter," rather than the seemingly opposite popular meaning of appearance as opposed to content or reality.

II

Can we, then, speak of a historical dream? If all dreams are formative in the sense I have been describing, the category of historical dreams becomes somewhat problematic. But I have used that concept in the case of dreams of Vietnam veterans. Here I want to discuss dreams that took place in the small "rap groups" that I and other psychological professionals held with Vietnam veterans in New York City during the early 1970s. Most of these veterans had come to oppose the war and were struggling with emotions they experienced both in Vietnam and upon their return. Any dream reported was responded to by other members of the small group and would become a fulcrum for collective insight—and for connecting their immediate situation with their Vietnam experience.

For instance, the men often discussed their images of dying in Vietnam—and, indeed, their rejection of that fate was in many cases the beginning not only of opposition to the war, but of additional personal transformation as well. In one such discussion in a rap group, a veteran recalled his feelings while in combat: "I wanted to die clean. It didn't matter if I died—but I just didn't want to die with mud on my boots, all filthy. Death wasn't so bad if you were clean." Another man strongly agreed, and told of a repetitive dream he used to have in Vietnam, always with the same terrifying conclusions: "I would end up shot, lying along the side of the road, dying in the mud."

There was intense response in the group, as one veteran after another told of similar fears. And in their associations it became clear that "dying in the mud" meant dying in filth or evil, without reason or purpose—without nobility or dignity of any kind.

Then the man who had said virtually nothing in the group for several weeks suddenly spoke up, and everyone listened with close attention as he blurted out a story:

> I heard of one helicopter pilot in Nam who was carrying a shit-house [portable toilet] on his helicopter. He crashed and was killed, and was buried under the whole shit-house and all the shit. I thought that if I was going to die in Vietnam, that's the way I would like to die. I didn't want to die a heroic death. That was the way to die in Vietnam.

The group again responded with comments and associations having to do with filth and excrement alone providing the appropriate burial ground in Vietnam. I, in fact, heard no more telling evocation of what they had come to view as the war's absurdity and evil.

And from there they went on to contrast that filth, and the bleeding and bodily mutilations of men in Vietnam, with the "clean" deaths portrayed in various expressions of the American mass media. "In Flash Gordon no one ever bleeds" was the way one man put it. Here we may trace a sequence in a dream's prospective potential: the original dream in Vietnam provides a beginning, but still largely inchoate insight about the futility and ugliness of dying in Vietnam. That dream is recalled a couple of years later in connection with the group's effort to deepen a more general understanding of ways of dying and the nature of the Vietnam enterprise. The dream in turn evokes an image of ultimate filth—the helicopter pilot being killed and buried "under the whole shit-house and all the shit"—through which they can confront some of the most painful aspects of their Vietnam experience. That image, in turn, leads to a critique of a more general false American mass media romanticism, in which "no one ever bleeds." The dream was clearly the key event in the sequence—and the associations of others in the group maximized its prospective potential.

And a Vietnam veteran, Michael Casey, echoes this sentiment in a poem entitled "On Death," from a prize-winning collection appropriately entitled *Obscenities* (1972):

> Flies all over
> It like made of wax
> No jaw
> Intestines poured
> Out of the stomach
> The penis in the air
> It won't matter then to me but now
> I don't want in death to be a
> Public obscenity like this

And the veterans brought to the group other related dreams, such as a fragment of one by a former marine: "I was alone in a garbage dump. There was nothing but garbage all around me. I made a fire by burning *Life* magazines and things like that." The dreamer and the rest of the group associated not only to actual garbage piles in Vietnam but to the accumulation of dead and the ultimate "garbage" there—not just because they were dead but because of their grotesque, premature, and unacceptable deaths. Again, the group was groping toward the insight that, for Vietnam, "garbage was truth," as opposed to any more romantic claim to nobility or "victory." And that sentiment was again expressed by a stanza of poetry written by a Vietnam veteran, H. Kohler (1972):

> The Holy Army trampled
> In the sun of Christmas Day,
> But when they passed, the garbagemen
> Took all the dead away.

Dreams, that is, can propel individuals and groups toward the most painful kinds of insight—and in that very function and in the ingenious imagery with which it is carried out, they can also resemble illuminating imagery of poetry.

Among these veterans, I encountered what I came to describe as an "animating relationship to guilt." Feelings of guilt, of self-condemnation, could be experienced and then converted into anxiety of responsibility—so that the initial guilt became a source of reflection, commitment to humane principles, and constructive personal change. During some of the group sessions, men would try to make inner contact with a sense of guilt they thought they should but could not feel. One such veteran kept insisting, "I just can't *feel* any guilt"—despite an incident in which he saw a grenade he had placed blow a Vietnamese person apart so that pieces of the corpse flew fifty yards into the air—and that at the time he remembered "just laughing out loud." When others suggested that his laughter might have been a way of covering up his feelings, especially ones of guilt, he merely shrugged his shoulders inconclusively. But just a few minutes later he reported a rapid series of disturbing recent dreams, including the following three:

> I was riding on some kind of vehicle—a bus, I think—down Fifth Avenue. Somehow it turned into a military truck—and the truck got bigger and bigger, until it reached an enormous size. I was a soldier on the truck—and . . . I fell off . . . and was killed.

> I was riding on a subway—underground—and somehow [along the course of the ride] I seemed to turn into a soldier in uniform . . . There was a lot of confusion and then there was a battle with the police . . . in which I was killed.

> I was in Vietnam and off in the distance there was a firefight. One of the guys near me panicked and kept telling me he thought he heard something . . . acting very scared . . . I was so disgusted with him that I said, "Why don't you light a flare?" Anyone who's been in Vietnam knows that that was ridiculous, and that I was only kidding him—because it would be crazy to light a flare since that would locate where you were for the VC. But this guy didn't know any better, being new in Vietnam, so he actually lit the flare . . . There was firing and he was killed. [The veteran explained that this last dream re-created an actual incident in Vietnam, in which he had actually advised a GI to light a flare as a kind of joke, which the GI did, but no harm actually resulted.]

The group responded actively to these three dreams, emphasizing the dreamer's fear of the military and especially the sense of guilt: the idea that he had done something wrong and had to be punished or killed—that he was not finished with the military or the war and still had important psychological work to do in connection with both; and also the idea of the dream being a message from the underground (suggested concretely by the subway) which had to do with the question of guilt, contradicting his surface (conscious) insistence that he was not experiencing any. (These last two interpretations were essentially my own.) The dreamer responded by saying, "Maybe I don't *want* to feel guilty—maybe I'm afraid to"—perhaps because, as he explained, he was already burdened with violent impulses and feared that feeling guilty would make things much worse and somehow undermine his control over his violence. I had the clear impression that he was moving closer to a recognition of a sense of guilt, but not to the point, he insisted, of *feeling* guilt.

But then something else happened. His sequence of dreams triggered another struggle with guilt in a former Marine sergeant. The latter, a forceful man with an aura of masculine strength, expressed antagonism to the idea of guilt, insisting that "guilt is just plain useless"; that he had no reason to feel guilty; that he had no malice toward the nineteen people he killed and had killed them because "I saw my buddies dead." But as he went on, he spoke, in a tone of extraordinary pain and bitterness, of "one very big mistake" he had made in Vietnam, that of trusting someone unworthy of his trust to lead a patrol and of not having given sufficiently precise orders to this man, with the result that twelve of his best men were ambushed and killed in the most grotesque fashion—so that some could not even be found. And this former Marine added:

> You know, when you see dead men—whether they're round-eyes or gooks, they're all the same. Their faces are screwed up—they're all fucked up . . . I don't know why it all happened—there was the damned fool war—and maybe I just wasn't old enough to have responsibility for so many men.

At that point this man got up and ran out of the room, explaining that he just wanted to be alone for a while; but it was clear to everyone that he was beginning to confront guilt feelings of the most disturbing kind. At just that point, the other veteran who had dreamed those three dreams spoke up, now in tremulous tones:

> You know, I'm shuddering . . . I'm shaking all over . . . because what he said hit me hard . . . Before . . . we talked about guilt . . . but I didn't feel too much. But now I really feel remorse. I feel very badly about what I did in Vietnam— and it's a terrible feeling.

This sequence had much to do with the group's continuing struggle with guilt and with the effort to form an animating—that is, a morally energizing—relationship to it. But what I want to stress here, once more, is the role of dreams as the pivotal psychic force in this shared effort. Dreams seemed to possess something on the order of mythic power, of special illumination, that in turn enabled the veterans—as individuals and as a group—to make their special psychic leaps into the most painful mental terrain.

Sometimes the sequence can move, so to speak, from dream to dream. A veteran appearing at a rap group for the first time told of a frightening recurrent dream, in which an NLF soldier would shoot and kill him. The figure in his dream was the same NLF soldier he had actually confronted in what was, literally, face-to-face combat: as each of them shot they could see one another clearly. The veteran was wounded in the leg, and, without quite making things clear, gave us the impression that the NVA soldier had been killed. The combat incident had occurred a year earlier, but the recurrent dream together with diffuse anxiety had been intensified by two kinds of experience—the veteran's increasing involvement in antiwar protest, and his having been surprised by a mugger near his home in Manhattan a short time before.

In the midst of these associations to his dream one of the other men suddenly asked him, "Do you feel guilty about being alive?" He answered without hesitation: "Yes. You're supposed to be dead."

Right afterward, another veteran reported a brief but pointed dream of his own: "I was arguing with myself. Then there were two separate selves, and one of them finally shot the other, so that I shot myself." The dream, and a few associations to it, epitomized the survivor conflict: an inner split that is both guilty and deadly; a simultaneous transgression and retribution—the self murdering the self. It also suggests the classic literary and mythological theme of the double, in which one self can represent life (sometimes immortal life) and its replica death (or mortality). Above all it is the starkest of images—at the same time concrete and metaphorical—of one as both victim and executioner.

Here the two dreams in tandem brought the veterans to the very heart of their overwhelmingly painful, war-linked existential dilemma. It was after such a discussion that one man told of killing a Viet Cong soldier with a knife and then added softly, "I felt sorry. I don't know why I felt worry. John Wayne never felt sorry."

The dreams in these sequences are clearly formative and prospective, in their early illumination of evolving insight and action. At the same time they are historical dreams, in their intertwining of personal and social change having to do with the shifting currents of their historical era.

III

In my final exploration of a particular dream sequence, I must move to a still more painful realm, that of the Nazi death camp, the source of three dreams of a particular Nazi doctor. In this case, the dreams, in their formative and historical characteristics, suggest a moral struggle and a direction of partial resolution.

I interviewed one doctor, a man in his late sixties, for a total of about thirty hours—five full-day meetings over a little more than two years (Lifton, 1986). Dr. Ernst B.—not his real name—came from an academic family of some standing, was as a child and adolescent in considerable rebellion against his father and the latter's wish for his son to enter medicine, and succumbed to that wish only after his brief effort at becoming an artist ended in dismal failure. He developed a modus vivendi of being liked and being very adaptable in a variety of environments. Thus Ernst B. got along well with fellow students and with the Nazis who quickly came to dominate the faculty and student structures—his standing greatly enhanced when he became one of the winners of a contest sponsored by a Nazi science group to discover a local product to replace imported ones in bacterial culture media. Though not a strong ideologue, he was impressed with some aspects of the Nazis, and certainly did not hesitate to join the party when advised to do so for the benefit of his personal and professional future. There were many aspects to his being called into the Waffen SS and assigned to Auschwitz—he had himself experienced some patriotic fervor and requested a military appointment; but one reason was undoubtedly the regime's perception of his ideological reliability. In Auschwitz he continued his pattern of getting on with everyone—with his Nazi medical colleagues, and also with inmates, especially prisoner physicians with whom he came to have close contact. This latter I confirmed through interviews with survivor physicians in different parts of the world—and through his having been acquitted in an Auschwitz trial on the basis of testimony of former prisoner doctors, to whom he had been particularly kind in Auschwitz and, in a number of cases, whose lives he had saved. He got on, then, with his captors when he became a prisoner; and then with his patients when he returned to medical practice in southern Bavaria; and, for the most part, with me, during our interviews. But the whole process was not quite as smooth as it may sound.

Upon arriving in Auschwitz, which he claims to have previously known nothing about, Ernst B. was appalled and overwhelmed and had a strong impulse to leave (which would probably have been possible). But he was taken aside by his immediate superior, who turned out to be an old friend who had helped him in the past. This friend told Dr. B., in effect: "Yes, Auschwitz represents the 'Final Solution' of the Jewish people; what happens here is not pretty but there is nothing we can do about it; and I need you here for my unit [the Hygienic Institute, which was outside the ordinary hierarchy of camp medical officers] and if you stay it will strengthen us greatly and we will be able to keep our hands completely clean." Dr. B. stayed.

A few days after his arrival in Auschwitz he looked out a window early in the evening and saw prisoners returning from their work outside the camp, marching double-time six abreast, and thought he saw among them a former classmate from his old Gymnasium (secondary school), named Simon Cohen. Ernst B. ran outside to find him, but the prisoners had already disappeared into their blocks. For the next couple of days he went desperately about the camp trying to locate Simon Cohen—and in the process learned at first hand about the killing and working arrangements at Auschwitz and about the status of Jews as nonpeople. At one point he went running into the office area he was assigned to and asked the prisoner physician working there whether he knew a Simon Cohen in the camp. The answer came back cautiously that "tens, thousands of Jews . . . come through," that "many of them were named Cohen," and that it would be impossible to find any such person. The prisoner physician answered that way, as I confirmed in a later interview with him, because he believed that the attempt to find such a person was hopeless and could be harmful both to him and to Dr. B. himself. And even though the Nazi doctor seemed compassionate, the prisoner doctor might have been worried about the intention of a man in an SS uniform inquiring about a Jewish prisoner. In the course of his fruitless inquiries, Dr. B. saw more clearly the labyrinthine, murderous nature of Auschwitz.

Later he came to wonder whether he had really seen Cohen—or whether it had been an illusion or perhaps even a dream. In any case, he immediately began to have a series of dreams about the incident that were really one basic repetitive dream with many variations. In every dream Simon Cohen's face would appear:

> He was always a very attractive young man. And now [in the dream] he had really deteriorated . . . And he looked at me with a reproachful, beseeching expression . . . sort of saying, "It can't be possible that you stand there and I am . . . [like this] . . ." or more like a disappointed expression: "How can you belong to those people? That can't be you." (Lifton, 1986, p. 306)

In telling me about these dreams, Ernst B. further explained that he and Cohen had been special friends during the early 1930s (the dream had occurred in about May 1943), having in common their mutual lack of interest in schoolwork and enjoyment of drinking alcohol. They took long bicycle trips together during vacations and remained personally close despite living quite far from one another and despite the already extensive general anti-Semitism.

Dr. B. had the dream most frequently after drinking and associated it at the time with what he called the "especially bad situation" in which he found himself in Auschwitz and with "my problem: Is it right to stay, or would it be better to leave?" On the side of staying was his feeling that "I could do something good here, . . . something humane."

And, indeed, the dream could be understood as a call to residual inner humanity—just as he recalled feeling, at the time he thought he saw Simon Cohen among the prisoners, that "if I can find him, I can make some kind of human contact."

These specific dream images are important: the identification with the "beaten down" or macerated face of the victim, who as a close school friend and a central character in the dream represented an important part of Ernst B.'s own self-process. And the pleading, reproachful look, together with disbelief—in effect, "That can't be you standing among them"—this representing B.'s own sense of unreality in, and partial removal from, the overall Auschwitz situation. And perhaps the formative aspect in the dream lies exactly there—in its consistency with his subsequent capacity to divide himself to the extent that he was, so to speak, both: one of them (them being the Nazi victimizers) and not one of them (in the sense of standing apart from them sufficiently to be a consistent source of help to prisoners— so much so that a later historian of Auschwitz described him as "a human being in an SS uniform"). The dream is also, of course, replete with historical imagery—concerning Germans and Jews, and the historical transformations that turn friends into enemies.

One could argue, of course, that Ernst B.'s decision to remain in Auschwitz instead of leaving violated that prospective dream message of calling forth residual humanity. And one could support this argument by Dr. B.'s own insistence to me that, despite the extent to which he was appreciated and even admired by the inmates, he belonged, after all, to the group of Nazi doctors—to the Auschwitz camp structure. Toward the end of our interviews, he expressed for the first time a certain nostalgia for what he considered a few positive features of the Nazi era. He did not cease, that is, being one of "them."

But it is also true that, during his time in Auschwitz, he was unique in his consideration for inmates, especially those prisoner doctors who worked in his unit—taking personal risks to help them in such small (but, in Auschwitz, very big indeed) matters as enabling husbands and wives among prisoners to meet and carrying letters and messages from inmates to people on the outside. So, at least in that sense, the dream's prospective call to personal humanity was by no means totally ignored. And that call had its greatest effect when it was most needed—during his nineteen months at Auschwitz—after which it did not entirely disappear but became much more infrequent.

A second dream Ernst B. described to me also emerged from the Auschwitz situation—though he insisted he never had the actual dream in Auschwitz, but only years later upon returning to his home in Germany. It concerned a young Jewish laboratory assistant who had worked at the Hygienic Institute. In the dream he fled with her from Auschwitz to nearby mountains, where they joined a group of Polish Partisans (anti-Nazi underground fighters). That was the central theme of a recurrent dream that he had in a number of different versions. Dr. B. gave me the impression that he had a special relationship to this dream, a kind of proprietary affection. He introduced it to me, in response to my asking about dreams other than the one about Cohen, by saying, "Perhaps there is one other dream, . . . a purely, deeply psychological question perhaps. Maybe it is a key. I can't exactly explain it."

And when describing the dream's few details, he quickly added, "That is the only other Auschwitz dream that has remained. I'm sure that there was no erotic background to this. In fact, . . . to the contrary."

An erotic component is of course very much present, but in a particular way. In discussing the dream, Dr. B. explained that this Jewish laboratory assistant had a certain artistic talent, which SS men took advantage of by having her make drawings from photographs, which they (the SS men) would then try to sell or make some other use of. All that, he explained, was part of the prevailing corruption in Auschwitz: everyone there was likely to be corrupted in some way: everyone, as Ernst B. put it in the German idiom, had "dirt on his walking stick" (Dreck am Stecken). And everyone knew about everyone else's "dirt."

Although to Ernst B. the girl "seemed so young and so primitive," she had an uncanny ability to vary the style of each drawing according to what she perceived the taste of individual SS men: drawing "simple red-cheeked" pictures for simple SS men and more delicate, aesthetically sophisticated pictures for more sensitive SS officers like himself—and, in fact, she did draw for him what he considered a "beautiful picture" of his wife and young children from a photograph he provided. He became preoccupied with this seeming dichotomy in her, suspecting that "she just fooled around during the day and then took the whole thing to an artist in her block every evening": "I just couldn't believe that this girl would be able to do these kinds of things by herself"—adding that precisely that kind of suspicion was "in Auschwitz the normal reaction." Eventually he became convinced that she did indeed do all the drawings herself; though when he further observed her and spoke to her, he was "again and again surprised at how primitive she actually was," and concluded that "she was a primitive, naturally talented person." The mountains to which they flee in the dream were near the area from which she had come; and in one conversation they had when he spoke of his possibly taking a drive into that area, she warned him not to because there were likely to be too many partisans there.

He managed to take the picture with him from Auschwitz and to retain it despite his subsequent years of custody and trial. Upon returning to medical practice, he first hung it in his office and later in his bedroom. But he eventually, as he explained, "took it out of the room to get rid of the dream"—though the dream persisted after he had removed the picture. As we talked about all this, he had his wife bring in the picture, which he looked at affectionately; and when I asked whether he still valued it very much, he answered, "Yes, of course—I had it in Auschwitz the whole time, you understand. And later I kept it here." He added that now, with more detachment, he could say that it was "really a very nice picture but close to being kitsch"—a word that usually means "shoddy, pretentious, and without artistic merit." But Dr. B. qualified that judgment, and somewhat defended the picture, by adding, "Many good artistic things, including Goethe's Faust, always move close to kitsch."

And he went on to associate the picture further with "this emotion I had in Auschwitz . . . my bad feelings to my family"—what he had described as a "bad conscience" toward his wife for his having initiated the steps (asking for military duty) that led him to be assigned to Auschwitz—so that when he managed to get away from Auschwitz briefly to visit his wife, "I had a good feeling and a bad feeling . . . I was of course very happy to be there but I hoped to make things good again."

Ernst B. was right in seeing the dream as a special psychological key, as it contains virtually every conflict and contradiction he experienced in Auschwitz. At the heart of the dream, I believe, is a doubling, rather than a splitting, of the self: that is, Dr. B had two virtually autonomous selves: the one, the older, relatively humane self of healer and family man; the other, the Auschwitz self (with its numbed adaptation and capacity to witness or participate in mass murder and continuous brutality). Characteristically, the older, more humane self was reinforced by visits to his wife and family, but his guilt toward his wife suggests that he was less able than many former Nazi doctors to carry through successfully this doubling process. Indeed, the image of affectionate and compassionate flight with the young Jewish inmate is a way of reconnecting erotic feelings with human acts, all within the context of Auschwitz itself—and, in that sense, is a rejection of the doubling process and an assertion of at least prospective wholeness. But the dream also contains his profound doubts about himself, while in Auschwitz and before, concerning authenticity (his discussions of kitsch and of the "primitive"—the latter with a strong element of German and Nazi worship of what is ostensibly primitive and natural) and his concern about corruption and corruptibility (his own "dirt on his walking stick") in Auschwitz particularly. I believe one reason he values this picture so much is its association for him—via the dream and his perception of the Jewish girl—with a struggle toward authenticity and humanity. And that struggle is the dream's prospective thrust: his message is to "go over to the other side"—to the side of those who would kill the killers, to the side of love and life enhancement. And that prospective message has to do once more with extreme historical currents engulfing Germans, Jews, Poles, and in important ways all others.

I cannot say that Ernst B. has, in his postwar existence, fully embraced this prospective message—but he has gone much further than most former Nazi doctors in that direction.

Ernst B. told me of a third dream—really a merest fragment of a dream, not even a clear image. But it is nonetheless important to us.

When held for trial after the war, he learned that the authorities had in their possession what he called "a room full of files dealing with the routine work of the [Hygienic] Institute"—his own working place in Auschwitz. At the judge's request, he agreed to study the materials and from them make a scientific projection of the relationship between caloric intake permitted the prisoners, the work they did, and the length of average survival of those not subjected to the gas chambers. The impact of the experience was profound—so much so that he stuttered somewhat in conveying it and mentioning his dreams:

> That room with all those files and the computations that occupied me and all that, . . . I still dream of it sometimes, somehow . . . Whenever I have a dream that is related somehow to Auschwitz, those papers will appear too.

He worked methodically, over months, with the files, which were remarkably detailed, and eventually demonstrated that the Auschwitz near-starvation diet created a general life expectancy of three months. He knew that these findings were not in themselves of the greatest importance, but rather that something else was:

> What is important is that for months I was alone in a room [a cell] with these files . . . And through dealing with these papers I established a special contact with Auschwitz . . . It was an absolute reflection [of what went on in Auschwitz]. All of a sudden I was in this room confronting the problem and the memory in a different way and not under pressure to suppress things in the face of these confrontations—so one could deal with these thoughts without constraint. And that was very good . . . You are dealing with the experience all the time with these files, so you couldn't waste energy in trying to forget.

He contrasted his approach to Auschwitz with my own:

> It is a completely different route to the camp itself. You are starting out now by identifying these things (or approaching this subject) on a theoretical basis—and you have no practical experience. And I started out on the practical side and later came to the theoretical point of view. (Lifton, 1986, chap. 16)

We may say that he, like most other former Nazis, has never been able to confront fully the directly human consequences of the Nazi project. But in undertaking this study, he could abstract those consequences—the deaths and the suffering—in a way that nonetheless brought them closer to his awareness. Of great importance was that he conducted the study as a physician and prepared from it what was essentially a medical-scientific paper. He could at least touch some of the Auschwitz cruelty and in the process reclaim more of his pre-Auschwitz self.

Significantly, he bracketed this overall experience with his earlier adaptation to Auschwitz—the transition into Auschwitz, during which he consciously sought to integrate himself with his colleagues and the overall camp structure. This was, so to speak, his transition out of Auschwitz, during which he was now reintegrating himself—under the reversed circumstances of being himself a prisoner—with the non-Auschwitz, the anti-Auschwitz world. The dream fragment of the papers and files represents the burden of having been part of Auschwitz—the prospective message here that of confronting the experience, evaluating it, putting it in terms of human beings, applying to it humane medical standards.

IV

A few conclusions—or rather, visions or dreams of conclusions. Let me state three principles:

> First, the dream is prospective; it prefigures psychological and frequently behavioral functions. More than that, it is propulsive—it helps propel one toward certain kinds of experience.

> Second, the dream has an immediate or proximate psychological level, where it records and contributes to the self's struggles toward vitality—toward connection, integrity, and movement.

> Third, the dream operates also at an ultimate level: it suggests conflicts and directions in the self's larger historical relationships, and in efforts to maintain or recast forms of symbolic immortality.

Thus the dreams of Vietnam veterans help propel them toward painful insights and hard-won individual change, toward a new vitality based on experiencing and moving beyond guilt, and an equally new world view with shifting relations to American historical currents. And the dreams of the Nazi doctor prodded him toward earlier standards of compassion and integrity amid murder and corruption (the dreams also, it must be added, had the more dubious function of helping him to adapt to those Auschwitz conditions), and ultimately toward confronting what Auschwitz actually had been.

If a dream can do all this—encompassing a trinity of propulsive psychic power, renewed vitality, and questions about ultimate concerns—then it must have even greater power and significance than we had imagined.

Indeed, my claim here is that the dream has a central, life-enhancing, evolutionary function. We can thus begin to view the dream less as a "cover-up" and more as an "opening-out" of the psychic domain that is both close to organicity and unique in imaginative reach. For dreams permit a perpetual dialectic between the most "primitive" psychic fragments and the most "enlightened" frontier of the formative imagination. Within this dialogue the dream flashes its powerful and yet fluid symbolizations before us, ours for the using according to the mind's readiness and capacity. And the dream's ingenious symbolizations are highly subversive to the psychological status quo. This is so because of the sensitivity of the dream process to the contradictions and vulnerabilities of existing psychic forms, which is what we mean when we say that dreams reveal inner conflicts. It is the reason dreams are so disturbing.

Thus in the dream we find, most profoundly, both clue to and expression of the human capacity for good and evil—for holding visions, for prospective imagination. More than ever, we must dream well if we are to confront forces threatening to annihilate us, and if we are to further the wonderful, dangerous, and always visionary human adventure.

The Collective Nightmare of Central American Refugees

ADRIANNE ARON

A Dream in Two Scenes

Scene One

"There are armed men coming after me. I am running, they are getting closer. I don't know what they look like but I can feel them behind me, preparing to kill me. And then . . ."

Scene Two

Mariana (Salvadoran, age thirty): ". . . I feel the heat of the blood running down my back, and realize I've been shot. Then I wake up."

Julio (Salvadoran, age twenty-four): ". . . they are grabbing me, beating me. I can see blood all around. I try to disarm them, but can't. Then I wake up."

Armando (Salvadoran, age twenty-three): ". . . I stop, because I have a gun. I turn around and take aim, and shoot at them. But the gun misfires. I wake up."

Inez (Guatemalan, age thirty-two): ". . . I'm shot in the arm, and can feel the blood flowing. We all keep running. I'm still running when I wake up."

This dream in two scenes is the late, late show of the Central American refugee. Invariant in its first scene, this same nightmare replays so often, in so many different bedrooms, that the clinician who works with people who fled the state terrorism of Central America in the 1980s learns to expect it. Only the end holds any surprise, for the second scene, customized by each dreamer, is somewhat different in each person's account. That second scene is the psyche's creative contribution to the drama—its response to the action of the first scene, whose unforgettable script was written back home by the Salvadoran and Guatemalan governments.

In this chapter we will look at this collective nightmare, with attention to three factors: (1) the traumatogenic conditions in the homeland that furnish the props for Scene One, (2) the conditions of uncertainty abroad that account for the dream's steady frequency of repetition in exile, and finally, (3) the specific circumstance that for each individual determines the plot of the dream's second scene. Our object is to better understand the relationship between this unhappy dream and the unhappy circumstances of the individuals who left Guatemala and El Salvador to escape a living nightmare.

Collective Nightmare, Collective Reality

A Political Nightmare

First, it is important to note that this is a political nightmare. Its content bears a direct relationship to the way power is distributed and exercised in the countries where the dream was born. Those armed men who are chasing the dreamer have been armed by the government. Although their faces are indistinct, it is understood that these are not creditors, or sociopaths, or bosses. They are not academic deans or abusive fathers. Nor are they figures who symbolize such things as the Antichrist, or poverty, or sexuality. These assailants are the Death Squads. They are the torturers. They are the hit men who carry out the government's campaign of psychological warfare against the civilian population. All the dreamers have been victimized in their waking lives.

We may accept with Freud that dreams, however vividly they might replicate a past experience, very rarely reproduce it in an unchanged and unabridged manner. The stylized, almost choreographed chase in Scene One of the refugees' collective dream condenses a past reality rather than rendering it with camera accuracy. Of the four individuals we are observing here, only two were literally pursued. Inez was part of a throng chased and fired upon by the police, and Julio was hunted like an animal for two years. He had hidden in the mountains to avoid being killed by the men who murdered his brother, two nephews, and two cousins, and subsequent to his escape killed another of his brothers and one of his brothers-in-law. Mariana and Armando did not actually experience pursuit because one was at home and the other at work when the soldiers came and took them away. In detention, they experienced great dread each time they were taken for interrogation and torture, but it cannot be said that they were ever pursued. The manifest content of their dream does not exactly duplicate a memory of an event, although it does of course re-create the anxiety of the events it compresses and distorts.

Neither for these individuals nor for the countless others whose sleep is repeatedly disturbed by this recurring dream does the nightmare originate in childhood impressions. It is not the typical dream of being pursued and falling in terror that Freud traces to spooky games played by children with their taunting uncles. It is, rather, a typical dream of post-traumatic stress, of an individual whose waking hours and sleeping hours alike are intruded upon by the traumatic events of the past, when the individual was only one step ahead of death.

A Shared Dream

The dream of the refugee comes to the clinician's attention spontaneously, as one of the complaints that leads the individual to seek psychological services. A symptom of the disease when the diagnosis is Post-Traumatic Stress Disorder, the dream of the traumatic instance is also an expression of the individual's dis-ease, the profound agitation attendant to sleeplessness and relentlessly terrifying sensations.

Of forty-four Salvadorans and Guatemalans examined between 1985 and 1992, thirty-three, or 75 percent, spontaneously complained of nightmares when asked during the assessment interview if they had any difficulty sleeping. Asked what the nightmares are about, twenty-one of them (or 64 percent of those who spontaneously complained of nightmares) told of repeatedly dreaming the nightmare of pursuit described above. Two others dreamt it, as well, but with family members as the victims instead of themselves.

So unlike the wishful dream of the immigrant for an idealized future, this standardized, shared nightmare preserves the horrific moments of the refugee's past. As such, it becomes a diagnostic sign of prior social experience, discriminating as accurately as a social history-taking between immigrants, who make a decision to leave their homeland for greener pastures, and refugees, whose relocation is involuntary, precipitated by armed assailants chasing them in hot pursuit.

The recurring nightmare reported by refugees from Guatemala and El Salvador belies the claims made by the U.S. State Department and the Department of Justice that these are people "seeking a better life for themselves by finding better employment" (Abrams, in Golden and McConnell, 1986, p. 45) or "peasants who are coming to the U.S. for a welfare card and a Cadillac" (Larrabee, in ibid.). The dream's mood, its content, and the remarkable fact of its being shared by large numbers of people make it incongruous to a voluntary immigrant population; the anxiety and violence it contains are not what we would expect to find in the dreams of peasants fantasizing *la dolce vita*.

If dreams enjoyed in law the status they occupy in psychology, they would constitute a principal piece of evidence in the case for granting Salvadorans and Guatemalans legal sanctuary in the United States. But politics count more than dreams in the law, and more than 97 percent of those who apply for political asylum are denied on the grounds that they have no well-founded fear of being persecuted if they are deported to their homelands.

Not a "Refugee" Dream, Per Se

The collective nightmare, it should be noted, is affected by the threat of deportation, though not created by it. Although a recurrent experience for persons who have left these Central American countries, it is not a "refugee" dream coetaneous with the arrival in exile. Rather, it is a dream that begins to occur in the homeland, during a time of mounting anxiety about being captured. Whereas the dreams of Czechoslovakians studied by Cernovsky (1988) expressed the anxiety felt in exile by persons at risk of punishment for having violated the "failure to return" laws, the nightmare of the Guatemalans and Salvadorans begins before emigration and continues uninterrupted in exile. It is not the dream of a person who is at risk for having run away, but rather of one who runs away because he or she is at risk.

At the same time, the Central American dream *is* a refugee nightmare, in the sense that it disturbs the sleep of people who are refugees. Persons who have left El Salvador without permission from the government believe themselves to be at greater risk of detention and abuse than those who never departed, and long after the signing of peace accords in their country continue to receive mail from relatives warning them it is unsafe to come home. Although data regarding the risk for returning refugees are inconclusive, a study conducted by the American Civil Liberties Union did document the torture and/or murder of 15–25 percent of the refugees returned by the United States to El Salvador in 1984, when approximately four hundred Salvadorans a month were deported by the Immigration and Naturalization Service (INS). In Guatemala, government attacks have been mounted on refugees returning from exile in Mexico. For exiles in the United States, the probability of deportation, which derives from the grim statistics on political asylum, intensifies the anxiety of being returned to the homeland, and thus keeps alive the threat that is enacted in the nightmare. Another aspect of the reality of exile that cannot be ignored as we examine the pursuit nightmare of the refugee is the presence of the INS, whose explicit purpose is to pursue, arrest, and deport all persons who have entered the country illegally. Although Temporary Protective Status was granted to many Salvadorans in 1990, no comparable measure was extended to Guatemalans. The undocumented Central American who escaped the outstretched arm of the Death Squads must keep running in exile to keep ahead of the outstretched arm of the INS.

Individual Differences

Turning to Scene Two of the dream, we can see a direct correspondence between this prototypical refugee nightmare and the biographies of those who dream it. Of special interest to psychologists, beyond the unusual circumstance of a single script being dreamed by large numbers of people, are the individual differences observable in Scene Two of the dream.

Although all four of the persons whose second scenes are reported here escape annihilation only by waking up, each has a slightly different experience prior to awakening. Mariana feels the heat of blood from being shot in the back; Julio feels the assailants beating him; Armando stops and shoots at them, but his gun misfires. Inez, even after being shot, keeps running. What is known about these individuals' circumstances that can help us understand their subjective responses to the intersubjective dreamed reality?

Mariana

Mariana, a young woman without any involvement in political affairs, was picked up on a Monday and informed that on Friday she would be killed. While isolated, starved, and blindfolded in detention, she heard other prisoners being tortured and shot, and she lived for four days with the anticipatory fear of being shot herself. On the fourth day her family bribed a guard and she was released. It was almost unbelievable to her that she survived, for she fully expected to be killed. The dream, which started for her after her release from detention, seems to reactivate her specific, frozen anticipatory fear that has still not been resolved. The nightmare re-creates the fatalism with which she awaited her death.

During her first two years in the United States Mariana awoke screaming several times a week. Only after gaining legal status through marriage to an American citizen did she begin to feel safe. After six years, the nightmare's frequency was reduced to once a month; the fear is attenuating.

Julio

Julio was nineteen when the other male members of his family were killed. He and another surviving brother went into hiding, but the brother returned home after a short time, for unlike Julio, he had never been involved in any political activities, and the family thought he would be safe. They were wrong. His mutilated body was found floating in a lake a few days later. Julio lived with the knowledge that he was a marked man. He was sure they would capture him, and sure they would kill him. In the dream he resists and tries to disarm them, but their power is overwhelming, just as it was in life, during the time when he was in hiding and expected every day to be his last.

From the time of his flight to the mountains Julio's sleep has been disturbed by nightmares approximately four times a week. For six years, until winning political asylum in the United States, he slept no more than two hours at a time. Subsequent to receiving asylum his condition began to improve.

Armando

Armando worked for the military after his discharge from the Salvadoran Air Force. His motive for going to work in the military armory was to be able to carry a gun and thus able to defend himself against the guerrillas, whom he feared. Early in 1985, when he was twenty years old, he was forced into detention by the Salvadoran National Guard, who accused him of stealing weapons for the guerrillas.

He was not collaborating with the guerrillas in any way, nor did he know whether anyone else within the armory was. When he tried to explain this to his torturers, it was of no avail. During his thirty-six days of detention he was tortured repeatedly. He was hung by his feet, completely naked, with his hands bound and his eyes covered—the "airplane" treatment. The soles of his feet were beaten and electroshock was applied to his tongue and genitals. He was submerged in scalding water, and his head and body were poked with pins and needles. Never could he understand why any of this was happening to him: he was an innocent man; they must have mistaken him for someone else; his protection—the law, his innocence—was failing him.

In his dream, as in the torture room, Armando's protection fails him. Neither weapons nor the law can counteract the government's capriciousness or save him from its indomitable power. Still, he has not lost faith. He continues turning and drawing his defective gun, believing it will fire, practicing in the dream the same denial that characterizes his waking life and that, for the present at least, helps him function.

After fleeing El Salvador, Armando's dreams of being tortured attenuated, though his recurring nightmare of being pursued continued to plague him. The presence of the gun in the dream augurs well for Armando, despite its persistent malfunctioning; following torture many people are not able to "re-arm" at all. Armando managed to win political asylum, which may give him the security he needs to get a better weapon for Scene Two of the nightmare and eventually turn off the harrowing re-runs altogether.

Inez

Inez, mother of a three-year-old child and former wife of a Guatemalan guerrilla, was at work in a pharmacy when the police began shooting into a demonstration that was taking place on the street outside. She went to close the door of the shop and was shot in the stomach. Amid flying sticks, shattered glass, and wounded people, she took off running down the street to get out of the line of fire. She dropped and lay on the street for hours before she was finally carried to a hospital, where she was placed in a filthy ward filled with the wounded from the attack. Hospital workers were on strike. Severely wounded patients lay unattended, bleeding and crying, without pain medication. Inez was operated on the next morning, without anesthetic. Seeking protection from the chaos and the danger, she fled to the United States as soon as she was strong enough to travel. She was successful in eluding the border patrol as she crossed from Tijuana to San Diego.

In her dream Inez is injured, but keeps running. Although she can feel the blood dripping down her wounded arm she continues running, as she ran from the police, the chaos, and the danger.

In San Francisco Inez' landlord began pursuing her for sexual favors, and when she spurned him, he reported her to the immigration authorities, who arrested her. While awaiting her political asylum hearing, she dreamed she was in the parking lot of the Safeway and her son came to tell her the police were looking for her inside the store. Her sense of vulnerability had not diminished in exile; it had expanded to include new dangers.

Common Trauma Blurs Individual Differences

Individuals vary in their dreamed responses to the act of being seized by killers. While the variance may be related to personality characteristics, coping styles, earlier experiences, and the like (factors warranting further investigation), it is very clear that the individual's dream response is linked to the particular conditions that applied as he or she hovered at the abyss.

Mariana, bereft of any resources for self-defense, cannot confront the attacker; she can only turn away, and be shot in the back. Julio undertakes a struggle, even knowing it is likely to be lost, just as in reality he defended himself by hiding, yet never believed in its efficacy. Armando dreams of himself aiming a weapon at his attackers, a counterpart—but equally ineffective counterpart—to the law that was "on his side" while he was being tortured. Inez keeps running, even after she is shot, as she in fact did when she was in Guatemala. Each individual symbolically re-creates the vulnerability of the victim before the insuperable and unrestrained power of the state.

Conclusion

The collective nightmare of the Central American refugee, of hot pursuit by police, soldiers, or government-organized Death Squads, is a post-trauma dream. It originates in the terrifying conditions of institutionalized political repression, and is carried into exile by persons who could not adapt to life in the homeland but cannot feel secure in exile, either.

Both the first scene of this recurring dream (the incessant pursuit) and the second scene (the victim's response) are inspired by the political experiences of the individual who is having the nightmare. The first scene, remarkably, is dreamed repeatedly by large numbers of Salvadoran and Guatemalan citizens who are now in exile in the United States. Not a "refugee" dream precisely, since its onset occurs prior to emigration, it is, however, a political dream, reflecting the political oppression endured by these individuals before their flight. It is a dream whose repetition and content can also be affected by political realities in exile. Refugees who have been granted political asylum report significant improvements in their sense of security, and a significant reduction in the frequency and intensity of their nightmares. In a truly safe environment—the ideal one being of course a homeland to which they can return and live in peace—the refugees would be able to look forward to the nightmare ending once and for all.

Jasmine: Dreams in the Psychotherapy of a Rape Survivor

KAREN HAGERMAN MULLER

As with Post-Traumatic Stress Disorder following other forms of trauma, nightmares are an almost universal symptom of rape trauma syndrome (Burgess and Holmstrom, 1974). Such nightmares sometimes literally re-enact the trauma (although close inspection will always reveal some distortions). With equal frequency, the dream content is not remembered when the survivor awakens in terror. Such dreams are especially common in the first weeks and months following the trauma, but may occur months and even years later. Nightmares of murder are common, consistent with the fact that many rape survivors fear for their lives. Among most of the one hundred or so rape survivors I have treated, the primary trauma was the brush with death. The sexual insult, however horrible, assumed second place by comparison.

As the months following an assault turn into years, references to the assault and the resultant damage to the survivor's psyche become more symbolic. The fear of sexual assault, other forms of violent assault, or threats of assault and dreams of the assailant become part of the fabric of the survivor's dreams, important threads, but no longer dominating the entire tapestry as before, paralleling the integration of the event into the dreamer's life. Dreams of rape or assault may recur for various reasons in the long-term survivor: around the anniversary of the event, for example, or after a news story or other external event concerning a sexual assault. Other kinds of insults such as job loss or rejection by a boyfriend may also be triggers for dreams of rape. A third category of trigger is extremely self-critical thoughts, such as those reported by a dreamer who had been working on a project for a year. One evening she was feeling so discouraged with how it was going that she decided to abandon the whole thing. That night she dreamed of being raped, reflecting the fact that her psyche considered the abandonment of the project equivalent to a sexual assault on herself.

How is a horrible event like a sexual assault ever integrated? How does one maintain a world view with any degree of optimism or feel in charge of one's life after being the victim of an act of misogynistic violence? In the course of seeing many sexual assault survivors in psychotherapy, I have seen various solutions to the problem of integrating sexual assault into one's life. I have seen many examples of unsuccessful integration: phobias or paranoia in cases in which the event is integrated as typical of a hostile, dangerous world. Sometimes the event is repressed or split off, not really integrated, but forgotten or denied as a way of maintaining a view of the world as a positive, friendly place. In this situation, the memory tends to intrude in the form of nightmares or isolated symptoms like migraine headaches, violent visual images, or physical sensations disconnected from affect or a context that would provide some understanding. In these piecemeal memories, it is as if the psyche has cut the memory into pieces, with the memory of a feeling stored in one spot and a bit of kinesthetic memory over here, and then a visual image somewhere else. Making little sense by themselves, these snippets of apparently unrelated memories contain the trauma encapsulated and condensed as a means of avoiding intolerable affect.

When the event is integrated as the fault of the woman, a common occurrence, the result is depression. Another common self-blaming integration that may accompany depression involves hiding one's sexuality by dressing in baggy, unattractive clothes that thoroughly cover the body. This defense is also often accompanied by weight gain, another way of covering and hiding the body, sometimes to the extent of morbid obesity and a full-blown eating disorder.

The rape survivor whose case I will examine in some detail is a woman I will call Jasmine. She has had some special problems integrating her assault for several reasons. She was neglected and verbally abused as a child by a cold mother who regretted having children and felt trapped in a loveless marriage and by a father who was given to unpredictable bouts of explosive rage.

Jasmine was coping with multiple rapes, a gang rape by strangers that occurred when she was twenty and a violent date rape that occurred at the age of thirty-three and brought her into treatment with me. The earlier kidnapping and gang rape was treated only briefly in a rape crisis center. An attempt to report it was not taken seriously by police, whom she felt did not believe her. This unfortunate experience, coupled with the fact that her problems were not taken seriously when she was a child, caused her to blame herself and avoid seeking help. The rapists even continued to harass and threaten her for two weeks after the actual assault, ceasing only when she left the geographical area.

She recovered only incompletely and slowly from the first rapes. She lived seclusively, became obese, and agoraphobic. She managed to work as a part-time store clerk, eking out a marginal existence. She constantly feared that the men who had kidnapped, raped, and harassed her would show up again to do the same and worse. She had nightmares of their return to murder her that were so vivid that she was unsure after waking whether they had, in fact, returned. After one such dream, she was afraid that her assailants were in the house. Unable to move, she stayed frozen with fear in her bed for hours, uncertain the entire time whether they had returned, but so paralyzed with fear that she could do nothing to check her perceptions or call for help. After five years of this misery, she got help at the local rape crisis center, where she saw a psychiatric nurse for eight sessions. Following this brief treatment, she was able to overcome enough of her fear that she was no longer a housebound agoraphobic, and lost some of the weight she had gained.

A further issue in her integration of these rapes was her profession. Jasmine is a jazz singer. She did very little singing for the five years following the first rapes. Her treatment at the rape crisis center freed her enough to sing more. Although it continued to be difficult, she was able to support herself solely by singing in nightclubs and touring for about three years. At the time she came into treatment with me, shortly after her second rape, she had turned down two opportunities to tour because she could no longer get up on stage and sing. Putting on an evening dress, fixing her hair, and putting on make-up made her feel she was "asking for it." Singing ballads, especially love songs, was also difficult or impossible for the same reason. The music that had been her life, her solace, and her joy when she was growing up became inaccessible because of the feelings of shame, guilt, and self-blame that her assault had engendered. A dream from early in her treatment reveals the fear of death and the feeling that being sexy caused the rape.

> In the first part of the dream I am an absent observer, like watching a movie. I see a woman being ritually raped and hanged. She was beautiful and dressed in attractive evening clothes. I feel her feelings, but not at their full intensity.
>
> In the second part, I was supposed to be singing in a concert, but I was having trouble finding the place. I didn't seem to have anything appropriate to wear, either. Everything seemed too revealing. When I finally found the hall, my father was on the stage. There was no room for me.

Like many self-blaming rape victims, Jasmine gained weight and sought to wear baggy, high-necked clothes that covered as much as possible. Yet such an adaptation was incompatible with being a nightclub singer. After being raped the second time, Jasmine was unable to work for several months, then worked at temporary clerical and accounting jobs. She took an occasional singing job when fellow musicians pressured her but did not pursue her music, turning down opportunities that included an offer to tour Japan and other parts of the Far East.

In Jasmine's life, as in the lives of other artists, it seems that self-development cannot be entirely separated from the development of the artistic gift. Working artistically is necessary to a feeling of well-being in people like Jasmine, who have a strong creative urge. But before that artistic work can be undertaken, a sense of adequacy or essential self-esteem must exist. Rape destroys basic self-esteem because it destroys the sense of bodily integrity: the physical boundaries of the body have been violently violated, often with an implied or overt threat to maim or destroy the body. If one does not have the right to control what happens to one's own body, the core of self-esteem is challenged, if not destroyed. A central aspect of healing from rape, therefore, is the re-forming and protecting of body boundaries.

During the acute phase of recovery from her second rape, Jasmine had many nightmares recapitulating her first rapes and combining events from the earlier gang rape with events from the more recent trauma. She tended to have more dreams of the return of her earlier rapists than dreams of the more recent rape, supporting the notion put forth by trauma researchers (such as Siegel in Chapter 12) that any given trauma brings up previous traumas, especially, but not limited to, similar traumas. The new trauma causes a recrudescence of unresolved conflicts from the previous trauma, and the content and conflicts of the two (or more) quickly become interwoven. Thus Jasmine's therapy following her second rape began with the telling of the stories of both rapes.

The remarkable healing power of the telling of the unholy secret, as well as the capacity of such secrets to cause illness, has already been hinted at in the considerable progress made by Jasmine after her brief treatment at the rape crisis center. An Irish fairy tale captures well what happened, not only in Jasmine's treatment but also in the early phase of treatment of any rape or incest survivor and any trauma survivor who carries the terrible secrets of trauma (Colum, [1918] 1958).

> There was once a king who had the ears of a horse. Now this king, fearful that he would lose his throne if the fact of his not-quite-human make-up were to get around, kept his ears carefully covered. The one person who could not help seeing his ears was his barber. Consequently, every time he had his hair cut, he had the barber executed. When this became impractical, the king hired a permanent barber who was sworn to secrecy. After a time, the barber fell ill. The village healer felt that his illness was caused by some terrible secret, and

told him to go and tell this secret to a certain willow tree in the forest. The barber did so and was cured.

Soon, one of the king's musicians was looking for wood to make a harp, and, as luck would have it, the willow tree suited his purposes perfectly, so he cut it down and made a harp. When he played the new harp at a state dinner, the harp sang out, "The king has the ears of a horse, tra la. The king has the ears of a horse!" Well, as the king had feared, he lost his throne, because the people did not want a king who was not altogether human.

This story illustrates the psychology of the terrible secret. The terrible secret always has to do with the animal, instinctual, or primitive aspects of someone (that is, the primitive rage of the rapist and the horse's ears of the king). The king in a fairy tale can represent the dominant force or quality in a culture or personality (the ruling aspect), but in the case of the rape survivor, the king is the assailant who assumes the position of authority over the woman's life by assaulting her, dominating her life for months or years afterward.

The weight of carrying the secret alone makes the barber ill, and the illness is cured by telling a tree, thus relieving him of the secret without breaking his vow of silence. By his telling the willow tree his painful secret, the secret might be said to be integrated into the flow of life, no longer split off. It is grounded and contained by the deep roots. Similarly, in the early treatment for sexual assault, the therapist listens like a willow tree, containing and grounding the horror and fear simply by hearing and thus sharing the burden. Like the tree, she bends without breaking, which is to say, she empathizes without becoming overwhelmed. I believe this kind of listening to be a central part of any healing process, because there is always the need in the patient to have someone hear without judgment what no one else has wanted to hear. By telling the terrible experience without overwhelming the therapist, the survivor feels less overwhelmed, and the pain is relieved. Depending on the severity of the trauma history of the individual survivor, this initial phase of treatment may be all that is necessary. This was not the case with Jasmine, however, who had suffered multiple traumas after a difficult childhood.

The other important principle illustrated by the story is the way that the secret manages, almost of its own volition, to come out. Such secrets do have a way of emerging, and their unfortunate bearers, trying to hide their own shame, protect only the guilty. The guilty king loses his power almost automatically when his true nature comes to light. This happens both literally and figuratively in the aftermath of sexual assault, as revelation brings criminals to justice and, as in Jasmine's case, the telling causes the assailants to lose their symbolic power as the survivor recognizes that they are not waiting for her around every corner.

About seven months into Jasmine's treatment, as her nightmares and the paralyzing fear that characterizes the acute phase of recovery from rape began to abate, our focus shifted to her relationship with her parents and to her childhood. She had been collecting unemployment and then disability, which was running out. She was beginning to be able to work at temporary clerical jobs, but her finances were in bad shape. She turned to her parents, who said they would help her, then reneged. As her father told her casually that he could not help her after all, he also mentioned that he was buying himself a new diamond ring. Understandably, this felt to Jasmine like a slap in the face. Jasmine had the following dream shortly after her conversation with her father:

> I was playing Monopoly with Dad. I had all the money and property. I put them down on the table. He took them and kept them.
> I went into the kitchen. The microwave door was open. It knocked me down and burned me. I called out, "Daddy! Daddy!" He didn't come. I lay on the floor, cold.

In the first part of the dream, Jasmine is winning at Monopoly. Since Monopoly is largely a game of luck, requiring only the simplest of strategies, one might speculate that life had dealt Jasmine a better hand than her father. This probably refers to his envy of her musical gift. Despite having been a musician himself, Jasmine's father rarely attended her musical performances, even in elementary and high school. Nor did he encourage her in any way. His only comment after attending the one performance he had heard in years was, "Well, you're no Ella Fitzgerald." The headline of a newspaper article on Jasmine that she had recently sent him called her a young Ella Fitzgerald. He is apparently so threatened by her talent that he is not only unable to encourage it, but must actively discourage it. Hence, he takes all the resources away from her and then refuses to help her when an accident severely burns her. The microwave burn seems to be a reference to her rape. In another dream around the same time, her father keeps her from going onstage because he wants the limelight all to himself. The dream shows how devastated Jasmine was by her parents' refusal of help—indeed, she seems to be dead at the end.

Another dream the same night:

> I was with my family. Something was wrong with my vision. Mother took me to a doctor who looked like you. There was nothing wrong with my eyes, but I was blind. They looked white. You put drops in them, then rinsed them and rinsed them. Then I could see again.
> Then I was on a train watching porno movies. We went way up and way down. At the end, I was alone with a lot of kittens.

This dream illustrates the beginning of Jasmine's realistic view of her family. As devastating as her parents' let-down of her was, she did not want to see that this was typical of their relationship; they made promises and didn't deliver. In fact, since childhood, she had taken care of them more than they had taken care of her. She did not want to face this painful reality, but didn't want to be blind either. Talking to me in therapy was cleansing her vision. Therapy is often represented as a trip to the doctor, sometimes with images of hospitalization or surgery, especially when people are engaged in the kind of examination of basic assumptions that Jasmine was starting to undertake.

The second part of the dream mentions some other issues that are part of her life journey. She is on a train, a collective mode of transportation, which suggests that she is not yet on her own individual path, which would be represented by a vehicle she was driving or a journey on foot. This fact is also evident in the action of giving all her money and property to her father, or allowing him to take them, in the previous dream. She is still giving away her power, her energy, and her resources. She is not really able yet to take responsibility for her own life. She might prefer the idea of rescue to the idea of solving her own problems. The porno films suggest her rape, since pornography is a crude and exploitative version of sexuality.

She is alone at the end with a group of kittens. Cats, being very self-contained and independent pets, often seem to represent the dreamer's instinctive healthy narcissism. Having kittens to care for represents a good step for Jasmine at this point, because her nurturing of her own nascent healthy narcissism is essential to the healing of her poor self-esteem, which in turn makes it possible for her to feel strong enough to take charge of her own life. The need to focus on herself, including her needs, wishes, interests, goals, and boundaries, was necessary to counteract the self-esteem-crushing effect of her sexual assault. The fact that her relationship with her parents tended to interfere with this process was demonstrated vividly by their initial consent to help her financially, followed by their casual refusal. Jasmine wisely reduced the frequency of her contacts with them, and began to rely on friends for support. She had some very positive, loving friends, and the difference in her mood, self-esteem, and even the clarity of her thinking was quite obvious after a month or so. She had the following dream after about six months of very little contact with her parents:

> I was visiting some people on a remote farm. I found that a little girl there was being sexually abused. I rescued her, deciding that I would take care of her myself. As we were leaving, I found a large, incredibly beautiful jewel in her hair. We both knew it was mine.

This dream seems to affirm Jasmine's need to distance herself from her family. Even in the dream, she reported some awareness that she was also the little girl. The little girl's abuse seems to suggest both her multiple rapes with their damage to her child self (both the vulnerable and the potential for the future aspects) and her abuse as a child.

The dream presents a question that we have been unable to answer: whether Jasmine may in fact have been sexually molested as a child. She has no such memories, but her dreams often depict the sexual molestation of a child, usually by the father. This might be explained by the intertwining of symbolism from various traumas that was mentioned earlier, or it might be literally true. Dreams can neither confirm nor deny what has literally occurred, but they do suggest that there was a feeling in Jasmine's childhood similar to the feelings she experienced as the result of the rapes. John Bradshaw, in *Creating Love* (1992), talks about a symbolic sexual abuse that occurs when a child is closer to one or both parents than they are to each other. The child becomes a spouse substitute for one or both parents. The abuse occurs in the child having to put his or her own needs second to those of the parents and in the pressure to grow up before her time. This was exactly the case with Jasmine. Her parents did not speak to each other for months at a time, using her a go-between.

She felt that the dream showed her to have rescued her own young self, and to be protecting herself from further abuse. She associated the gem with her intrinsic value and with her musical talent. Gems are also quintessentially feminine, in their beauty and in their earthy origins, as is her particular artistic expression. The dream also reflects the beginnings of her movement away from self-blame, in that the child is innocent and the feminine gem is recognized and valued as beautiful. Jasmine knows that the gem is hers although it seems to come from outside her. She has always had difficulty owning her intrinsic value, her femininity, and her musical gift, owing to both her rapes and her early family messages. So the dream message seems to be that these qualities do belong to her and come from her child self, whom she is obliged to rescue, protect, and nurture.

The next dream occurred four years later. During those years, she was in treatment most of the time, taking a couple of brief hiatuses of one to three months when her work schedule made it difficult to get to therapy. My maternity leave of three months was another hiatus. During those years, she supported herself via clerical work, singing intermittently. She had two relationships with men, one of whom, an abusive alcoholic, she briefly married and divorced. Both men were compared to both her father and her assailants in her dreams. In the previous six months, she had decided to think of herself as a singer, rather than considering it a hobby, as she had tended to do in the past. In this period she had the following dream:

> I was at a club with a full house. The band was playing a song I was to
> sing. I went up to join them and sang the song. There was no applause,

but I thought it was good. The band took a break. I went to the table of a backwoods family. It was the birthday of their daughter, Ella. She was obese, with long, gray hair, plain, baggy clothes, and no make-up. They had invited me to join them because they thought we were so much alike. I did not think we were.

I went to the bathroom. There were two stalls with no door between them. I was too embarrassed to use the toilet. I saw an address book on the floor. It looked like mine, but I didn't pick it up. I tried to put on lipstick, but it wouldn't stick, and the lipstick broke. A young blonde came in and asked who I was. I told her, and said I was singing. She said I must be really obscure, because she knew everybody.

I returned to the table with the family. I thought, "I have to get back on stage—the break must be over." I saw two men who looked like the men who kidnapped and raped me. I thought they would abduct and rape me. They heckled me like construction workers, "Hey, Baby, come on over here!" I kept walking. I felt okay. I took off my high heels and walked as fast as I could.

This dream shows the intertwining of childhood conflicts with rape-related imagery. In the beginning of the dream, she is onstage singing. Her continuing conflicts about musical performance are clear in that she is late getting onstage, since the band is already playing the song she is to sing. She is also late in that she has not been doing a lot of performing for the past few years. Almost being late to performances is a recurring image in her dreams. She then gets no response from the audience. Often in her dreams, someone or something keeps her off the stage. In one dream, it was her father. In some dreams, she sings, but is heckled by men in the audience. It is only a slight improvement that she is able to sing and feel okay about it, although she gets get no response from the audience.

After she sings, she goes to visit with the members of a backwoods family who are celebrating the birthday of their frumpy old daughter, Ella. I mentioned before the comparison between Ella Fitzgerald and Jasmine. The "backwoods Ella" seems to represent Jasmine's fears about her appearance, her programming from her "backwoods" family about how she is supposed to look, and perhaps, most important, her fears about who she really is. About a year into treatment with me, she lost forty pounds and has maintained a svelte figure since, so she has not been obese, or even overweight, in several years. Although she is able to counter the family's comparison between her and Ella initially, the following events in the dream betray the fact that it is still hard for her to think of herself as an attractive performer. In her own mind, she still fears, or often fears, that she is a fat, old, frumpy hick.

In the next part of the dream, she is unable to use the bathroom because it is too exposed. Using the toilet usually seems to relate to processing negative feelings—especially anger, but any kind of shadow material that must be discharged. Perhaps because she denies any feelings about the lack of audience response and the family's comparison between her and fat, frumpy Ella, she is unable to process and thus get rid of her negative feelings, probably hurt and anger. Those feelings must be dealt with adequately to keep the shadow from becoming too powerful. The deterioration that occurs in the rest of the dream shows that the shadow has indeed taken over. She doesn't pick up the address book that is probably hers, suggesting that she fails to make the contacts she knows she needs to make to continue her career. She can't get her lipstick on, which is to say that she probably feels ugly or feels she can't maintain her persona, the image she wants to present to the public.

A young woman tells her she is obscure, which is to say unimportant, another reference to the small-town frump she feels like. This procession of events leads to her being threatened with abduction and rape again. This threat is most likely of the internal variety, since she had just made the decision to start pursuing singing again, but does not have the positive self-esteem essential to maintain a view of herself as a singer. An alternative possibility is that she sees herself as either a mousy frump or cheap bimbo. Since she has just performed and refused to identify herself as a frump, the alternative may be the feeling that she is "flaunting herself and asking for it" when she dresses the part of night club performer. She escapes with heckling, a considerable improvement over the violent dreams of rape and murder of a few years ago.

The last dream of this series is a very recent one. It repeats the precious stone imagery of the first dream, and has a fairy-tale quality.

A girl and a boy live in a small, closed community. They are in love, and want to leave because people are being treated unkindly in the little town. They met at a restaurant where she was a waitress. They flee to the mountains and eventually, to another town. As they walk through a clothing store there, a couple stare at her hair because it contains two beautiful peridots. When the boy sees this he gets angry and walks away. She follows him back to the town they came from. He is angry because he thinks she is using him to smuggle the gems. It is forbidden to take these gems from the little town, on penalty of death, although they are common there. She took them in ignorance of the law. He heads out of town again, through the mountains where the gems are mined, and she follows him, although she knows now that her life is in danger.

As in real life, this story has no ending. Several important facts remain obscure. Will the girl be able to convince the boy to trust her again? She seems to keep the jewels, although she now knows it is forbidden. Of the many jewels that appear in Jasmine's dreams, there is usually some uncertainty about ownership—here, the girl takes them although they are not hers. In a different jewel dream, she is supposed to care for her grandmother's things, but not touch or use anything for herself. In another dream, her grandmother gives her jewels, suggesting a feminine legacy from a grandmother she didn't know. In another dream, another girl has jewels in her hair. Jasmine thinks the girl has stolen them from her, but then finds she has her own jewels in her hair.

Will the fact that the jewels in this dream are stolen cause the girl's downfall? In other words, will Jasmine's downfall be her inability to recognize the gem she truly is: her essential value, beauty, femininity, and musical talent? That has been her downfall so far, and the dream shows that the potential is still there, because the basic self-esteem problem remains. Since jewels are mined from the body of mother earth, I think it is reasonable to presume that earliest form of the problem is in Jasmine's early relationship with her mother. The cold mother who frequently proclaimed that she regretted having children has given Jasmine the message that she is without value and will not escape the isolated family alive. In fact, in another recent dream, Jasmine is a child and her mother shouts at her that she is worthless, that her life means nothing, and that she is a failure. Her only approved role is as a waitress, taking care of her parents, and any attempt to escape whole will be punishable with death.

As we peel away the layers of the results of her multiple assaults, I think we have now arrived at the layer that dynamically similar to the outer layers, might be referred to as the premorbid personality. For Jasmine, rejected by her mother from birth, the abuse suffered at the hands of her father, her assailants, and her husband seem to her to be her due. She is able to glimpse only infrequently the jewel she truly is, keeping it hidden. Even when she sees it, she is not sure it belongs to her. I have heard her describe over and over the difficulty she goes through to sing. When she does sing, she almost always gets raves from both the audience and other musicians. She reports these rave reviews, but never really believes them. The jewels seem to belong to someone else, because she cannot imagine them to be her own. The dream seems to say that she has decided to keep the jewels and leave behind the family that has treated her badly. But until she is convinced that the jewels belong to her, it will be a struggle to survive, let alone to allow the light of her jewels shine forth.

Dreams of Firestorm Survivors

ALAN SIEGEL

On Sunday morning, October 20, 1991, a small brush fire ignited high in the Oakland, California, hills. Parched terrain, unseasonable heat, and hot Santa Ana winds were the perfect incubator for wildfire. Within minutes, a 2000-degree wall of fire, at times a hundred feet high, roared through the hills of Oakland and Berkeley. As the swirling inferno advanced deep into residential areas, many stunned residents were forced to run for their lives, clutching family photos, jewelry, computer disks, or whatever they could hastily grab (Adler, 1992).

Tens of thousands evacuated, seeing the explosive flames threatening and later watching live footage of their neighborhoods burning on network and local television. Dozens suffered burns and twenty-five died in the hellish maelstrom, overcome by fumes, trapped in burning cars, or succumbing while trying to save others.

Many of the evacuees did not learn the fate of their homes and in some cases of their loved ones for one to three days, as the fire burned in areas cordoned off by officials. When the residents returned, they saw smoldering destruction that was comparable to that of wartime firebombing. Over three thousand homes were reduced to ash, and more than five thousand people were left homeless.

Occurring almost two years to the day after the massive Loma Prieta earthquake damaged the San Francisco Bay Bridge and destroyed a huge freeway structure in Oakland, the devastation of the East Bay Firestorm went far beyond the statistics on property loss and personal injury. For thousands of victims and hundreds of thousands of "lucky" survivors in Oakland and Berkeley, their basic trust in life was again shattered, leaving the whole community vacillating between numbness, intrusive anxiety, and survivor guilt.

Dream Journal Research

In the wake of the second natural disaster in the San Francisco Bay Area in two years, my collaborators (Barbara Baer and Karen Muller) and I initiated an investigation designed to analyze the patterns of unconscious responses to a disaster. A further intention of our project was educational and therapeutic—to offer psychological assistance to the participants and education and guidance to the community of Firestorm survivors.

Two weeks after the East Bay Firestorm, we sent a press release to the local newspapers and posted notices at places frequented by survivors. Subjects were also recruited by friends and colleagues. Volunteers ranged in age from twenty-three to sixty-eight and were primarily Caucasian and well educated. They represented a diverse economic spectrum, from affluent people with full insurance to low-income renters with no insurance. The forty-two experimental subjects included twenty-eight who lost their homes (Fire Survivors) and fourteen others who lived in the burn zone but whose homes were miraculously spared from destruction (Fire Evacuees). A control group of eighteen individuals who lived outside the evacuation zone also participated.

All subjects were given standardized instructions for completing a "Two Week Dream Journal" (Siegel, 1983, 1992a). Subjects completed their journals from three to fourteen weeks following the fire. Most had never kept a dream journal.

Each subject participated in a one- to two-hour interview. It included an emotional review and debriefing of their experiences in the fire and its aftermath. Part of the interview was also devoted to a qualitative exploration of one or more of their dreams.

Subjects also completed a questionnaire focusing on pre-fire stresses and post-fire losses and coping responses, the Beck Depression Inventory (1967), and the Horowitz Impact of Events Scale (1979), which measures post-traumatic reactions. A follow-up questionnaire was administered two weeks before the first anniversary of the Firestorm. All subjects were invited to participate in a series of three follow-up workshops three, twelve, and fifteen months after the fire. To further the goal of community education, results of the study were published in local newspapers (Gihvan, 1992; Myers, 1992, Rufus, 1992; Siegel, 1992a; Warren, 1992) and aired on radio and television and a series of public forums were presented at hospitals, churches, clinics, and community centers.

Dream Content Analysis

Content analysis of each dream was accomplished with the Composite Dream Rating Scales (CODERS), which consisted of 133 discrete themes. Scales were combined primarily from the Hall and Van de Castle (1966) system but also included other validated scales (Winget and Kramer, 1979) and specially designed scales intended to tap unconscious response patterns to natural disasters. To control for the length and quantity of dreams, the first five dreams containing between 25 and 300 words were used for quantitative content analysis measurements. The content analysis compared 215 dreams of the Survivors with 70 dreams of the Evacuees and 90 dreams of the Controls.

Within the CODERS scale, emphasis was placed on characters, settings, objects, architecture, disasters, death, sensory experience, heat and fire, natural disasters, injury and illness, instincts, character interactions, emotions, threat, masochism, ego mastery, food, shelter, clothing, finances, and common themes such as flying and falling.

Group comparisons were made between the Survivor, Evacuee, and Control groups' dream content. All significant themes in the quantitative comparisons were subjected to qualitative analyses following the approach described by Brenneis (1975).

Unexpected Traumatic Reactions of the Evacuees

An unexpected finding of our study is the profound and largely unacknowledged reactions of the Fire Evacuees—people who lived in the burn zone but whose homes were spared. Their unremitting survivor guilt, depression, intrusive thoughts, and nightmares were more distressing than that of the Fire Survivors. In addition, the Evacuees' dreams were more focused on death, bodily injury, and disaster and had more manifest content references to the events of the Firestorm than the those of the Survivors, who actually lost property.

Statistical analysis established that ten dream content categories occurred significantly more frequently ($p < .05$) in the Fire Evacuees dreams when they were compared with the Control Group. These included Disasters, Death, Dreamer Injured, Fire/Heat, Man-Made Disasters, Dead Person Comes Alive, Teeth Falling Out, Natural Disasters, Communication, and Friendly Interactions. Only two content categories occurred more frequently in the Fire Survivors when compared with the Controls: Finding Valuables and Events at Times out of Control. For the Evacuees, six other dream themes showed trends toward significance ($p < .1$). These included Separation Anxiety, Damaged Body Parts, Events out of Control, Father, and Familiar Persons. Six themes tended toward significance as well when the Survivors were compared with the Controls.

The predominance of the Death, Disaster, Fire, and Injury themes in Evacuees' dreams raises intriguing theoretical questions. Were the survivor guilt and the community denial of their invisible trauma more devastating to the Evacuees, resulting in morbid preoccupations? Or were the Evacuees less traumatized and therefore more readily able to tolerate the recall of morbid themes? A further hypothesis is that Evacuees who volunteered for the study were motivated by deeper distress than the Survivors.

Interview and questionnaire responses strongly corroborated the severity of the Fire Evacuees' post-traumatic responses. The loss of property was not necessarily the most devastating aspect of the Firestorm. Feelings of relief and celebration at the salvation of their homes were perceived as secondary. And apart from retaining their home, the Evacuees had parallel experiences during the fire; a terrifying brush with death, hours believing their homes had burned, and finding out that friends had suffered injury, death, or loss. In addition, they faced living in a charred landscape for months to come. For the Evacuees, as for the Survivors, unresolved traumas of the past were reactivated and a potent strain of survivor guilt took root.

Andrea, a Fire Evacuee, fled the flames with her husband but returned to find that her intact home was the only standing structure left in her neighborhood. Her haunting dream suggests both survivor guilt and a residue of unresolved terror from the Firestorm.

The Fire Seed

What I recall is an absolutely terrifying nightmare in which the fire had developed an organic consciousness. It was the embodiment of evil. It hid itself very well up on the hill in a pile of brush where it waited for all the fire departments to leave. Then it came back to get the houses it had missed. Somehow it had marked these houses with a fire seed and all it had to do was pass by the fire seeds for the house to ignite. I woke up screaming because I saw our "fire seed" begin to swell. In the dream, I was alone in the house.

Depressed and wracked with survivor guilt, Andrea felt that she was marked by the "fire seed" symbolizing in part the hidden post-traumatic wounds that could reignite at any moment. In Andrea's dream the mark of the fire seed signified the inevitability of retribution by nature, punishment for her home being spared. The "Fire Seed" dream was unusually clear in its manifest representation of survivor guilt and punishment. Other subjects whom we judged to be suffering from survivor guilt did not have easily identifiable guilt and punishment themes in the manifest content.

Survivors who lost homes had an external focus to their recovery requiring immediate activity: finding temporary shelter, purchasing necessities, fighting their insurance company, deciding and/or planning to rebuild, and so forth. Despite their horrible fate, they had a map of external steps to take that centered on establishing shelter and stability. They could deny or delay their inner anguish by immersing themselves in rebuilding their lives. Survivors were also the recipients of sympathetic reactions from friends, family, and the general public.

In contrast, Evacuees garnered no such sympathetic reaction. They were similarly traumatized during the fire. They had no map of activities, however, to chart their recovery and distract them from their inner preoccupations. At the same time, they believed they had no right to be upset. Their woes were not adequately validated by sympathetic reactions from friends and family. In this climate of denial, the Evacuees felt they had to shamefully conceal lingering reactions.

Results of our study suggest that special attention be given to the hidden wounds of the "lucky" survivors of a trauma. They may not suffer injury or lose property but may require extended emotional support or professional help to resolve post-traumatic reactions. These findings are relevant to survivors of natural disasters such as hurricanes, floods, or earthquakes who do not sustain losses or injury. Survivors of accidents and siblings of victims of violence and abuse may also bear these hidden wounds.

Furthermore, our results suggest that people who have "near-miss" encounters with trauma may be especially vulnerable if they have a history of multiple or severe loss, trauma, or deprivation. They may suffer full-blown symptoms of Post-Traumatic Stress Disorder, exacerbated by a lack of recognition of the basis of their condition.

Early Post-Fire Dreams

Dreams recalled within the first few weeks proved to be excellent indicators of whether a person was fixated on the trauma or had turned the corner and moved onto a path of recovery. A favorable sign was dreams portraying a direct confrontation with the Firestorm trauma (or its symbolic equivalent) and some attempt at mastering the threat within the dream sequence. In contrast, the dreams of survivors with past trauma or multiple life stresses at the time of the fire had meager evidence of mastering threats and more vivid images of violence, destruction, injury, and death.

One of the most haunting dreams in the entire collection was that of Rebecca, a forty-year-old Fire Survivor. Her family home had burned down when she was a child of ten, and her mother-in-law with whom she was close, died a week before the fire. She was emotionally devastated after the fire and immediately sought psychotherapy, troubled by repetitive dreams like the following one from her Two Week Journal.

Burnt Alive

I had an appointment with a psychiatrist I used to see twenty years ago. I waited and waited. He finally left with a young man. I then was suddenly watching a woman burn alive in a building. I was watching her. There was nothing I or anyone else could do. She was terrified as she clutched the front of the charred building—flames all around her. She had blond hair. She couldn't scream—just looked out terrified for help.

There is little resolution here—only an image that would make a Munch painting seem tame. Rebecca was still unconsciously fixated on the trauma of the fire as well as unresolved trauma and grief of the past and present.

The dream begins with a search for help. Rebecca returns to a psychiatrist she saw briefly many years earlier. Her unconscious is perhaps seeking the understanding and compassion that she sensed with her old doctor. But she is left waiting, unable to establish contact and then helplessly watching the grotesque incineration of the mute blonde woman.

The imagery of "Burnt Alive" appeared to reflect the recent and childhood traumas that she reported on her questionnaire and during her post-fire interview. At a follow-up session, one year after the fire, she explored this dream further and found roots deeper than the Firestorm. To a small group, she revealed that she had been ritually physically and sexually abused as a child. She had only remembered the details after years of repression were painfully dissolved by the Firestorm.

The images took on different meanings. The trapped woman in the dream not only represented her own terror during the Firestorm but her hideous memories of witnessing other children confined, burned, and tortured even to death in one instance and her own experiences of being brutally abused and not being able to obtain help from any understanding adults.

The nature of her grisly dream was, therefore, only partly explained by life stress before the fire, terrifying experiences during the fire, and adjustment problems related to loss of home and property. Her dream opened a door to a black hole of childhood trauma. Fortunately, Rebecca sought the kind of help that was unavailable to her in childhood. Through her dreams and recovered memories she was painfully engaged in confronting both her fire losses and her recovered memories of abuse.

At the one-year follow-up she was still troubled by nightmares and intrusive images from the fire and childhood. Despite psychotherapy, support from friends, and continued attempts to resolve her anguish, she reported, "I am just beginning to experience my anger and cry over my losses." She had a dream indicating her continuing inability to escape the trauma of the fire.

Trapped by the Silver Wall

I saw the house to my left in flames. I stood next to the house facing a tall shiny silver-colored wall. I couldn't climb over it.

At the final follow-up meeting, fifteen months after the fire, Rebecca had improved visibly. She talked about finally getting angry and "working through my grief cycle." She reported a dream after attending a party for a neighbor's newly rebuilt house.

Escaping Unhurt

I was at a friend's house. She was having a gathering of women friends at her new home in the burned area. One of them said, "Did you hear about Rebecca?" They lost one entire wing of their house in the fire, but they escaped unhurt. The hills were barren but had a few, new yet unpainted homes here and there.

Rebecca felt this dream represented a breakthrough. She was with supportive friends who were paying attention to her, and only part of her home had burned. The key image for Rebecca was escaping unhurt. During the childhood abuse she was trapped by groups of women, unable to escape. In the Firestorm, too, she did not escape from emotional injury. Getting emotional support, escaping injury, and seeing the new construction in progress were symbolic solutions to her previous unconscious fixation on the experience of being trapped without exit.

In contrast, the fire disaster dreams of some Survivors showed early indications of mastery. Helen, a forty-nine-year-old teacher, wrote the following vivid dream in her journal six weeks after the fire.

Escaping the Flames

I am in Tilden Park in the Berkeley Hills with two women friends who were also burned out. We are in a condominium complex at the edge of the park and suddenly see gigantic flames coming rapidly toward us. Somehow we manage to escape and find ourselves in downtown San

Francisco—from where we can watch the flames with awe. We aren't afraid but excited by the spectacle.

Helen had little time to evacuate the day of the fire. Her family lost everything but a few photo albums, some artwork, and jewelry. In her dream she experienced the terror of the swift and deadly flames but succeeded in eluding the flames and getting a visual and emotional perspective on her harrowing escape.

A tamer but thematically related mastery dream occurred at the end of her Two Week Journal. In this dream, while on a camping trip, she was exhilarated when she managed to turn off some hot water at a campground. Helen associated to the camp trip setting as an activity that requires self-sufficiency but exposes one more directly to the elements. She saw this as a metaphor for her homeless status after the fire, staying with friends and living out of suitcases. This later dream depicts a less direct confrontation with mortally dangerous flames—the heat of the water is less wild and more decisively controlled than the actual Firestorm that burned her house.

At the end of her Two Week Journal, Helen's dreams showed intermittent signs of mastery that reflected favorable waking life circumstances—full insurance, supportive friends, and strengthened family bonds. The fire had not shattered her life nor touched any emotional nerves from the past.

It should be emphasized that not all of Helen's dreams were uplifting or hopeful. An analysis of the ten dreams recorded in her Two Week Journal revealed themes of grief—a friend's father dying, melancholy images of her long dead father and grandmother, and a dream of being homeless. In contrast, other images included joy at becoming unexpectedly pregnant and finding many green sprouts in her charred garden. The alternation of hopeful images with persistent struggles to overcome the trauma is a typical configuration early in recovery. This mixture points to the need for gathering a series of dreams rather than relying on one dream to assess recovery from a trauma.

Nine months after the Firestorm, while her house was being rebuilt, Helen had recurring dreams of discovering unexpected new rooms "much larger than I expected—almost like a hotel" with parties of friends to celebrate the new house. Three days before the first anniversary of the fire, she dreamed that she was traveling in Hawaii and found "a beautiful place to live—surrounded by flowers, with orchids lining the path."

On the anniversary follow-up questionnaire, Helen rated her adjustment in all areas as better than before the fire. A painter in her spare time, she had lost most of her own artwork in the fire, but had engaged in painting again after the fire to master her lingering anxieties. At the anniversary follow-up meeting, she was excited about an exhibition of her recent oil paintings based on photographs of the fire.

Loss and Grief Dreams

Dreams portraying dead and dying people and pets, searching for or grieving over lost objects, were common in the dreams of Fire Survivors and especially for the Evacuees. Associations linked these loss and grief dreams to emotional wounds stemming directly from the fire. For many Survivors and Evacuees, however, memories of the death of a parent, family member, or friend provided the central imagery in their dreams.

Post-fire dreams reawakened preoccupations with grief from earlier epochs. With healthy defenses weakened by the trauma, unresolved losses of the past became an emotional achilles' heel—areas of psychological vulnerability that flared up and weakened the survivor's coping ability.

Content analysis revealed that Death and Dying themes were significantly greater for the combined Evacuee/Survivor groups when compared with the Controls ($p < .04$). The Evacuee group accounted for much of this difference, however, and its members' death dreams were even more ubiquitous compared with those of the Controls ($p < .01$). Seventeen percent of the Evacuees' dreams had death themes, 11 percent of the Survivors', and 5 percent of the Controls'. Salient subthemes for the Evacuees included dying in their own dream, a dead person from the past appearing, and a living person dying or appearing dead in a dream. Both Evacuees and Survivors had dead animal themes; the Controls had none.

Survivors and Evacuees suffering multiple stressors at the time of the fire or who were the victims of childhood trauma were especially susceptible to dreams with death themes. Connie, a twenty-four-year-old single graduate student, was living in the home of a couple who were surrogate parents for her. Smelling the smoke, she tried to rescue the extensive art collection of her landlords. The fire was advancing too rapidly and her desperate attempts to douse the flames licking at the trees surrounding the house was in vain.

Connie had no insurance and lost everything but a few hand-carried valuables. In addition to severe financial losses, she felt tremendous guilt over not rescuing the artwork and possessions in the house and was especially depressed about the loss of contact with her surrogate parents, who chose to move out of the area after the fire.

Prior to the fire, she had suffered from a troubling parasitic infection that had forced her to take a semester off. Connie's father had died when she was ten, and her mother had difficulty caring for her afterward. She spent her teenage years with relatives, visiting but not living with her mother.

Connie's grisly dream six weeks after the fire reprised the memory of her father's death that had led to her being orphaned and abandoned a dozen years earlier.

Touching the Corpse's Rotting Hair

I was with an old military man who wanted to bury his superior officer in a finely esteemed way. We carried the body in a station wagon all around the cemetery. I was tired of carrying the stretcher with the dead body because my hands kept touching the dead man's head of rotting hair.

Connie's father and grandfather had in reality served as military officers and she recently had memories of her father's moribund face before his death, gaunt and ravaged by cancer and nearly bald from chemotherapy.

In the metaphor of the dream, Connie is attempting to lay to rest her grief for her father in a formal, ritualistic manner. The emotional burden of carrying the grief has been overwhelming and horrifying to her—emotionally untouchable, like the corpse's rotting hair.

For Connie, discussing the "dream corpse" stirred up grief for her long-dead father and a recently ended love relationship. She related the fire experience and especially the loss of her close relationship with her surrogate parents to her grief and loss of security after her father died. Exploring the dream helped make more explicit the connection between her grief for her father, which ended her stable family life, and the loss of her surrogate parents in the Firestorm.

Other dreams in Connie's Two Week Journal revealed parallel morbid preoccupations. Two days after the Rotting Corpse dream she dreamed that her mother was dancing with a viper snake that bit her repeatedly until she convulsed and died. One week later she dreamed that she was caring for a gravely ill woman with sores on her body. In the dream she was rebuffed by a childhood schoolmate whom she knew at age ten, around the time of her father's death.

After completing her Two Week Journal, Connie was suffering from moderate depression with occasional thoughts of suicide, guilt, and recurrent somatic concerns. On the Impact of Events scale, her score on the Intrusion subscale was extremely elevated, indicating that she was suffering from Post-Traumatic Stress Disorder.

During the Two Week Journal period, Connie recorded fifteen dreams and felt that the journal was both enjoyable and therapeutic. On the questionnaire she spontaneously wrote that keeping the journal gave me "insight into my own mind's working out daily life problems and their relation to past situations."

Just before the anniversary of the Firestorm, Connie continued to suffer from serious emotional difficulties, including frequent nightmares, emotional numbness, and intrusive thoughts. On her follow-up survey, she reported a disturbing dream of "fear, houses burning, destruction, everything desolate." By this time her dreams, like those of other Survivors, had begun to focus more directly on fire imagery.

Connie's dreams and many others in our study support an information-processing view of dream formation, which postulates an unconscious search-and-match mechanism as an individual struggles to adapt to a current trauma. Dreaming activates memories and images of parallel wounds from the past as the unconscious searches for symbolic solutions, "whether defensive, magical or realistic," to pressing emotional conflicts (Breger, Hunter, and Lane, 1971). Thus for Connie, her grief dreams echoed back to profound past instances of loss as she struggled unconsciously to resolve her present losses.

Survival Needs Dreams

Dreams of searching for or needing food, shelter, or clothing were common in Survivor and Evacuee dreams. Themes of financial troubles, problems with insurance reimbursement, and searching for valuable items were also prominent.

On the objective level, these dreams mirrored real deprivations. Subjectively, these themes suggest powerful feelings of neediness and hunger for emotional support and security. Those who lacked proper insurance or who were financially devastated by the fire had many dreams of neediness. The imagery, however, tapped into deeper issues than a mere reflection of conscious monetary concerns.

Hannah, a thirty-five-year-old administrator, had less than half an hour between seeing the smoke and fleeing for her life, singed by flying embers. Although she did get a few important belongings into her car, she had no insurance on her rented apartment. In the aftermath of the fire, her steady relationship broke up, causing additional stress. She had frequent repetitive nightmares of her house and trees around it engulfed in unstoppable flames. In the first of thirteen entries in her Two Week Journal, she recorded a disturbing dream image.

The Haunting Homeless Figure

There is a small homeless person draped in rags, head completely covered, pushing an empty shopping cart.

Although she did experience a significant financial loss from the fire, Hannah was by no means destitute. For Hannah the empty shopping cart represented her own feeling of emotional depletion. Not only was the dream figure homeless but its shopping cart was empty. She had no emotional resources left.

Discussing her feelings about the rag-draped homeless person was very upsetting to Hannah. She felt, however, that exploring the meanings of the stark image jarred her awareness of how emotionally destitute she had become.

Her emotional adjustment improved steadily, but nine months after the fire, Hannah had a recurrence of anxiety symptoms. She joined a support group for survivors who were all having similar flare-ups of symptoms. Despite the dramatic benefits of the support group, for the entire month of the anniversary, Hannah suffered a recurrence of her depression.

Fifteen months after the fire, Hannah was neither depressed nor anxious. She was feeling optimistic and contemplating a career change. She felt the passivity of being victimized by the cataclysm of fire had stimulated crucial insights into her chronic tendency toward passivity in love and work. She was experimenting with a dramatic new level of assertiveness. Her dreams featured recurrent images of discovering new rooms. One dream was emblematic of deep inner changes—a repetitive dream of replacing the floral wallpaper in her childhood home. In another dream, she was working with an architect to design an expansive and modern new gymnasium. She related this dream to structural changes in her outlook and a newfound autonomy and direction that had emerged from the gloom of the Firestorm.

An early example of a more hopeful survival needs dream was that of Laurie, who lost both her home and her home-based business.

The Food Line and Our New House?

I am waiting in line for food. I finally get to the cashier who accepts my food voucher and gives me spaghetti. All the fire victims cheer loudly. My daughter sits in my lap and I stroke her face. Then I am walking on a burned-out hillside and see a few trailers that didn't get burned. A friend's house burned but has been rebuilt looking toward the coast. I go to look at it but worry it doesn't have a good foundation. It creaks and moves as we walk. It seems like a peculiar house but at least it is a house so we take it.

In this dream Hannah's emotional and physical needs are modestly fed with a soup-line spaghetti dinner. Then she nurtures her daughter and finds shelter. At this point in her recovery, Laurie's emotional house is still unstable—the foundation is weak and the floors creaky—but at least there is some shelter and nourishment available. A symbolic house, albeit a "fixer-upper," for building her recovery with her family has been found.

Body Integrity Dreams

Dreams depicting physical injury and/or disability to the dreamer or others were related to attempts to master the unexpected mortal threat the fire posed and the disorganizing impact on the experience of the self. Dream characters suddenly contracting fatal illnesses—especially AIDS—and dreams of physical injuries and of losing teeth all speak directly to unresolved concerns about both the physical threat and the grave emotional injuries the dreamer is attempting to resolve.

Susan, a forty-four-year-old woman who smelled smoke and had to run for her life within fifteen minutes, had the following nightmare six weeks after the Firestorm:

I Lose My Weakest Tooth

I see the wrong dentist. He makes a mistake and accidentally knocks out my weakest tooth. I am devastated! I weep and then feel grim and angry.

The dentist reminded her of the insurance adjustor trying to extract more money from her settlement. Dreams of lost or crumbling teeth frequently symbolize physical injury, narcissistic wounds, or impotence. The loss of the aggressive, cutting power of a tooth for this survivor was a debilitating dream injury symbolizing damage to the self.

Natural Disaster Dreams

Natural disaster themes occurred significantly more often in the dreams of the combined Survivor (11 percent of total dreams) and Evacuee (19 percent of total dreams) groups compared with the Controls ($p < .03$). Specific images included heat and fire damage as well as floods, mudslides, and other disasters.

Disaster dreams with apocalyptic themes were reported by a number of participants in the early days after the fire. Three weeks after the fire, Michael, an Evacuee, whose house had been miraculously spared from certain destruction by air-dropped fire retardant, dreamed of a flood of biblical proportions.

Parting of the Waters

In my house watching the flood waters rise. Soon I look out the window and the ocean waters are coming right up to the edge of the house. I start getting worried. Ultimately the waves start splashing against the house and water starts leaking in. I take my computer, unplug it, and start to carry it upstairs. More water starts to leak in. I tell my wife we may get flooded and she gets worried. Then as I watch out the window, the flood recedes like in the movie the Ten Commandments. Mary, a friend who has bad fire damage, is wet and upset. I quickly receive two tennis warmup jackets from friends to help me recover.

Images of flood waters and mudslides represented the destructive violence of the Firestorm in some Survivors' dreams. Michael's dream reflected what felt like a divine reprieve from destruction. Just when the dream flood waters were about to destroy his house and drown him, he was saved. The tennis jackets represented the warmth of friends, and he felt that his wet, burned-out friend Mary might represent the emotional damage he suffered, despite the saving of his house.

Tidal waves and floods in dreams are often connected to overwhelming and out-of-control emotions that the dreamer is facing in waking reality. For Michael, the flood also symbolized severe anxiety symptoms that flooded him the day of the fire, when his house appeared doomed, and for weeks afterward.

In the flood dream, Michael, an Evacuee, is passively saved from the apocalypse that threatened his house. Ten months after the fire, he had a dream that suggested more active mastery over a group of environmental terrorists threatening the forests in his neighborhood.

Fighting the Destruction of My Neighborhood

I am returning to my house in a huge wooded area with other houses on large lots. As I approach I see hundreds of back hoes tearing down the forest around my house. I can hear their engines throttling. It reminds me of pictures of the destruction of the Amazon rain forest. I run up to the foreman and shout at him, "You are destroying my house and my whole neighborhood." I was outraged and started ringing all my neighbors' doors, urging them to join me in fighting back. I organized a protest group to sit in front of the bulldozer. I was pissed off to the point of violence. The police came to break it up, but it became violent and they began chasing and beating people. Finally the cops agreed to stop the destruction of trees and houses. I felt satisfied.

In this dream Michael is more active in confronting the destruction of his neighborhood. In reality, his immediate neighborhood had been virtually destroyed, with houses burned on three sides of his lot. He was living daily with the construction noises of rebuilding and the barren landscape that had been lush before the fire.

At the time of the dream, he had begun to master his post-fire anxieties and his life was stabilizing. His active role in mastering the destructive threat in this dream echoed his increasing conscious sense of mastery over Firestorm anxieties.

Anniversary Reactions in Disaster Survivors

Firestorm Survivors suffered profound reactions to the impending first anniversary of the fire. There was a dramatic resurgence in nightmares, intrusive fantasies, and an unshakable sense of dread. Many Survivors reported that their Firestorm-related anxieties were equal or even greater than in the aftermath of the fire. Survivors who previously had not dreamed directly about fire and destruction were plagued with flaming nightmares.

To add to their jittery nerves, in the weeks prior to the anniversary, weather conditions mimicked the day of the fire with unseasonably hot, gusty days. Shortly before the anniversary, a house in the fire zone that had been rebuilt burned down.

One factor that was working against both Survivors and Evacuees was their sense of shame. They believed erroneously that they should have been well beyond the disorienting flashbacks, anxiety, and depression they were experiencing on the eve of the anniversary.

Terri, a twenty-seven-year-old law student, lost virtually everything in the fire. Two weeks before the anniversary, she was having frequent nightmares, early morning awakenings, headaches, and constant intrusive thoughts about the Firestorm. Her grades had dropped, and she rated her coping level as much worse than before the fire. Terri's preanniversary disaster dream depicted her continuing feelings of distress and isolation.

My Private Earthquake

I am standing with a few friends and the ground begins to shake. I start to panic, thinking to myself, "I knew it. I knew there'd be another earthquake." I look at my friends and they don't seem to notice anything. I tell them, "We are having an earthquake," and it seems like the world is going to end. My friends imply that I am crazy and there is no earthquake. I know I am not being paranoid and wonder how they could be so clueless.

Terri immediately connected the lack of empathy in the dream to her friend's waking response to her renewed distress. No one close to her seemed to understand that she was still experiencing intermittent periods of severe anxiety and depression. She wondered if she was abnormal or if her condition was worsening.

Two days before the anniversary, she had a further nightmare that featured an encounter with an old boyfriend. In the dream, he had deteriorated personally, had gained weight and was chronically abusing drugs.

Rescuing My Stuff from the Fire

My boyfriend appears and I know he is high on drugs. He kneels in front of me and slowly lights a fire. Everyone panics, leaving behind their belongings. I begin to flee but realize I've left everything behind. I start to feel in control of the situation. I grab everything, knowing I left nothing behind me. I know this event will not traumatize me in the future.

In contrast to Terri's near-total loss of her belongings in the Firestorm, the dream enacts a symbolic rescue of what she had lost. And although Terri rated this dream as a nightmare, she felt it left an afterglow of accomplishment—a feeling that she could finally control the dread of the fire and her rage over her losses. For Terri, the anniversary provoked both a regression and a quantum leap toward resolving her lingering traumatic reaction.

Factors Affecting Recovery: Echoes of Earlier Traumas

Of all the factors shaping coping and recovery, one invisible dimension of the Survivors' and Evacuees' experience was dominant—the lingering emotional impact of earlier losses, traumas, and deprivations. Three subjects (two Survivors and one Evacuee) remembered previously repressed sexual abuse from childhood in the aftermath of the fire. Others found themselves inexplicably stuck in melancholy ruminations on long-dead parents, the death of a child, divorces, or past tragedies.

For those who suffered childhood abuse, loss of a parent to divorce or death, previous disasters, accidents, or unresolved losses, the Firestorm set off a disturbing alchemy—blending the pain of past losses with present traumatic anxieties. Those with more profound backgrounds of trauma were more severely affected and slower to recover. Their dreams after the fire and around the anniversary of the fire frequently used the metaphor of their earlier traumas to depict reactions to the Firestorm and its aftermath.

A number of other critical factors also had an impact on the Firestorm Survivors' and Evacuees' perception of the magnitude of the trauma. These included the amount of warning they had had before evacuation, the perceived degree of mortal threat to themselves and their family members, the perceived severity of financial loss, and the degree to which irreplaceable objects were lost, such as photos, writings, original works of art, home-based businesses, and business records. Many family members and roommates had to split up and live separately, at least for a time.

Factors mitigating the impact of the trauma included continuing emotional support from family and peers, flexibility and understanding on the part of employers, participation in therapeutic and self-help groups, restoration of a stable living situation, and good insurance coverage. For a small number of Survivors, changes provoked by the fire opened up new career opportunities, brought families closer, or resulted in positive new friendships or love relationships.

Conclusion

Dreams open a window to observe the evolution of recovery from a natural disaster. For disaster survivors, remembering and exploring their dreams provides access to earlier emotional wounds that shape their post-traumatic response patterns. For the clinician and for the dreamer, making linkages between the present trauma and its emotional roots in the past can stimulate vital insights that may promote the resolution of both present and past traumas.

Dream images are sensitive indicators of impasses in recovery from a trauma. Survivors who suffer from repetitive nightmares or frequent dreams of undisguised brutality may be in need of immediate psychological help to resolve the post-traumatic syndrome before it becomes entrenched. Nightmares are a cardinal feature of Post-Traumatic Stress Disorder, and when repetitive dreams dwell on the disaster for months afterward there is a danger of fixating on the trauma.

Most of the participants in our study felt that keeping the Two Week Journal and participating in individual and group meetings to discuss their dreams and link them to fire experiences was therapeutic. There was an expectation of being helped by the ritual of remembering, sharing, and exploring their dreams. They also experienced an emotional catharsis and a sense of reassurance that their nightmares, grief, and guilt were legitimate and human rather than shameful, bizarre, or pathological.

When mental health resources are limited in a disaster, dream journals can serve as a self-help tool and a focus for discussion in support groups. It is important for mental health specialists to reassure disaster survivors that disrupted sleep and recurrent nightmares are part of the psyche's normal response to trauma.

Disaster survivors (or their psychotherapists) who are cataloging and exploring their dreams can identify core conflicts from the present and past. They can see and experience images evoking hope and recovery as more dreams emerge with themes indicating partial mastery, rebuilding, rebirth, new discoveries, or growth.

A series of dreams often shows a progression toward mastery as a trauma is resolved. Nightmares that are like graphic memories of the trauma gradually fade, giving way to dreams less focused on the trauma and more mixed with other concerns (Hartmann, 1984).

For months and years afterward, disaster survivors continue to be hypersensitive to subsequent life crises and stresses. Psychotherapists must pay special attention to anniversary reactions, episodic regressions, and other delayed post-traumatic reactions. For some, emotional regressions occurred only after substantial progress had been made and signaled a breakthrough in the ability to face the most abhorrent memories and emotions of the Firestorm.

Post-disaster dreams are compelling and infect the listener with a contagious anxiety that triggers fears for our own security and mortality. For the clinician who shows sympathetic interest, the exploration of dreams can transform disaster survivors' nightmares into a powerful vehicle for insight and resolution of post-traumatic reactions.

PART THREE

Traumas of Normal Living

Dreams and Adaptation to Divorce

ROSALIND D. CARTWRIGHT

Divorce is a trauma of normal living that comes along all too often. It does, however, provide an opportunity to look into the two questions that have been raised about dreams throughout history: Do dreams have meaning? and Do they perform some function?

Freud faced the same two questions when he wrote *The Interpretation of Dreams* ([1900] 1965). In his words, those in the exact sciences view the activity of dreaming as analogous to "the ten fingers of a man who knows nothing of music wandering over the keys of a piano." He concludes that on this basis a dream would be something wholly and completely incapable of interpretation, but "if we adopt the method of interpreting dreams that I have indicated here, we shall find that dreams really have a meaning and are far from being the expression of a fragmentary activity of the brain, as the authorities have claimed" (p. 110). In the content of every dream "we will find a link to a recent daytime impression" (p. 601). "Unsolved problems, tormenting worries, overwhelming impressions, all of these carry thought activity over into sleep" (p. 593). In other words, Freud believed that dreams not only are related to waking experience, but "are only concerned with what seems important to us and interests us greatly" (p. 624).

Freud was also clear that dreams deal more often with experiences that are accompanied by distressing emotions, with displeasure rather than with pleasure. In fact, he quotes the Hallam and Weed (1896) study, finding only 28 percent of dreams to be pleasant. As to their function, Freud agrees with Robert that in dreams "all kinds of harmful things are made harmless." In present-day parlance this has become known as the adaptive function of dreaming (Garma, 1946; Bonime, 1962; French and Fromm, 1964; Jones, 1970).

A good deal of research has been undertaken to test the ideas that dreams have meaning in terms of current emotional issues and an effect of reducing the negative affect they induce. Mostly these studies have relied on one of two designs. In the first, the subjects are exposed to some high and/or low affect-inducing manipulation prior to sleep, such as movies of circumcision rites versus travelogues, followed by a night of dream collection in the sleep laboratory to test for the appearance of the experimental stimuli in the dreams (Rechtschaffen and Foulkes 1965; Witkin and Lewis, 1967; Cartwright et al., 1969; Cohen and Cox, 1975). In the second type of study, some waking experimental condition is followed by different sleep conditions (one including REM time, the other with little or no REM time), and the effect of the opportunity for dreaming is calculated on a difference in the following waking behavior (Greiser, Greenberg, and Harrison, 1972).

The first design focuses on the dreams, the second on their effect as measured by some change in the waking level of affect or in the response to the original stimulus on a second occasion. The first work is addressed to the question of understanding the relation of dreams to the previous waking experience, its meaning, and the second to the question of function. When these are combined in the same study the question is: if the dreams include some direct representation of affect-arousing experimental stimuli, will that have an effect of "rendering these more harmless"?

Despite a number of innovative studies of this kind, there is not yet a clear consensus about the findings. One reason for this is that there is some confusion and confounding about what is being tested, dreaming or REM sleep. These two are usually synchronous in occurrence but they may become dissociated on occasion, especially when REM time is reduced. Under these circumstances dreaming may be intensified in other states, such as stage 2 (Cartwright, Monroe, and Palmer, 1967) or waking (Fiss, 1979), and so frustrate the attempt to establish a difference that dreams make in waking response. One lesson to be learned from these studies is that it is better to leave sleep intact if the focus is on the function of dreaming. Then at least we know how to locate and retrieve the major portion of the dreams by making the awakening close to the time that they are naturally occurring.

A second problem with this work arises when the subjects bring to the laboratory their own concerns. Then they often ignore the intended target topic, which is less important to them than it is to the experimenter (Cartwright and Kaszniak, 1991). They just go on with their own dream agenda. It is easier to demonstrate a direct influence of some presleep event on the dreams when the subjects are in a naturally occurring emotional situation, such as anticipating surgery (Breger, Hunter, and Lane, 1971) or childbirth (Winget and Kapp, 1972).

The best test of whether dreams have emotional meaning, and produce some real change in waking behavior, requires that the subjects be undergoing a life event that creates genuine affect, preferably one that can be expected to persist for some time. Such an event is a marital separation with the intent to complete a divorce. Some people weather this upset in their lives well; others are bogged down for very long periods of time in hurt, anger, despair, and self-pity. This offers an opportunity to look into the dreams of those who are doing well and those who are not, while they await the legal termination of the relationship they expected to be a lifelong, loving partnership. Do these two groups demonstrate differences in their dreams that relate to this transition? And is there any positive effect on the waking adjustment to the new circumstances from dealing with this issue directly in the dreams?

To help answer these questions I assembled a team to interview a large group of volunteers, to assess them on psychological tests and a standard psychiatric evaluation interview, the Schedule for Affective Disorders and Schizophrenia (SADS) (Endicott and Spitzer, 1978), for the presence of a mood disorder or any history in their own lives or of others in their family of a mood disorder. Two hundred and fourteen people responded to our ads offering to pay a small fee to individuals going through divorce for participation in a sleep and dream study. Male and female, rich and poor, black, white, oriental, and Hispanic, they came and told their tales of how their marriage began, got into trouble, and died. Most cried. Even those who had sought the separation did not feel cheerful about this turn of events. If we were looking for a trauma that creates genuine affect that is long lasting, this turned out to be a good choice. Thirty-one percent, more women than men, were suffering from a major depression, although none was on any medication for this disorder.

We selected seventy to enter the sleep studies, thirty-five men and thirty-five women. Forty of these (twenty of each sex) were depressed as a consequence of the breakup of the marriage, and thirty were managing the stress without showing the symptoms of an affective disorder. Each slept for three consecutive nights in the laboratory, with the third one being a night of REM interruptions to collect the dream material. Almost all produced four dream reports that night. Sixty-one of these people, thirty women and thirty-one men, came back one year later and repeated the interviews, psychological testing, and sleep studies. Most were no longer depressed according to the Research Diagnostic Criteria (RDC) (Spitzer, Endicott, and Robbins, 1978), only 11 percent still met diagnostic criteria, and most, 69 percent, were also divorced.

What did they dream and to what effect? The dream reports were all tape recorded at the time of the REM awakenings, and the subjects answered a standard series of questions about each dream before they were allowed to go back to sleep. The dreams were then transcribed and given code numbers so that judges could do their analysis of the content without knowing who was depressed or even whether this was an initial set of dreams or a set from the one-year follow-up session.

The first analysis of the dream content asked whether the mood disorder was reflected in the dreams: Do depressed people have more unhappy dreams than those who are experiencing the same stressful event but keeping their mood response within normal limits? The judges found significantly more negative-feeling dreams among the depressed subjects than in those who were not depressed. When asked to rate each of their own dreams at the end of their report, the depressed subjects themselves called 39 percent of their dreams "unpleasant," whereas this was true for only 14 percent of the dreams of those who were not depressed. It seems the waking mood has a real effect on the affective tone of the dream.

The second question we addressed was whether the dreams would include the about-to-be-former spouse as a character. Here we chose not to accept anything except a straightforward inclusion of the real person without any need to interpret. This time the interest was on the question of function: would dealing with the marriage partner in the dreams relate to some working through of the feelings about the divorce and contribute to the subject's making a good waking adjustment to the single life?

We first looked at the initial set of dreams of the group of sixty-one for whom we had one-year follow-up data. Twenty-one of these, 34 percent, included the spouse in at least one of their four dreams that were recorded on the third night of their initial study. Seventeen of these "incorporators," 81 percent, were classified at the time as depressed. This classification was based both on the SADS interview and on a self-report test, the Beck Depression Inventory (Beck, 1967), on which those scoring 14 or more were considered depressed. Looked at another way, only 17 percent of the twenty-three who were not depressed originally, and who returned one year later to report on how their life was going, had included the spouse as a dream character. This is in contrast to 45 percent of the thirty-eight depressed subjects for whom follow-up was available. Depression, unpleasant dreams, and dreaming of the spouse all seemed to occur together.

This part of the investigation was supported by a closer look into the content of these dreams. The dreams that included the spouse of those who were depressed displayed the negative feelings associated with this relationship quite directly.

> Me and my husband and my sister went out to a restaurant like a pharmacy and sat in a booth and a co-worker was there who asked for lager if they would warm it. I went to do it and when I came back my husband said,

"I'm divorcing you. Leaving you," and got up and walked out. I was *stunned* and *embarrassed.*

My ex-husband told me to go to the hospital for a problem. It turned out I didn't have a problem. *He was just giving me a hard time.*

I had to tell my boyfriend I couldn't see him because work has to take priority because of the financial mess my husband left me in. I was *upset* and thought, "*You bastard,* you got in the way again."

I was having a fight with my husband. *Yelling and angry.* His not taking good care of himself, overworking. He was running to me, not feeling well. Started collapsing. I was in a phone booth trying to make a call. I sat him down on a pile of something. I was persuading him to stay put while I call a cab to take him to the hospital. I was holding him up and said, "I have to go back and close the door."

I was in Europe with my boyfriend and husband. I was sleeping alone in a bed. Then my husband joined me. I was *irritated* that he messed up the sheets. I had been sleeping alright before with another woman, who was also me. Before that I dreamed a friend joined me at a table and the two men sat at another table, that way I didn't have to choose between them who to sit with. I was doing fine on my own.

My ex-husband was *yelling* at me, blaming me for following him and disrupting his life.

Not all the dreams were angry in tone. Some were dreams of sadness and loss.

. . . So then my wife called the army, General MacArthur to try to get them out. And after a long while all I *wanted* to do was just *be alone with my wife,* just to be able to be with her, just to make love and that's it.

Somehow me and my husband are visiting old friends of ours and he's wearing an earring in his left ear to prove he is not gay. He's really good looking. And my husband was there and I *wanted to get back at him* but he didn't care. So I jumped into John's arms and he was holding me. I had my feet wrapped around his body. And we were kissing passionately and my husband was standing around kinda indifferent.

The dreams of the nondepressed that incorporated the spouse had a different tone. The subjects and the judges rated them as more pleasant or neutral. The theme was often the end of the relationship, the recognition of the separation.

She and I had been out together. I dreamt of her closing a window when we arrived home. She wanted to close a window; the frame was old, made of small pieces of stone that fit together very precisely: cotswald stone. It wasn't my home. It might have been her home. —Before that an image of an empty dishwasher.

I was with my ex-wife again walking through an exhibit of a scientific project that dealt with the historical discovery of one people by another. All kinds of artifacts dating back to this time. Before that an image of a plot of land where a school was torn down. I was dreaming of being in front of it after it was torn down and made into a park. We walked in from daylight into darkness, like an eclipse. The discoverers who came over were murdered by being buried alive or walled up inside a wall and left there to die. The exhibit was behind glass a diorama. All the exhibits clean and new.

Taking a Christmas tree in my car to throw it out. I was in the truck my wife and I owned and the fender got bent. I was complaining you have to pay so much for things and they don't hold up right. It felt like tinfoil.

I was invited to dinner by a friend and she said, "Sorry Pat (my ex) is not coming, so no dinner." So I went home to bake a cake for myself.

Serving different flavored cakes at a party for me, my ex-wife and different people I'm dating and friends were there. We were marking them. It had something to do with sex. Ordering them by how close I felt to each woman. The flavor represented each person. I picked G.F.'s flavor over my wife's to be number 1.

We were playing a memory game, going from room to room in a house we bought back in 1977. My former wife was not playing, but went to take a nap and we had to turn on the light briefly to remember what you could see in each room. She said, "Give me a break."

The third analysis had to do with the outcome at follow-up. At the time they returned for their annual check-up, the subjects were interviewed about how they were managing their lives. Many areas were touched on. In what way was their life now different? Were they working? Did they change jobs, move, go back to school? How was their health, how were the kids, were they dating, how were they doing financially, did they see the former spouse? At the conclusion they were asked, "On a scale of 1 to 10, where do you think you are in getting over the divorce if 1 represents not over it at all and 10 is completely over it?" The interviewer also made a rating independently, and a blind rater later went through all of the transcripts of these interviews and made a 1 to 10 rating. Agreement among these ratings was very good.

The thirty-one subjects who had been depressed and incorporated the spouse into their initial dreams had a better adjustment at follow-up than those who did not (more rankings from 6 to 10). This was a significant difference. Although it would not be correct to assume that the direct incorporation of the problem into the dreams was the cause of the working through of the negative feelings so that a better adjustment could be made, it is suggestive that dreams do relate to ongoing emotional issues and may contribute to some regulation of the associated negative mood. If so, this would help in the overall ability to cope more effectively.

The study is suggestive. There are many ways in which it could be faulted. There was only one night of dream collection, and some who did not dream of the spouse that night might well be experiencing a great deal of incorporation of the problem of this relationship on other nights. Also there was a very long gap between that one night of dreaming and the follow-up interview, during which many new reality factors would have intervened. In addition, of course, those who dream of the spouse at night may be doing a lot of waking work directly on the problem as well, which may be the more powerful variable. Those who did not dream of the spouse may have completed their dream work on the relationship before we saw them. Despite all of these caveats, the main findings stand: those who are depressed have more negative dreams, and more often dream of the spouse. Among the depressed those that dream of the spouse have a better outcome.

Major life events are a fruitful field for the study of the role of dreams in psychic life. This at last is receiving the attention it deserves if we are to have a full picture of the work of the mind (Cartwright and Lamberg 1992).

Dreams in Bereavement

PATRICIA GARFIELD

Methought I saw my late espousèd saint
  Brought to me like Alcestis from the grave
. . . . .
Came vested all in white, pure as her mind.
  Her face was veiled, yet to my fancied sight,
  Love, sweetness, goodness, in her person shined
So clear, as in no face with more delight.
  But O, as to embrace me she inclined
  I waked, she fled, and day brought back my night.

JOHN MILTON

The death of a loved one is a trauma that each person must eventually endure. Researchers on the topic of bereavement report a period of sleep disturbance and nightmares that survivors almost inevitably experience following a death (Tatelbaum, 1980; Worden, 1991). Yet professionals in the area of grief counseling, with few exceptions (Kast, 1982; Von Franz, 1986; Kennedy, 1991), rarely describe the nature of these disturbing dreams or offer the mental health worker guidance in what to expect and how to help clients respond to their nightmares about the deceased in a constructive manner.

The dead live on in our dreams long after they die. We see them, yearn for them, love them, fear them, hate them, agonize about them, embrace them, or listen to their advice. The type of dream about the dead varies with the survivor's stage of mourning, the recency of the loss, the nature of the death, and the relationship of the deceased to the survivor.

Phases of Mourning Are Mirrored in a Series of Dreams: The Seasons of Grief

After a physical trauma, the body undergoes a process of healing that is reflected in the injured person's dreams (Garfield, 1992). Likewise, after an emotional trauma such as the death of a loved person, the survivor's dreams reflect the process of bereavement (Kast, 1982). Investigators into the topic of grief describe at least three general phases of mourning (Kubler-Ross, 1975; Staudacher, 1987; James and Cherry, 1988; Worden, 1991):

1. Numbness. Characterized by shock or denial of the death. Survivor usually feels dazed, as though events are unreal.

2. Disorganization. Emotional chaos occurs, typically including anxiety, fear, grief, anger, fury, guilt, relief, and/or anguish. Also common are restlessness and behavior that suggests searching for the deceased. In cases of violent death, hatred, horror, or revulsion may be experienced.

3. Reorganization. Survivor develops new roles, skills and relationships, or resumes former ones. Survivor readjusts, treasuring memories of the deceased but able to emotionally reinvest in life.

These phases are not discrete; they ripple back and forth like waves.

Worden (1991) has developed the concept of "tasks of grief." He asserts that this formulation helps the mourner to play a more active role during bereavement, rather than simply passing through stages. He describes four tasks of grief:

1. To accept the reality of the loss.

2. To work through the pain of grief.

3. To adjust to an environment in which the deceased is missing.

4. To emotionally "relocate" the deceased and move on with life.

The goals of the mental health worker are to assist the client in successfully accomplishing these tasks.

When a person is bereaved, his or her dreams may help or hinder accomplishment of the tasks of grief. It is important for the mental health practitioner to be able to point out the relationship between current dreams about the deceased and the tasks of grief.

Folk traditions hold that our ancestors and lost loved ones speak to us through dreams. The scientific view is that aspects of ourselves animate their images, based on memories and activated by psychological needs. Survivors themselves often feel that they have had actual contact with the spirit of the deceased in a dream. Elisabeth Kubler-Ross agrees, calling dreams of the dead "true contacts on a spiritual plane" (Kubler-Ross, 1975). Regardless of the explanation of the source of dreams of the deceased, the dead have messages for the living. The living also have messages for the dead that can be delivered and resolved in the meeting point of the dreamworld.

Some workers in the area of grief have observed dreams that forewarn the dreamer of the imminent death of a person close to them (Kast, 1982; Linn, 1991). Common dream themes preceding the death of a loved person include preparations for a journey (Smith, 1984; Von Franz, 1986; Garfield, 1992), natural catastrophes, and drastic changes in climate. Here I focus on dreams following the death of a significant person in the survivor's life, mainly drawn from three samples of bereavement dreams:

1. A collection from my dream journal during the two years following my father's death, consisting of twenty-six dreams in which the deceased was "present" and eighteen dreams in which he was mentioned, for a total of forty-four bereavement dreams.

2. A collection obtained from my in-depth, face-to-face interviews with fifteen bereaved women, totaling about thirty hours, plus numerous follow-up dream reports by letter. Assorted other dreams were described to me by participants in various bereavement support groups (Hilton, 1992).

3. A collection of 101 bereavement dreams gathered by Patricia Keelin from people who answered advertisements (Keelin, 1992).

Dreams during the Phase of Numbness

Alive-Again Dreams

Definition: In Alive-again dreams, the deceased appears and the survivor is surprised to see him or her alive. The death is often explained away as a mistake. During the dream, the survivor may or may not realize that the person is actually dead.

In the early stages of loss of a loved one, dreams about the deceased often involve the theme of shock at seeing the deceased alive again. Barrett (1992) classified these as "Back-to-life" dreams, and noted that they occur soon after a death. A typical example of these Alive-again dreams from my collection of bereavement dreams comes from a woman in her forties who had remarried after her husband's lingering death from cancer. The dream recurred in several variations. In this one, she was wandering around the house where she and the deceased first lived. She was surprised to find it stocked and cooking going on. She felt like an outsider, when:

> Suddenly my husband walks into the kitchen looking just as he always did. I am astonished. I run to him, hug him and am ecstatic that he is alive. I am full of questions. I ask him where he has been and why he hasn't tried to contact me. I tell him of my loneliness and about what a difficult time I have had without him.

So far this dream had the usual Alive-again theme. However, it continued with a disturbing element:

> He does not really answer and seems somewhat distant. Another woman walks into the kitchen. She seems shocked to see me embracing him. He then tells me that he has remarried and that this is his new wife. I am utterly stunned. I ask him why he did not try to find me. I simply cannot believe that he abandoned his search for me, we were so much in love and so happily married. There wasn't a moment when we felt doubts and I find this whole scenario almost impossible to believe. I awaken feeling betrayed, deeply sad and shaken.

In addition to wishing her husband were alive again, this survivor was expressing her own feelings of guilt over having remarried. She was undergoing a complicated grief reaction that had not yet been resolved. She thought her first husband might be "trying to make me let him go" in these dreams.

"Alive-again" or "Back-to-life" dreams appear to help the dreamer in the first task of grief, that is, to accept the reality of the loss. They are not always successful. During the dream, the survivor is typically overjoyed to find the deceased alive, believing that some sort of mistake was made. When the survivor awakens from such a dream, he or she is often overwhelmed once more with the pain of the loss. Its reality is accentuated. Sometimes the recognition that the deceased is dead occurs within the dream, as in this case from a woman whose mother had died a few months before:

> I am very surprised to see my mother alive. I ask, "But didn't we hold a funeral for you?" She replies, "Yes, but I don't want anyone to know, so don't tell."

The woman reported that this dream was "fun" and made her feel good when she awakened, as if her mother continued to be with her. Alive-again dreams occur for a long time after death, past the phase of numbness. The dream quality may become pleasant, as in this dream.

Occasionally a resolution can occur within the Alive-again dream, as in this one from the author's collection that occurred about four weeks after the dreamer's grandmother died:

> I'm in the lower level of a hospital or morgue in a waiting area. My dad has gone to do something and I am waiting to confirm Mom's [dreamer's grandmother] death. I go around to the nurse's station to ask something and Mom is there, sitting in a wheelchair. She is alive! She looks pretty good and is just sitting there. I say, "Mom! You're alive!" She looks at me but doesn't talk. She sits like she is waiting for something or someone. She has some sort of physical impairment around her head and arms, but is not in pain or upset. I go back to meet Dad to tell him she's not dead. I tell him over and over again and he doesn't believe me . . .

Later, the dreamer, her father, mother, and the deceased grandmother, on a gurney, were leaving the building in sunny daylight. Then the grandmother appeared more spiritlike, with a clear, beaming face, radiantly smiling at her daughter (the dreamer's mother). The dreamer awoke with a feeling of healing from this dream. She had been angry at her mother for not being present at the grandmother's death. In this dream, the survivor felt that since the grandmother had forgiven her mother, she, too, could forgive her. Here we see the beginning of attempts to accomplish task 2, dealing with the painful emotions of grief.

The survivor is not always happy after the shock of seeing the deceased alive again in a dream. One elderly widower described to me a dream of seeing his wife alive, playing cards. He was furious with her, wanting to berate her about "all the trouble you put me through while you were actually out having a good time." This type of Alive-again dream belongs more to the second phase of mourning.

In cases of violent death, the survivor may be terrified to see the deceased alive in a dream. A young widow, whose husband had recently died after being crushed in an industrial accident, told me of an intensely frightening dream of her husband, who was moving stiffly toward her in a navy coat, "almost not alive." In other dreams, she saw him very far off, and thin, "like a soda cracker." In yet another, she dreamed of looking into a mirror and seeing her husband's face, appearing as if it "had been scribbled on and erased." Such dreams echo the fear of ghosts common in past times. They reflect the sense of distortion and irreality that follow recent traumatic deaths. This woman ceased dreaming about her husband directly and substituted a symbolic image, discussed below.

In general, Alive-again dreams seem to represent wish fulfillment. On another level, they help the survivor accomplish the task of accepting the reality of the loss. Barrett (1992) found a high frequency (39 percent of seventy-seven dreams about the deceased) of this category of dreams of the dead coming back to life. The mental health worker can assure a bereaved person that such dreams are quite common, and although they may be exquisitely painful and temporarily enhance grief, they also help the survivor accept the reality of the loss.

Dying-Again Dreams

Definition: In Dying-again dreams, the deceased is once more suffering the symptoms that caused death, either as they were in actuality, greatly exaggerated, or profoundly distorted.

Dying-again dreams is another category of dreams that is common during the first phase of mourning. A recent death may be replayed especially if the survivor was present, or if the circumstances were sudden or violent. Several widows described to me disturbing dreams in which they saw their husbands in the agony of dying, their own desperate attempts to prevent it, and other aspects of the death. Here is a typical example from an elderly widow:

> My husband fell to the floor—just as he actually did when he died. I called 911 and the paramedics came but they couldn't revive him. I kept trying to get him to open his eyes and speak to me, but he was dead. I woke up crying.

This type of dream is characteristic of many types of post-traumatic stress, where nightmares about the trauma recur, whether of an injury (Garfield, 1992), accident, catastrophe, or war trauma. Sometimes the dream "replay" is much worse than the original event.

Kast (1982) describes the dream of a young women the night after her sweetheart died from a second heart attack. In it, the survivor held her lover, felt close to him, and was overwhelmed by tenderness, when:

> Suddenly I feel him become colder and colder. He dies in my arms. I am filled with despair. I know that nothing can bring him back again, that I can no longer embrace him, no longer feel him.

Cold, snow, or ice are frequently mentioned in disturbing dreams of the dead.

Dying-again dreams, like Alive-again dreams, also seem to assist the dreamer in accepting the reality of the loss. When grief is not resolved, Dying-again dreams may continue for a long time. Like other post-traumatic nightmares, replaying the event helps desensitize the survivor to it, eventually allowing him or her to bear the unbearable. Among the dreams I had in which my father was "present," 15 percent were of the Dying-again type.

A variation of the dying-again dream is one in which the deceased person becomes deformed and monsterlike. One of the women I interviewed reported that she had no dreams at all for the first few weeks after her father died. Then she began having disturbing dreams about three weeks after her father's death:

> I see my dead father and my dead uncle walking with my mother, flanking her two sides. They did not want me to tell them that they were dead and if I so much as mentioned it, their faces began to melt and twist strangely, like ghouls.

In another dream of this type, the survivor reported a nightmare that her father had turned into a monster. This kind of distressing dream is most common when the dying process is prolonged and accompanied by many physical changes that are difficult for the survivor to witness.

Here is an unusual variation of the Dying-again dream, described to me by a woman in her thirties after her grandmother's painful death:

> My grandmother is suffering terribly from cancer. Tumors are popping up like mushrooms all over her body. I run my hands across and through her energy fields, trying to heal her. I imagine her being healed, but my efforts have little, if any, effect. She goes on suffering. I suffer with her. I am crying with great wracking sobs as she dies. I wake up crying but without wet tears.

The survivor had this dream a few years after her grandmother's death occurred. She was experiencing a complicated and prolonged grief, as expressed in these final stanzas from a poem she wrote based on the dream (Evans, [1985] 1992):

Grandmother, for nine years
you have visited my dreams.
I have watched you die
over and again.

Release me, I cannot let go
this grief I failed to recognize
your dying took so long.

This survivor had not yet been able to complete her tasks of grief, but by expressing her dream in poetic form, she was beginning to come to some resolution.

The mental health worker may be able to assist survivors in coping with the disturbing emotions expressed in any Dying-again dreams that take ugly forms by pointing out, when appropriate, the way in which they symbolize the physical transformation that was witnessed and do not refer to the character of the deceased.

In general, Alive-again and Dying-Again dreams seem to help the survivor in grief task 1, accepting the reality of the death, and may initiate grief task 2, helping the survivor to work through the painful emotions of grief.

Dreams during the Phase of Disorganization

Once the period of numbness wears off somewhat, a phase of chaotic emotional responses surges through the survivor. These intense feelings are often accompanied by certain themes in dreams about the dead person. Sigmund Freud, in his classic 1917 paper "Mourning and Melancholia," originally described this process, particularly in reference to depression, naming it "grief work," without showing how it was expressed in dreams (Freud, [1917] 1959).

Saying-Goodbye Dreams

Definition: In Saying-goodbye dreams, the deceased appears and takes leave of the survivor. This category of dream often includes physical contact, the exchange of loving feelings, and an affectionate goodbye.

Survivors frequently dream of the deceased appearing to say goodbye. Barrett (1992), who calls this category of dream "Leave-taking," reported that 39 percent of her sample of seventy-seven dreams of the dead were of this type. She observed that these dreams were usually positive and often helped survivors resolve their grief. She noted that they occurred more often later in mourning. In contrast, a Saying-goodbye dream was the first dream I had after my father's death in which his image directly appeared. The difference is probably due to differences in definition of categories.

This example from my dream diary took place about six months after my father's death from a second heart attack:

> I am on a train, sitting on the right-hand side of the car, near the aisle. My mother comes and squeezes between me and the seatback in front of me to get to the vacant seat near the window. I feel almost squashed . . . Later I get up to leave the train and go to the door. Near it, on a sideways seat,

is an old man. He stands up, wobbly and bent over, supporting himself with a cane. His shoulder is bumpy and distorted. I know it is my father, even though he doesn't resemble him in the slightest. I kiss him goodbye and feel a wave of sadness. I wake up weepy.

Among the numerous emotions depicted in this dream is the sense of pressure I was feeling at the time from my widowed mother and the mood of nostalgia I felt over having been deprived of my father's elder years by his early death at sixty-two years of age. This was one of only two dreams during the first year after my father's death in which he was "present." During the second year of mourning, he appeared in twenty-four of my dreams.

Saying-goodbye dreams, whether it is the deceased who appears to give a final farewell or the survivor who initiates a goodbye, often give a sense of completion. This type of dream, too, helps the survivor accept the reality of death, and expresses some of the emotions of grief.

Taking-a-Journey Dreams

Definition: In Taking-a-journey dreams, the deceased is taking a trip on a train, bus, airplane, or ship. Travel by car usually falls into the category of Daily-activity dreams, unless the trip aspect is emphasized. Occasionally it is the survivor who is setting out on a journey.

People in the process of dying frequently dream of preparing for a journey (Von Franz, 1986). Likewise, their caretakers sometimes have similar dream themes (Kast, 1982). Survivors also often depict the deceased at some point of departure, taking off on a journey. Usually a barrier or border is pictured between the survivor and the departing deceased. This typical Taking-a-journey dream is from an elderly widower. It took place about two months following the death of his wife, who was the dominant partner (Garfield, 1988):

My wife and I are going to the airport. We reach a gate through which I am not allowed, but she is. When she has almost reached the airplane, she turns and waves goodbye.

Although there is a goodbye gesture in this dream, the emphasis is upon the trip that is undertaken. The widower felt great relief. He told me it was as if his wife had simply gone on ahead and he would join her later. He was able to actively engage in life once more, even to the point of remarrying. This dream helped him in task 3, that of adapting to an environment in which the deceased was missing.

Airports, train stations, bus stations, and docks are common settings for Taking-a-journey dreams. So is traveling down a river or crossing it. Even if the deceased is not directly seen, dreams involving journeys seem to symbolically represent the separation from the deceased.

In the group of dreams in which my father was present, 15 percent involved trains or railroad stations. This one from my dream diary occurred about seventeen months after his death:

> I am teaching a class when I get a telephone call from my father asking me to meet him at a railway station to help him with tickets for a trip. I talk with others on the telephone about this, too, and it doesn't seem necessary for me to go. When I finally get off the telephone, the students in my class are restless and resentful. I manage to get them attentive again.

This dream reminded me of when I tried to teach class the day after my father's death. I got in front of the class and found I was unable to talk, dissolved into tears, and dismissed the class. The dream seemed to be saying that I no longer had to attend to the details of my father's journey, that I must now concentrate on my work. In addition to the train station mentioned in this dream, another common image in dreams of the dead is a telephone call from the dead person.

Telephone-Call Dreams

Definition: In Telephone-call dreams, the deceased telephones the survivor or is already speaking to him or her on the phone. The survivor may also telephone the deceased.

An intriguing type of dream about the dead that is typical is one in which the survivor dreams of receiving a telephone call (or a letter) from the deceased. This example from my collection of bereavement interviews, from a woman in her thirties whose father had died five months previously, shows how powerful such dreams can be:

> The phone rang, so I got up out of bed to answer it. On the other end of the line was my dad. My father had had a laryngectomy, and spoke with the aid of a mechanical device that made his esophageal speech sound strange. In the dream, his voice was clear and normal, his "real" voice. He said, "Hi, it's me. I need to talk to you." I told him how glad I was that he called because I was worried about him. He told me, "I know how you worry, so I wanted to let you know everything is all right. I'm whole again. They gave me back my voice." "I know," I replied. He said, "No, you don't understand, it's me. I'm talking. I'm well again. Everything is going

to be all right." I said, "I know, Daddy, I really do know." He said, "I don't think you really understand what I'm trying to tell you. I want to tell your mom that I'm okay. Never be afraid of dying. Being dead isn't a terrible thing. This is such a good place to be. She won't believe me. You understand [psychic things]. You tell her." I agreed.

When the survivor awoke, she felt as if she had received a real communication from her father, the experience was so vivid. She felt "peaceful and complete." Four days later she called her mother to tell her about the dream and was surprised to find that her mother described a similar dream. Categories of dreams may overlap. This dream is also classified as a Young-well-again and Advice-comfort-gift dream.

In this woman's dreams shortly after her father's slow death, he spoke with the same "mechanical" sound that he acquired as a result of the surgical removal of his larynx. In later dreams, like the one above, her father spoke to her in natural, clear tones. Another woman's father had been confined to a wheelchair the whole time she knew him; he died when she was nine. After his death, this young woman's father walked in her dreams and assured her that he no longer needed a wheelchair, that he was well and they would be together someday. Grieving survivors have begun to heal when the deceased appears in normal health in their dreams.

Telephone calls are sometimes attempted from the survivor to the deceased in dreams. In one of my dreams of this type, about twenty months after my father's death:

I am trying to telephone my father from a train station. I want to ask him to come pick me up. The telephone is out of order and I lose my coin. In this case, I seem to be expressing my frustration at being out of emotional communication with my father, want his support, and lose something of value.

Dreams of telephone calls are more common in bereavement dreams than in general dreams. Only 3 percent of general dreams contain telephone calls (Barrett, 1992). In contrast, I found that 12 percent of the dreams in which my deceased father appeared involved telephone calls. Barrett (1992) found that 53 percent of the category she called "State-of-death" dreams involved telephone calls from the deceased, while telephone calls appeared in 24 percent of the dreams about the dead in her other categories. Many such dreams and waking reports of apparitions of this type are reported by Rogo and Bayless (1979).

Receiving a telephone call from the deceased appears to be a metaphor for communication with the spirit of the dead person. Telephone-call dreams seem to help survivors accept the reality of death, may help them believe that communication with the dead person is intact, and that the deceased is at peace.

Dreams during the Phase of Reorganization

As survivors begin to adjust to their changed environment, one in which the deceased is missing, their dreams reflect their emotional adaptation.

Young-Well-Again Dreams

Definition: In Young-well-again dreams, the deceased appears in an image that reflects the way he or she looked or acted when young or healthy. Clothing is often described as flowing, hair as shining, and face radiant. Infirmities caused by illness or injury have vanished.

This category of dream characteristically appears as the survivor reaches the last stage of mourning. It usually produces a very positive feeling and sometimes brings a sense of peace, as in this example from my collection, from a woman in her forties whose father had died several months before the dream:

> I was at a dance at the high school, standing outside the door, talking with my father. The sky was a vast, clear velvet overhead, studded with stars. I held an adorable little girl on my hip. My dad was healthy and young, vibrant, like I've never seen him except in old sepia photos of his high school days. He was in a great mood, smiling, like he rarely did, his face light, as if it were a party. The little girl wanted to go back into the dance. I took Dad's arm and said, "Come on, Dad, let's go dance," but he turned pale as a corpse and said, "You know I can't do that." And then I remembered that he was dead.

The emphasis in this dream is on the health and vibrancy of the father, who was often depressed when he was alive. The survivor "had a great time talking with him." She associated the dance in her dream with the world. This was the same woman who, in earlier dreams of her father, saw him in a ghoulish way, with his face melting and twisting. In this dream, she felt she had experienced her father in a wonderful way, the way she liked best. She wrote a poignant poem based on the dream, which gave her a great sense of satisfaction.

Another woman in her forties told me a series of three dreams she had following the death of her grandmother. In the first two, she simply saw her grandmother standing in a light in the corner of the room. In the third,

My grandmother told me this was the last time she could see me. After this, I'd have to come to her. She led me through corridors where there were people all crippled up. It scared the wits out of me. Then I saw her sitting on a chair, wearing a light lavender gown. Her hair was up, white and glowing. She was just beautiful!

Although lavender was a favorite of the woman and she loved its aroma, she associated it with death. She had planted English lavender on the top of a grave of a relative, and her grandmother was buried in a lavender dress. The beautiful appearance of her grandmother in the dream gave the survivor a feeling that all was well with her grandmother's spirit, and helped her feel at peace.

Approval-Disapproval Dreams

Definition: In Approval-disapproval dreams, the deceased is depicted as severely criticizing the survivor. In the contrasting form, the deceased appears to strongly approve of the survivor.

People whose relationship with the deceased was highly ambivalent frequently still yearn for their approval in dreams. The British writer Virginia Woolf had this type of relationship with her father, both admiring him and resenting his treatment of her sister. After his slow, arduous death she was obsessed with feelings of guilt, in contrast to her sister's feeling of relief. Four years later, when she first began to try to write a novel, Woolf dreamed that she showed her manuscript to her father, who was himself an accomplished writer (Woolf, 1908). In her dream, Woolf's father read her work, snorted, and dropped it onto a table. Woolf awoke melancholy and discouraged. The "disapproval" form of Approval-disapproval dreams may occur during the disorganization stage of mourning, while the "approval" form is more associated with the reorganization stage. In complicated grief, both forms may go on for years.

The Swedish philosopher-mystic Emanuel Swedenborg, living in the eighteenth century, also had a conflictual relationship with an authoritarian father. Swedenborg's father was a minister and bishop who had always wanted his son to follow his own religious career, instead of science. Some nine years after his father's death, Swedenborg recorded in his Journal of Dreams an entry that made him feel he had finally succeeded in winning his father's approval (Kirven and Larsen, 1988). In it, he saw his father tying the lace cuffs that he—Emanuel—wore. At that time lace cuffs were only worn by the laity, not the clergy. To dream of his father assisting him in this manner suggested to Swedenborg that his father had finally accepted his son's chosen role as scientist. Although Swedenborg had not become a minister, he had had a powerful spiritual experience that prompted him to use his scientific skills to probe the spiritual world. Probably this greater emphasis on spiritual life allowed him to dream of his father's approval.

Modern-day mourners replay the same theme of parental approval and disapproval in their dreams about the deceased parent. One woman described to me frustrating dreams in which she argued relentlessly with her deceased mother. It infuriated her that she continued to be plagued with such dreams long after the mother's death. Another woman reported a dream she had the night after her mother's death in which the deceased scolded the survivor furiously for having divided up her belongings. A widow described a dream of receiving approval from a portrait of her deceased husband before she remarried. A young man told me about being able to confront his dead father in a dream and feel forgiven. Old battles continue to be fought—and sometimes won—in bereavement dreams.

Advice-Comfort-Gift Dreams

Definition: In Advice-comfort-gift dreams, the survivor receives a message from the deceased, one of comfort, such as, "Don't worry, I'm fine," or advice, such as not to sell the house, or a "gift" such as an inheritance, a message about where to find something that has been hidden, and so forth. Rarely, the survivor offers advice, comfort, or gifts to the deceased. This category of dream often has a high emotional charge and is described as exceptionally vivid or "real." These dreams can have the intensity of a visitation.

This type of dream is among the most pleasant for the survivor. Advice-comfort-gift dreams tend to take place during the last stage of mourning, as in this typical example from a woman, taken from Keelin's (1991) collection of bereavement dreams:

> My aunt appeared to me. She was smiling the most beautiful smile as she said to me, "Don't worry about me. I am just fine." I woke from the dream with such joy and happiness. My heart was bursting with an overwhelming feeling of love. I felt as though if my arms were only long enough I could have encircled the entire world with a hug. [The survivor regretted that her aunt was cremated so that she did not have a chance for an official goodbye. This dream occurred about a month after the aunt's death.]

The survivor's mood of happiness carried over into the following days. She relived her wonderful memories of her aunt, instead of dwelling on how cheated she felt at not being able to see her body. She believed that her aunt sensed the deep distress she was experiencing and wanted to comfort her.

The following example is from the series of dreams I had after my father's death, toward the end of a long, complex story:

> My father is holding my hand, delivering me to my husband's house to be married (although we're already wed). He wants to give me an inheritance paper, sensing that he is going to die. He holds me in his arms tenderly, saying, "I love you, baby." I reply, "I know, Daddy." I wake weeping.

This dream took place about eighteen months after my father died. In the group of dreams in which my deceased father was present, 23 percent were of the Advice-comfort-gift type. The exchange of loving feelings in a dream can seem so real to the survivor that they are intensely satisfying.

A woman in her thirties whose father had died about six months before this dream derived much comfort from it:

> I'm sitting on the ground, my legs folded under me, wearing a long, blue, flowing gown. My hair hangs down. I'm holding my father, as an adult, his torso, and rocking him.

The survivor described blue as her favorite color, the color of her father's eyes, and the soft blue of the sky. She thought of having her hair down as "my mother image" in contrast to going to work when she wears it "done up for the world." She was providing the comfort she felt her father needed because of his rejection of religion.

When survivors dream of being "visited" by the deceased, their grief is usually greatly eased. A widow in her sixties told me a dream she had about a year after her husband died from a long, painful illness:

> I am in the walled garden, adding some flowers. My husband comes to the gate. His face is very red (meaning he's ill). He says, "I'm not going to work anymore. I'm going to spend all my time with you." We talk about driving up the coast to a favorite beach of ours. I wake feeling comforted.

Such a dream clearly contains a wish for the presence of her husband and to be able to enjoy life together. Yet the fact that the survivor is gardening, a waking-life activity she finds pleasurable, suggests more. By planting new growth while her husband remains on the other side of the gate, she is beginning to reinvest in her own life, grief task 4.

As mentioned earlier, dreams about the deceased often contain a barrier of some sort between the living and the dead, such as the gate to the walled garden. It is frequently a doorway or hallway in which these dream meetings with the dead take place. In one of my dreams about my father after his death, his arrival was announced by the banging of a screen door. In other cases, it was the ring of the telephone or someone calling out, "Your father is here," as in this dream I had about my father approximately a year after his death:

> I'm at a house where I'm trying to get everything organized, especially sewing material and pins. There is so much to be done to get things in order. Someone says to me that my father has just arrived. I go flying down the stairs to meet him, so happy to be able to see him after such a long time.

This dream depicts my attempts to "get my house in order," as well as still wishing for the presence of my father. I had the dream on almost exactly the anniversary of his death, a phenomena that many survivors share.

Carl Jung (1963) has described a powerful dream of the Advice-comfort-gift type, seeing his deceased wife in her prime, about thirty, wearing the dress that had been made for her by his cousin the medium, the most beautiful she ever wore. Jung wrote:

> I knew it was not she, but a portrait she had made or commissioned for me. It contained the beginning of our relationship, the events of fifty-three years of marriage, and the end of her life also. Face to face with such wholeness one remains speechless, for it can scarcely be comprehended.

"Gifts" from the dead may be remarkably meaningful to waking life. William Blake, the British mystic poet-artist, was deeply disturbed by the death of his younger brother, Robert. While he was searching for an inexpensive means to engrave his illustrations, Blake dreamed that his brother Robert appeared and taught him an innovative method of engraving (Bellin, 1988). Awake, Blake carried out these dream suggestions and found that they were the perfect answer to his dilemma.

Advice-comfort-gift dreams are often extremely soothing to the survivor, especially when they contain a message relevant to the dreamer's current life. Mental health workers can stimulate such dreams by suggestion at the appropriate time.

Passionate-Encounter Dreams

Definition: Passionate-encounter dreams are a variation of the Advice-comfort-gift dream in which the survivor dreams of a romantic or passionate encounter with the deceased, who is usually a former spouse or lover.

The sculptor/artist Käthe Kollwitz, at seventy-four, recorded a poignant dream rendezvous in her diary about nine months after her husband's death:

Recently I dreamed that I was together with the others in a room. I knew that Karl lay in the adjoining room. Both rooms opened out into an unlit hallway. I went out of my room into the hall and saw the door to Karl's room being opened, and then I heard him say in his kind, loving voice: "Aren't you going to say good night to me?" Then he came out and leaned against the wall, and I stood before him and leaned my body against his, and we held each other's hands and asked each other again and again: "How are you? Is everything all right?" And we were so happy being able to feel one another.

The opening door in Kollwitz's dream is a common symbol of the barrier between the living and dead being temporarily suspended. The unlit hallway seems to be a borderland between these worlds.

One elderly widow described to me a dream of dancing delightfully with her deceased husband, and another in which she and he were making love. She awoke laughing with pleasure. To be able to lovingly embrace a deceased mate in a dream can give great comfort to the survivor. Comforting Passionate-encounter dreams are characteristic of the latter stages of mourning.

Deadly-Invitation Dreams

Definition: In Deadly-invitation dreams, the deceased appears to reach out and draw the survivor toward death. Rare but serious indicator.

This type of bereavement dream is important for the mental health worker to recognize. It indicates severe depression and may signal danger to the survivor's life.

In one such dream, a young woman whose fiancé had recently died had recurrent dreams as long as a year later that her sweetheart was beckoning her to follow him (Hilton, 1992).

In another case, a woman in her fifties whose husband had died dreamed that she was at the cemetery, sitting on his gravestone, when two hands came up, one putting its bony fingers into her heart and the other squeezing her throat, making it hard to breathe. She awoke with a rapid heartbeat, pain in her heart, and a spasm in her throat. The woman had experienced a myocardial infarct one month before the dream, so on one level the images depicted her physical symptoms. Yet on another level she was expressing her fear of, or possible wish for, joining her husband in death.

Dreams of this type that involve an invitation to accompany the deceased into death are warning signals for the mental health worker. Like the legend of the Flying Dutchman, who was said to lure his love to her death, they portend danger for the dreamer.

Daily-Activity Dreams

Definition: In Daily-activity dreams, the deceased is seen performing his or her routine actions, such as shopping, fishing, driving a car, or cooking. There is no unusual emotional charge, but a pleasant feeling may prevail. The deceased may simply be present.

This final category of dreams of the dead is typically found when the tasks of grieving have been fulfilled and the dreamer returns to the more usual style of dreaming. In my collection of dreams in which my deceased father was present, 39 percent fell into the category of Daily-activity. At this stage, the deceased person has been incorporated into the survivor, without the intense pain of the period of bereavement.

Dreams Vary with the Nature of Death

Dreams not only change throughout the mourning period, but vary according to the nature of one's loss. When Annie, in her late twenties, lost her husband, father, and brother within one year, she could barely get up out of a chair to cross the room. Such multiple deaths complicate grief. In Oklahoma, a family and friends were traveling by limousine in a funeral procession to the burial of a man when they were struck head-on by a pickup truck. Four relatives of the man being buried were killed, including his widow; five others were injured. Such a catastrophe creates complex grief responses and violent nightmares. Healing from such trauma takes longer than from a single death.

Multiple deaths, violent accidents, murder, and suicide all involve complicated grief. Sometimes, as in John F. Kennedy's assassination or in the explosion of the spaceship Challenger, a whole nation or a large segment of the population may be plunged into mourning. Disasters such as earthquakes, volcanic eruptions, fires, and wars also usually create widespread grief and subsequent nightmares.

The nature of the particular death affects the survivor's dreams. All the categories of dreams I have described may occur, but the feelings emphasized vary with the type of death.

Dreams about Violent Death

There were 93,500 accidental deaths in the United States in 1991. Among people aged fifteen to thirty-four, accidents are the leading cause of death. The survivors of those who died accidentally, especially if in a sudden or violent way, have dreams about the deceased that are characterized by intense emotions.

Traumatic deaths lead to more traumatic dreaming. Sudden, unexpected deaths of a significant person—whether by accident, suicide, or homicide— share the element of shock. Phase 1, numbness or shock, is prolonged in comparison to deaths from natural or expected causes. During phase 2, disorganized emotions often include guilt, blame, helplessness, and rage (Worden, 1991). An eighteen-year-old woman who lost her fiancé in a drowning accident when they were white-water rafting was not permitted to see his body when it was recovered. For months afterward, she told me, she was tormented by nightmares in which she saw her fiancé alive, but he had amnesia and was unable to recognize her.

"Replays" of a traumatic death are common in dreams. Although the loss may never be replaced, the pain does lessen. These repetitive dreams about the circumstances of the death occur less often and begin to change in character; finally the loss is accepted and dreams resume their more usual form.

Dreams about a Suicide

Approximately 30,000 people in the United States commit suicide annually; throughout the world, 1,000 commit suicide each day. When a significant person commits suicide, survivors are likely to respond with more feelings of shame, guilt, anger, feelings of rejection, and fear for themselves than in other types of death. A man in his forties who had survived the suicide by hanging of his identical twin at age eighteen told me a horrific nightmare he had the night before his second marriage. In it, the twin became entangled in barbed wire that severed his head; the decapitated head then asked, "Now are you sorry?" The man said he thought he probably felt guilty about being happy. Grief over suicide is usually prolonged and complicated, with therapy indicated.

Dreams about a Homicide

There were about 23,440 murders in the United States in 1991. Survivors of these murder victims often depict the murderer in their dreams about the deceased. When someone has been murdered, a sense of horror and/or rage predominates. The inevitable involvement with medical and legal authorities can lead to severe frustration. All these feelings are reflected in the survivors' dreams.

Dreams about Miscarriages and Abortions

Survivors of abortions and miscarriages grieve as well as parents who have lost older children. Profound guilt feelings may be experienced and expressed in dreams.

One woman in her early thirties, shortly after an abortion, dreamed that her garage doors were torn off and her car stolen. The land around her house was being torn up by bulldozers. These images reflected the damage the survivor felt had been done to her body (the garage doors and the land) as well as her grief over the missing fetus (symbolized by the stolen car).

Another woman in her early thirties was already on an emotional seesaw when she learned she was pregnant for the first time because she was told that she was carrying twins, one of whom had died. A few weeks later she was informed that, in fact, both were alive and were boys. Just before her sixth month, she went into premature labor. Medical intervention personnel were unable to save the firstborn son; then the second was lost. The blow was crushing.

This woman and her husband were wise enough to want to see their tiny boys, to hold them, name them, and have a funeral for them. Such acts, excruciating as they can be, help grievers accept the reality of the deaths and carry through the other tasks of mourning.

Many of this woman's dreams contained "double" images. Her two pet dogs became symbols in her dreams for the lost twins. In an early dream after the deaths, the woman came home and went into her yard, where she found that her two dogs had been shot. In another dream, she herself was shot by an intruder. In a later dream, one of the dogs was in a crib, the other trying to climb in. Other troubled dreams included her house being "torched" and destroyed from a fire. Her body felt damaged; her sense of vulnerability, loss, and destruction was acute.

Months later, as she neared her projected due date, this woman described a comforting dream. In it, she saw a little boy in a meadow up on a hill with her husband. The child was a small blond-haired boy happily playing softball, an activity she and her husband had planned to do with the twins. The scene was "almost heaven-looking." A year later, she was happily pregnant with a son.

Parents whose children die at a later stage of development cast their dreams about the deceased child in forms characteristic of their personalities, interests, and the circumstances of their death.

Dreams about Sudden Infant Deaths (SIDS)

Over 7,000 babies die from Sudden Infant Death Syndrome each year in the United States. Dreams of the surviving parents are often characterized by guilt and blame; divorce rates for couples are high (Worden, 1991). Survivors' dreams share much with those of survivors of miscarriages and abortions. They, too, grieve the loss of the child's future.

Dreams about Deaths from AIDS

A whole new form of death has struck in the past decade. It is believed that some 500,000 people will die from Acquired Immune Deficiency Syndrome (AIDS)–related disorders in the United States by the year 2000 (Worden, 1991). Dreams of the survivors of people who have died from AIDS-related problems emphasize vulnerability, fear for themselves, guilt, and stigma as well as sorrow. These survivors are likely to experience multiple losses, thus complicating their grief experience still further.

Dreams Vary with the Relationship to Dreamer

Dreams about the Loss of a Pet

"Whenever was the first moment we learned of death? There must have been a time?" asks a character in Tom Stoppard's play *Rosenkranz and Guildenstern*. For children, the first experience of death may be the death of a beloved pet.

A married woman in her fifties was deeply involved with her four Saint Bernard dogs, who died one by one. In dreams about her last, favorite, dog, she hugs his shaggy mane and smells his "dogginess." The sense of smell is primitive; it is attached to our deepest emotions. Many grievers report the poignancy of smelling their lost loved ones in dreams.

Paradoxically, some people allow themselves to grieve the loss of a pet more openly than the loss of a person. Pet cemeteries, such as the one on the grounds of the Presidio Army base in San Francisco, speak to the passion people often feel about a pet's death. Grief over the death of a pet can be complex, as in the case of a nine-year-old girl whose pet hamster was killed by a cat on the same day that her father died.

Dreams about the Loss of a Grandparent

In general, people have less conflictual relationships with their grandparents than with their parents. Therefore, dreams about the loss of a grandparent tend to represent qualities the survivor idealizes. To the Oregon poet Alice Evans, her grandfather was the ultimate "wise old man." He represented high standards and good taste, hard work, responsibility, and uprightness. She valued his energy and his trustworthiness, which were expressed in a touching poem about "Grandfather Eagle."

Alice's dreams about her grandfather became the basis for several poems (Evans, 1992). In these Advice-comfort-gift dreams, her grandfather visited her, pointing out well-crafted objects, polished figurines, a bookcase, and a grandfather's clock. She felt certain that it was his spirit body who was present in the dream about the clock, rather than simply a dream representation of him. Alice thought his spirit was trying to communicate that she was running out of time (represented by the grandfather's clock) to accomplish work of value (symbolized by the fine craftsmanship). Perhaps Alice's own well-crafted poems—her grandfather was a highly skilled engineer—are her product of value. This dream was most comforting to her.

Another griever who was very close to her grandmother found it agonizing to watch the elderly woman's painful death. Eventually she was able to see her grandmother in a reassuring dream, with her face clear and beaming, spiritlike. In another comforting dream, she saw her grandmother as a young girl, smiling and talking in the sunshine. Mental health workers can help survivors learn lessons from the lives of their grandparents, and then let them go.

Dreams about the Loss of a Parent

When a parent dies, the effect is profound. Many people experience the death of a parent as the removal of a buffer between themselves and their own death. There is not only the pain of the loss of the person, but a new anxiety about one's own mortality (Worden, 1991). Adults may feel "orphaned." The loss is particularly striking for children under the age of eleven (Worden, 1991).

In many ancient and primitive cultures deceased grandparents, parents, and other ancestors are believed to guard and to guide their living descendants. Our fairy tales retain this theme, as in the original version of the story of Cinderella, who prays at her mother's grave for a year, leading to the later appearance of her fairy godmother. Modern grievers have much to discover in their dreams of their deceased parents that can similarly guide their waking lives. Mental health workers can assist survivors in resolving conflicts with the image of their dead parents in their dreams, and show how good dreams about a deceased parent can improve the survivor's life.

Dreams about the Loss of a Child

The death of a child or infant is one of the most painful of griefs. Life seems unnatural, thrown out of kilter. Older people are supposed to die first. It seems to many people bereaved over the loss of a child that life in general or God in particular has been unfair. Parents who suffer the loss of a child go through an extremely difficult mourning. Yet even this great loss can be healed, and the surviving parents can find value in continuing their own lives. Dreams about the dead child are poignant and may be supremely disturbing. The survivors grieve the loss of the future as well as the specific child.

Dreams about the Loss of a Spouse or a Lover

The death of a spouse or a lover is exceedingly hard to bear; some experts attribute the highest degree of stress to this experience. Like the loss of a child, losing a spouse cuts a chunk out of the center of the survivor's life. Women are the most frequent survivors; the ratio of widows to widowers is a startling five to one. Dreams about a dead spouse or lover are usually lifelong.

Dreams about the Loss of a Friend

Depending on the degree of intimacy, the death of a friend may trigger as much grief as the loss of a sibling, cousin, or other relative. When death dissolves an intimate relationship with a contemporary, one's own life seems vulnerable.

Symbolic Dream Images of Death

When the person who has died appears in dreams during mourning, we easily recognize that the dream is about our grief. Yet a large number of grief dreams do not contain the image of the deceased. This is when our dream skills are most useful. Mental health workers need to learn the language of dreams for depicting loss and recovery. Scenes of destruction often parallel grief, just as they do with physical damage; scenes of regeneration accompany re-investment in life tasks, just as they do in physical healing (Garfield, 1992). Through the techniques of dream interpretation, active imagination, poetry therapy, and art therapy, dreams symbols can form the foundation for inner work that leads to recovery from grief. Some abbreviated samples follow.

The Tree of Life

In the folklore of many peoples of the world, a tree is identified with the "tree of life." Dreams about the destruction of a tree seem to be associated with death. I had such a dream following my father's sudden death. He had had one unexpected heart attack in the autumn, but appeared to have made a full recovery; the second heart attack, just after Christmas, killed him instantly. The night of his death, I dreamed that all the big trees on the lawn of an old people's home had been chopped into tiny bits. I was very distressed that they didn't leave a few for shade. The sheltering presence of my father was sorely missed.

Kennedy (1991) describes a strikingly similar image in a dream two nights before her father died, in which a large redwood tree outside her house crashed to the ground, scarring the earth. In the dream, she told a neighbor that he had no right to cut down a tree on her land.

I have found it useful to ask survivors, "If your (father, mother, spouse, etc.) were a tree, what kind of tree would she/he be?" Their answers provide clues to the perceived personality of the deceased as well as to recognizing the deceased in their dreams. Visualizations that involved planting new growth or making something from the residue of the destroyed tree also prove helpful.

The Journey of Life: Ships, Airplanes, Trains

Dreams about a journey frequently mark the passage of a loved one, as we have seen. Ships, like trains and airplanes, often appear among the dreams of people mourning the death of a spouse. One elderly widower, who had lost his wife of many years, told me his dream of being on a cruise ship "like the loveboat." On the main decks, everything was shipshape. When he went down the "companionway" to the lower decks, he found that the ship was a "rust bucket," rotting and falling apart. Like many people in deep grief, he was struggling to keep afloat. On the surface (represented by the main deck), things looked good. But underneath (symbolized by the lower decks), because of the pain of the loss of his wife (indicated by the references to the "loveboat" and the "companionway"), he felt he was disintegrating (as seen in the bad condition of the lower decks).

A few months after her husband died from cancer, a woman in her forties dreamed she was in a little boat on a stream when a funeral barge crossed her path at right angles. In it, she saw a relatively young woman with long dark hair, carrying a bronze cremation urn in her lap. (She told me she felt some discomfort over having chosen a concrete urn for her deceased husband because it was cheaper.) In the dream, the woman felt much sympathy toward the other woman for losing her husband so young. She continued on in her own boat, not knowing her destination. Images of rivers appeared in several bereavement dreams.

Mental health workers can assist survivors in finding ways to steer themselves through the sea of life, charting their own destination. One group of bereaved persons found it useful to draw a ship, equipping it with all they might need for the remainder of their journey through life.

The Soul Animal

The image of an animal may become a substitute for the deceased in dreams.

The woman mentioned earlier whose husband died in an industrial accident, who stopped dreaming directly about her husband, was later greatly puzzled by disturbing dreams about fish, such as an avalanche of dead fish. When I asked her to describe a fish to me as though I were a little child who didn't know what it was, she explained that a fish was "an animal that can't breathe out of water." As soon as she said the words, the widow gasped. In giving this description, she remembered that the last thing her husband said to her as he was dying was, "I can't breathe!" She had substituted the image of a fish for the disturbing images of her distorted or unreal husband. Understanding this substitution helped her to comprehend her dreams and begin to heal.

In my collection, dogs, cats, and birds have become symbols for the deceased person. Asking survivors, "If (the deceased) were an animal, what kind of animal would he/she be?" often provides clues to dream symbolism. Survivors may need to be helped to see the connection between the animal in their dreams and the deceased.

Cold and Warmth

Snow, ice, and cold often accompany images of the dead in the early stages of mourning, such as in a dream in which I saw my family asleep, inside the old family house, covered with snow. Warmth is more characteristic of later stages of mourning.

Dark and Light

Images of darkness in dreams often represent the confusion a person feels in the face of death. When one of his best male friends died, Frank had a nightmare about struggling to find his way in the dark. After Jo's cousin died of an accidental drug overdose, she felt "as though a black hole opened up"; she feared falling into it herself. In one of the early dreams after my father's death, I saw a black carriage pulled by horses draw up to the family home.

Positive dreams about the dead often contain images of light surrounding the deceased, or shining from their faces, hair, or clothing. The image of light appears to be associated with the "spark of life," the soul or spirit of the deceased.

Conclusion

Dreams about the deceased—whether they directly include the image of the dead person or involve symbolic images of death—offer mental health workers diagnostic clues to the stage of mourning the survivor is experiencing. The recently bereaved person's dreams contain more negative images of the deceased, often with the themes of Alive-again and Dying-again. Later stages of mourning tend to be characterized by greater numbers of comforting dreams about the deceased, such as those in the Young-well-again and Advice-comfort-gift categories. Traumatic deaths lead to traumatic dreams about the deceased, which may continue for years if the tasks of grieving remain unresolved. Dreams of the Deadly-invitation category alert counselors to survivors who are at high risk. Personal dream symbols of death and reinvestment in life can be used as a focus for completing grief tasks.

Dreamers may find that they experience both nightmares and comforting dreams about the deceased. Nightmares are founded on more than the trauma of a death and grief reactions to it. Ancient beliefs that the ghosts of dead people are capable of harming the living still linger today. The Grim Reaper, the ferryman across the river Styx—mythological and folkloric underpinnings concerning death, dying, and grief—are important to understand because they influence our dreams about the dead. Dreams of guidance have their ancient counterparts in beliefs that the ancestors guard their descendants and warn them of danger. Myths, legends, and fairy tales all contribute to the modern dreamer's thoughts and feelings about death and grief, and these ideas are still active in our dreams, whether or not we are aware of them.

Dreams about the dead sometimes contain images of a life hereafter. Regardless of whether or not there is an afterlife, as survivors accomplish the tasks of grief, they accompany the deceased on a rite of passage through life's greatest mystery. Dreams are the guiding star.

Neurological Dreams

OLIVER SACKS

However dreams are to be interpreted—the Egyptians saw them as prophecies and portents; Freud as hallucinatory wish fulfillments; Crick and Mitchison (1983) as "reverse learning" designed to remove overloads of "neural garbage" from the brain; Jouvet (1980) as rehearsals for complex motor programs and behaviors—it is clear that they may also contain, directly or distortedly, reflections of current states of body and mind.

Thus it is scarcely surprising that neurological disorders—in the brain itself, or in its sensory or autonomic input—can alter dreaming either quantitatively or in striking and specific ways. Every practicing neurologist must be aware of this, and yet how rarely do we question patients about their dreams. Though there is virtually nothing on this subject in the literature, I think such questioning can be an important part of the neurological examination, can assist in diagnosis, and can show how sensitive a barometer dreaming may be of neurological health and disease.

I first encountered this many years ago while working in a migraine clinic. It became clear that there was not only a general correlation between the incidence of very intense dreams or nightmares and migraine auras (a correlation now well established by EEG studies) but also, not infrequently, an entering of aura phenomena into the dreams. Patients may dream of phosphenes, or zigzags, of expanding scotomas, or of colors or contours that wax and then fade. Their dreams may contain visual field defects, or hemianopias, or more rarely the phenomena of "mosaic" or "cinematic" vision (Sacks, 1985b, pp. 98–99). One patient of mine with an occipital angioma knew that if his normally black-and-white dreams were suddenly suffused with a red color, if they "turned red," he was in for a seizure.

The neurological phenomena may, in such cases, appear direct and "raw," intruding into an otherwise normal unfolding of a dream. But they may also, given a chance, combine with the dream, fuse with, and be modified by, its images and symbols. Thus the phosphenes of migraine are commonly dreamed of as firework displays, and one patient of mine often "embedded" his nocturnal migraine auras in dreams of a nuclear explosion. He would first see a dazzling fireball with a typical, iridescent, zigzag margin, coruscating as it grew, until it was replaced by a blind area with the dream round its edge. At this point he would usually wake, with a fading scotoma, intense nausea, and an incipient headache.

Another patient, who had focal sensory and motor seizures, once dreamt that he was in court, being prosecuted by Freud, who kept banging on his head with a gavel as the charges were being read. But the blows, strangely, were felt in his left arm, and he awoke to find it numb and convulsing, in a typical focal fit. But the most common neurological or "physical" dreams are of pain, or discomfort, or hunger, or thirst, at once manifest and yet camouflaged in the "scenery" of the dream. Thus one patient, newly casted after a leg operation, dreamt that a heavy man had stepped, with agonizing effect, on his left foot. Politely at first, then with increasing urgency, he asked the man to move, and when his appeals were unheeded, he tried to shift the man bodily. His efforts were completely useless, and now in his dreams, in his agony, he realized why: the man was made of compacted neurons—neutronium—and weighed six trillion tons, as much as the earth. He made one last, frenzied attempt to move the immovable, then woke up with an intense viselike pain in his foot, which had become ischemic from the pressure of the new cast.

If there are lesions in the visual cortex, patients may observe specific visual deficits in their dreams. One patient with a central achromatopsia remarked that he no longer dreamt in color (Sacks and Wasserman, 1987). When dreaming, patients with prestriate lesions may be unable to recognize faces, a condition called prosopagnosia. If there is diffuse damage to the occipital cortex, visual imagery may vanish completely from dreams. I have encountered this, on occasion, as a presenting symptom of Alzheimer's disease.

The central effects of blindness can manifest themselves in dreams: there are few or no changes in dream imagery for a year or two after becoming blind; there then tends to be a loss of color in dreams, then a loss of recognizable faces and places; and finally, as the patient enters "deep blindness," a complete loss of all visual elements. This probably corresponds with a slowly progressive secondary (Wallerian) degeneration of the visual cortex.

Patients may sometimes dream of the onset of a disease. One patient, stricken with an acute encephalitis lethargica in 1926, had a night of grotesque and terrifying dreams about one central theme: she dreamed she was imprisoned in an inaccessible castle, but the castle had the form and shape of herself; she dreamed of enchantments, bewitchments, entrancements; she dreamed that she had become a living sentient statue of stone; she dreamed that the world had come to a stop; she dreamed that she had fallen into a sleep so deep that nothing could wake her; she dreamed of a death which was different from death. Her family had difficulty waking her the next morning, and when she awoke there was intense consternation: she was parkinsonian and catatonic (Sacks, 1990).

Another patient was admitted to the hospital three days before surgery to remove her gall bladder due to gall stones. She was placed on antibiotics for microbial prophylaxis; being an otherwise healthy young woman, no complications were expected. The day before surgery this patient had a disturbing dream of peculiar intensity. She was swaying wildly, in the dream, very unsteady on her feet, could hardly feel the ground beneath her, could hardly feel anything to her hands, found them flailing to and fro, kept dropping whatever she picked up.

She was distressed by this dream ("I never had one like it," she said. "I can't get it out of my mind")—so distressed that we requested an opinion from the psychiatrist. "Preoperative anxiety," he said. "Quite natural, we see it all the time." But within a few hours the dream had become a reality, as the patient became incapacitated by an acute sensory neuronopathy (Sacks, 1985a, pp. 44–45). One must assume in such cases that the disease was already affecting neural function, and that the unconscious mind, the dreaming mind, was more sensitive to this than the waking mind. Such "premonitory" or, rather, precursory dreams may be happy in content, and in outcome, too. Patients with multiple sclerosis may dream of remissions a few hours before they occur, and patients recovering from strokes or neurological injuries may have striking dreams of improvement before such improvement is "objectively" manifest. Here again, the dreaming mind may be a more sensitive indicator of neural function than examination with a reflex hammer and a pin.

Some dreams seem to be more than precursory. One striking personal example stays in my mind. While recovering from a leg injury, I had been told it was time to take the next step, to advance from using two crutches to just one. I tried this twice, and both times fell flat on my face. I could not consciously think how to do it. Then I fell asleep, and had a dream in which I reached out my right hand, grabbed the crutch that hung over my head, tucked it under my right arm, and set off with perfect confidence and ease down the corridor. Waking from the dream, I reached out my right hand, grabbed the crutch that hung over the bed, and set off with perfect confidence and ease down the corridor (Sacks, 1984).

This, it seemed to me, was not merely premonitory, but a dream that actually did something, a dream that solved the very motor-neural problem the brain was confronted with, achieving this in the form of a psychic enactment or rehearsal or trial: a dream, in short, that was an act of learning.

Disturbances in body-image from limb or spinal injury almost always enter dreams, at least when they are acute, and before any "accommodation" has been made. With my own deafferenting leg injury, I had reiterative dreams of a dead or absent limb. Within a few weeks, however, such dreams tend to cease, as there occurs a revision or "healing" of body-image in the cortex (such changes in cortical mapping have been found in Michael Merzenich's experiments with monkeys). Phantom limbs, by contrast, perhaps because of continuing neural excitation in the stump, intrude themselves into dreams (as into waking consciousness) very persistently, though gradually telescoping, and growing fainter with the passage of years.

The phenomena of parkinsonism may enter dreams. One patient of mine, a man of acute introspective ability, felt that the first expression of parkinsonism in him was a change in the "style" of his dreams. He would dream that he could move only in slow motion, or that he was "frozen," or that he was rushing and could not stop. He would dream that space and time themselves had changed, kept "switching scales," and had become chaotic and problematic. Gradually, over the ensuing months, these Looking-Glass dreams came true, and the patient's bradykinesia and festination became obvious to others. But the symptoms had first presented themselves to him in his dreams. Perhaps parkinsonism itself is potentiated in dreams.

Another patient of mine, who has Tourette's syndrome, felt that he frequently had "Touretty" dreams—dreams of a particularly wild and exuberant kind, full of unexpectednesses, accelerations, and sudden tangents. This changed when he was put on haloperidol, and he reported that his dreams had been reduced to ". . . straight wish fulfillment, with none of the elaborations, the extravagances of Tourette's."

Alterations in dreaming are often the first sign of response to L-dopa in patients with ordinary Parkinson's disease, as well as in those with postencephalitic syndromes. Dreaming typically becomes more vivid (many patients remark on their dreaming, suddenly, in brilliant color), more emotionally charged, and more prone to go on all night. Sometimes the "realness" of these dreams is so extraordinary that they cannot be forgotten or thrown off after waking.

Excessive dreaming of this sort, excessive both in sensory vividness and in activation of unconscious psychic content—dreaming akin, in some ways, to hallucinosis—is common in fever, after many drugs (opiates, cocaine, amphetamines, etc.), and in states of drug withdrawal and REM rebound. A similar unbridled oneirism may occur in other organic excitements, and at the start of some psychoses, where an initial mad or manic dream, like the rumbling of a volcano, may be the first intimation of the eruption to come. Dreaming, for Freud, was the "royal road" to the unconscious. Dreaming, for the physician, may not be a royal road, but it is a byway to unexpected diagnoses and discoveries, and to unexpected insights about how one's patients are doing. It is a byway full of fascination, and should not be neglected.

Integration and Ambivalence
in Transplants

ROBERT BOSNAK

When Claire Sylvia, a recipient of a heart and lungs transplant, and I, a Jungian psychoanalyst with a passion for dreams, co-led a monthly group of seven people with the hearts of others in New Haven for a year and a half, we were struck by the fact that the recipients often referred to themselves as "transplants." "I am a transplant." A participant who'd had open heart surgery with the usual baffling array of bypasses that made his insides look like the spaghetti of Los Angeles highway overpasses was adamant in telling us that a transplant is of a qualitatively different caliber than surgery in which the old organs are being repaired. Maybe that explains patients' identification with the transplant operation. A transplant is a transformation of identity; in part, it becomes one's identity for a while. Hence "I am a transplant."

One of the striking outcomes of our group's conversations was the discovery that each heart transplant recipient had at some point or other spontaneously experienced the donor/organ as an "other" with whom some form of communication was taking place. Even the person who vehemently denied that she had ever experienced the new heart as "other" told us that right after the operation she had told her new heart: "You used to belong to someone else, but now you're mine." I focus here on the meeting deep in the psyche's interior of the old self and the new arrival and upon the eminently ambivalent experience of the transplant, consisting of exultation and horror.

D. is an extraordinary young woman. Saying this about any transplant is a pleonasm, since their lives are played out inside the extraordinary, but D. was unusual even in this pioneering group of people with new hearts. She had been the fourth woman in the world to carry a baby to term and give birth while living with the heart of another. She tells us about the ghosts she sees.

"It started out with images in my mind," D. begins. We can hear the pressure in her voice. She had just told us that she wanted to tell the parents of her heart that she is taking good care of it. But she didn't know who they were or how to reach them. Frustration had pervaded this part of her story. Since the transplant, now over four years ago, she had been convinced, though no one had ever told her, that the heart she had received belonged to the mother of a young child.

"What kind of images?" I ask.

"Images of a woman and a man carrying a young child. Not an infant. I couldn't tell you the age. And then I see this woman lying in bed on the respirator with her parents around her. I just know they are the parents. I see gray hair. That's about as deep as that goes. Those are images when I am awake. And then it started to happen also at night when I didn't sleep. I haven't slept since the beginning of all this. And when everyone is asleep and when I turn the TV off I look in the doorway and I see one image of a white shadow which is, I believe, the donor. It's a woman."

"What does that shadow look like?"

"She comes toward me, never touching the ground, never having feet. No face. No face involved. Just a very cloudy image that doesn't frighten me. And it will come close to me. Then it disappears."

"Does it have an intention?"

"I can't figure it out." She sits quietly for a moment, a happy expression on her face. This is obviously a benevolent shadow. Here we encounter the life-giving aspect of the transplant. Suddenly her face contorts and her voice sounds shaky. "Then, many other times, there are two more images that come, that are dark. And they scare me. They have knives or a gun or an ax or something that wants to hurt me. They keep coming closer and closer and then usually I'd wake up my husband before they'd go away. They would come in the doorway and they would stand over my bed as though they're trying to tell me maybe I shouldn't be there. That I shouldn't have lived. I don't know. They would always follow behind the nice image. The cloud image. The friendly white cloud image is trying to tell me something and the dark images are just trying to scare me."

Here we see the ambivalence toward the transplant. On the one hand, it has given her life, and she feels kindly toward the young mother whose heart she carries; on the other hand, the demons want her to die. I am reminded of the mythical doctor Asclepios who contracted the wrath of the underworld after reviving a patient from the dead. He had overstepped a boundary. D. seems to experience the same wrath of the underworld for her "transgression." She shouldn't have lived.

"Can you tell a little bit more about the identity of these black beings?"

"They're hooded. They don't really have a face, no definition of arms. It's really hard to describe."

"You say they have knives. With silver blades? Do you see?"

"I really don't see a distinction of color. Everything is black. I always get a chill when I see these. I always get a chill. They never touch the ground, they're always in the air. They come from my daughter's bedroom across the hall." D. refers to the room of the daughter who was conceived and born after the transplant. "The bathroom is in between. And they always start from that bedroom. Sometimes I would get up and run over to my daughter's bedroom to see if she's all right. I know that they are going to her because they feel she shouldn't have been born in the first place. But she usually is sleeping quietly. Sometimes they would start from the hallway. Otherwise, if they start from the hallway they come very quickly to the door. And then it's very slowly from my doorway to my bed. And then they would come over my bed and sometimes they would even stay by the light above my bed."

"Is there any other sensation besides seeing? Do you hear anything, smell anything, feel anything?"

"No. I just have a sense that they want to harm me. That they want to warn me and tell me. They stand above the light. The light would be a sense of security for me. If I turn on the light they'd go away. And I freeze. I can't move. I don't move and I'm telling myself I want to move. I want to yell. And I can't make any sounds. I turn to my husband and ask him 'Did you see that?' "

"Has he ever seen them?"

"No." D. sounds disappointed. "He never did."

"And is their presence as tangibly real as this chair or is it another kind of reality?" I ask, pointing at the furniture in the New Haven hotel room where our transplant group meets monthly.

"Another kind. I can almost see through them."

"So they are phantoms?"

"Yes, like a ghost; that's what I was going to say."

Claire Sylvia has her own experiences with ghosts. We had started out our work as an ordinary kind of psychoanalysis, but had decided after a while to research her conviction that another was present within her since the transplant; to see if others had similar experiences. Late one night during the summer she calls me. It is not her habit to call me at this time of night, so something drastic must be going on. She sounds hysterical, hyperventilating. After some time I can make out that she has seen the movie "Ghost" and it has terrified her.

"I identified totally with the ghost. Especially when he was going through the wall. It was exactly like the dream I had just after the transplant. When I came home I felt completely like a ghost. I had no body. It was so frightening. I was so scared I had to call you." Claire is experiencing the ghost from the perspective of the dead person in the movie and of the dead boy whose living heart and lungs are now hers.

The dream she refers to stems from four months after her transplant:

> I walked through a wall. It was easy. I just willed it so. I stood up against it; gently, very gently my body leaned into the wall, tentatively at first, then I applied light pressure with my body—and off to the other side I went. I awakened from this dream and recalled the transplant. It was just like that. I crossed to the other side and came back into this world, familiar and yet so foreign.

The movie "Ghost" is about a man who dies but cannot leave this world. He remains on earth in a kind of subtle body, only able to communicate with the living world by way of a sensitive medium. Before he finds the medium, however, his attempts to communicate with the world around him are excruciating, because he doesn't know how to reach the living who are going about their business all around him. The poor ghost feels utterly alien in his familiar world. Because his body is made not of gross matter but of a subtle substance, portrayed by Hollywood's special effects as transparent, he can go through walls. The first time he does this, he behaves exactly like Claire in her dream, almost two years prior to the movie. He leans into the wall very gently, and with a little bit of pressure he moves through it.

Claire's ghost dream portrays a life that takes place on both sides of the hitherto impenetrable wall of death. The theme of crossing from one side to another is a frequent theme in her dreams. For example, three years after the initial ghost dream, Claire dreams of a young man, very cavalier, with a cape. She inquires where he is going, and he says: "I just go over to the other side and die." She asks him what it's like, and he replies: "Oh, I come right back."

Claire writes: "There were no longer boundaries. In a way I could walk through walls. In a way I was no longer just a mortal—I had tasted death! I cheated death! I am invincible! I can do anything—this is superhuman." Claire experiences both dread and exultation.

Claire's experience shows us that the transplant is unconsciously experienced from two perspectives: that of the living recipient and that of the dead donor. I don't mean this in the metaphysical sense; I don't know whether the spirit of the actual donor is involved in these experiences. I refer to a perspective that is felt to be that of the donor. I take my cue from a man who'd had a heart transplant. He dreams right after it, still in the intensive care unit:

When you die your soul goes into someone else's body. When I woke up in the body of another, everything around me was totally strange, very bright and colorful. It was the scariest moment of the entire transplant. I was incredibly frightened.

It seems as if this dream had been experienced from the point of view of the transplanted heart, this soul now suddenly in a strange body.

With this paradoxical experience of elation and horror as a basis, it is obvious that the transplant constitutes a severe psychological trauma. A relation to this trauma has to be established. In Claire's dreamworld this took place about four months after the operation. As can be seen in the work on the dream, however, it took much longer to consciously feel the painful impact of the experience. During the first year after her transplant Claire experienced only the elation, not the horror. One dream was of a man full of scars whom we came to call the Scarman. He is carrying the scars of the transplant operation. He portrays the trauma.

I am sitting in a chair and there is a man sitting directly behind me. My back is to him. He talks with me, loves me. But he does not let me turn around and look at him. He won't let me see him. I wonder if he is part of a mob, if it would be dangerous for me to see him, or what is wrong. Finally I convince him, or he begins to trust me enough, to let me look at him. When I turn and see him, I see that his hands and face are all scarred. He is very deformed and afraid that I would reject him. I don't find it ugly or repulsive at all. In fact, I caress his face and hands and find him wonderful and beautiful. From that point on we have a very healing relationship.

In the next scene we are living together. We're in some kind of relationship. We embrace and rock each other. Others see us. There is a picture that is important to him: a triptych, religious, colorful, archaic; from another era. I keep rearranging it, bring it to the table. Then we eat. He teaches me many things. In a very accepting and loving fashion he tells me about my annoying ways. He's very bright and astute, teaching me much.

When we worked on the first section of this dream quite some time after the actual dreaming, details were still vivid and clear. The dream occurred a year before the beginning of analysis.

"I'm in a room," Claire begins, eyes closed, recalling the moment of dreaming.

"What kind of room?" I inquire.

"It seems empty. I just see the two of us in chairs with him behind me."

"How far from each other are you?"

"We're quite close."

"Are you touching?"

"No."

"Are you talking loud or soft?" I ask. These questions serve to coax her memory into revealing itself. This way the presence of the dream image can become almost as real as during the actual moment of dreaming.

"The way we're talking now. Normal." Our conversation feels intimate. Her reference to the present makes me realize that the relationship between Claire and the dream figure "Scarman" is similar to our own. "Do you remember what clothes you are wearing?"

"No; everyday clothes."

"What is the floor like?"

"It seems like it's gray."

"And is the ceiling high?" I ask, getting a sense of height from the image that has emerged.

"Yes." Now we're connected. I can feel her image from within, as it were.

"What is the atmosphere in the room?"

"Quiet, still."

"And you look in front of you. Or is your gaze inward?"

"I look in front of me."

"Can you concentrate on your back? What do you feel in your back when you are sitting there?" By moving attention away from the visual center toward the back, the physical location closest to the other figure, consciousness becomes more visceral, less mental. Eyes cannot see what goes on behind the back.

"I feel him touching the back of my chair."

"Is it a straight-back chair?" I can almost feel the straightness of the chair in my back. I open my eyes and see Claire sitting up very straight, nodding.

"Comfortable or uncomfortable?"

"Comfortable."

"What is the voice of the man like?"

"Deep and resonant."

"Friendly, unfriendly?"

"Friendly, very confident."

"What do you feel at this moment?"

"Calm. I feel in a pleasant and safe surrounding."

"And does he tell you to turn around?"

"I don't think he verbalizes. I just sense it." We are now deeply into a visceral kind of knowing.

"And do you want to turn around?"

"Yes, I feel an urge to turn around. But I will not turn until he allows me to."

"What does it feel like, that desire to turn around and holding it back?"

"I'm a little bit anxious. It's a little frightening because I don't know what I will find. Why doesn't he want me to see him?"

"Can you concentrate on the fear for a moment?" I request, trying to slow down the moment just before consciousness. Claire is becoming aware of the Scarman, whoever he may be. "Ego" (our familiar self-image) is usually scared when a new awareness enters. Especially with someone like Claire, who ever since childhood has learned to deny painful realities and prefers to see the positive side in everything, feeling the darker emotions, like anxiety, is vital. Usually a transformative insight is frightening in some way or other. This is Claire's first response as well: she imagines the mob. It is frightening to think that a mobster is sitting behind you if you're unfamiliar with mobsters. This is the fear of the alien, an anticipation of something new and different that "Ego" will have to adjust to, resist, or flee from.

"Yes. I feel shaken within my body, within my stomach. My muscles are tense." I pause for a moment to let the discomfort sink in.

"What do you feel in your stomach as you begin to turn around?" I can feel the torque on my own spine as I begin to turn. I feel frightened.

"Excitement, like butterflies. Nervousness. The unknown." Claire doesn't make mention of fear, and my own fear intensifies into dread. It feels as though she is actively resisting this fear that now seems to be lodged inside my innards. My stomach twists in a pain that doesn't feel mine. I guess that I'm feeling the pain Claire is oblivious to. It happens often in intimate relations that the fear one person is unable to experience is pressed into the partner.

"What is the first thing you see?" I continue, realizing I'm on my own with this upset stomach.

"A very scarred man. I believe he has a beard."

"What kind of scars?"

"Well, his face is scarred. His cheeks and his forehead. And his hands are also very scarred."

"And what do his eyes look like?"

"They seem to be very kind and loving, and old and very wise." My discomfort is getting worse while Claire is all aglow.

"Can you move your hand and touch his shoulder?" Now that there is such a strong contact between Claire and Scarman, I'm curious how the dream develops from here on. This technique is called active imagination: a way to have the dream unfold.

"What is that moment of the touch like? Can you feel it?"

"I feel warm."

"Warm?"

"He's receptive."

"Upset in any way?" I ask, remembering the dream description of the Scarman who was afraid of being rejected for his scars.

"No, he is just very patient and waiting."

"Is he afraid that you won't accept him?"

"No, otherwise he wouldn't have allowed me to turn around. He must have known that I would accept him." This is the Scarman after he's been seen by the eyes of the mind. The one who could only be gropingly felt in the back, the one who is afraid of rejection, is gone. This feels important to me, as rejection is the primary form of death for a transplant organism.

"What does his acceptance feel like?"

"Like a warm embrace."

"What does it feel like to have those scars?"

"It feels wonderful."

"Try and feel the scars in your body."

"I've lost it," Claire says as we open our eyes simultaneously, disconnected from the dream image.

At this point Claire is not yet able to feel the pain of the scars, the pain of the death of her own heart, the scars left behind by an operation that has affected her whole being. The primary conscious experience is that of acceptance. The other side is probably held off by the fear of rejection, the primary cause of death for transplants. They die because the host organism perceives the transplanted organ as an intruder and eliminates it. The biological acceptance and rejection must have a psychological correlate. Rejection means that one organism doesn't want to have anything to do with another organism. This is true on a physical level as well as psychologically. In the analytical relationship between Claire and me it gets played out as emotional ambivalence. Sometimes I am identified with her strong new heart, her new passion for life, in which case we feel like we're in love. At other moments she feels that I am rejecting her, don't want her or love her. Then she feels isolated and I feel terribly burdened by her demands.

The scarman dream portrays Claire's relationship to the scarring event. It is the first dream that stays with her after the transplant. As such it can be seen as an initial dream, showing propensities and potential directions. If we look at an initial dream as a calendar for upcoming events, we get a useful picture.

The first phase of the post-transplant era, according to the scarman dream, is one of fear of rejection, of being rejected for one's deformity (being a freak), as well as the fear of physical organic rejection.

Phase two is about seeing what is going on. In the first part of the dream as written down by Claire in her dreambook, she uses the verbs "to see" and "to look" six times in the first seven sentences. This portion deals with observing the scars left behind from the traumatic event.

Phase three speaks of relationship, of getting on intimate footing with the traumatized being, the part of the self that was deformed by the invasive operation, and communing with it. In the dream Claire says "we eat": eating together has long been understood as a form of sharing in the substance of life.

Phase four is about getting the picture. The triptych, if properly arranged, brings about a meaningful picture. This is important to Scarman: getting the pieces of the picture into some kind of order.

Phase five is about lovingly learning how annoying you are: having a mirror held up to your negative side, because you're no longer just by yourself.

And as befits the dreamworld, these phases are going on simultaneously as well as subsequently in any order. The sense of sequence seems to be different from that of the dayworld. In the dreamworld events seem to take place simultaneously, reaching consciousness in random order.

Having seen that ambivalence is at the bottom of the transplant experience, we must strive in analysis to keep this sense of paradox and ambivalence as vividly conscious as possible. This is painful but can possibly lead to a mutation. In the middle of profound ambivalence about whether to contact her donor family, whose name she found through leads in dreams, Claire dreams:

"On a boat or train traveling. Very congenial—many people—eating and playing together. I'm involved with a family. Parents and two young boys. The younger one and I have a special rapport. He draws me a gift, a red rose.

"It becomes known on this voyage that the younger boy has died, but no one will talk about it. I know it had something to do with me.

"I'm lying next to a dark-haired virile handsome man. He had been the father but became the eldest of the two brothers, now the third. He is helping me tell my story to the world. I ask for something. There is a tremendous feeling of closeness between us. Of desire and of sadness about what had happened with the little boy who had given me the rose. We don't speak of this sadness directly. I caress him lovingly. We will soon make love.

"I'm on some kind of cruise. On vacation. In terms of the clothes it was like in the Twenties. I see a flapper kind of dress. It was like the movie 'Murder on the Orient Express,' very luxurious; beautiful people with furs, elegance, and the feeling that something was going to happen, almost like a Hercule Poirot story by Agatha Christie. It's a big ship in the middle of the ocean somewhere, sailing along."

"It's not particularly going anywhere?" I ask, wondering where we're going.

"It is, but I don't know where. It feels, maybe, like we're on our way to Europe. I could be a governess on a job. I don't know. In the dream I'm just there on the boat and it's moving along. We're at a table in the dining room having dinner. It's large and there are a lot of people at different tables. No, that's wrong. We're up on one of the decks. I just see this table with these people I'm involved with. I'm not actually sitting at the table. I'm looking at this family in the dining hall from one of the decks. They're at a rectangular long table; no one is at the head of the table. They are sitting on the long sides: the father, the mother—his wife—is next to him. There are two young boys, one is younger than the other. Now I'm sitting at the table too. One of the boys might be sitting next to the mother, and the other boy is sitting next to me. The young boy is dark-haired with kneesocks and short pants with a jacket. Like boarding-school-type clothes in the twenties, and hair kind of parted in the middle. Very good looking. The boy has a very sweet, gentle expression. He's a loving very sweet boy, very handsome. He has a crush on me. I have a special feeling, a relationship with him. We're close. He must be about eight. I now see the eight-year-old to my right and I'm sitting at the head of the table. Things seem to shift that way because the boy gives me a gift. It's a piece of paper, he's drawn a rose on it. I drew a rose many years ago on a piece of paper and I think I wrote something on the back and gave it as a gift to my husband at the time. It has a kind of special meaning. I wrote a poem or something like that. That's the rose I'm seeing now."

"What was the intention when you gave it to your husband?"

"With love from my heart. With all my heart."

"In a way the little boy is giving you his heart?" I question her.

"Yeah." She sounds completely certain. Her positive reply feels like a conclusion: she's aware that this little boy and "Tim" (Claire's image of the donor) are one and the same.

"What do you feel right now?"

"A lot of sadness. I'm all choked up. It's a very deep and very painful sadness. I can feel it in my stomach, my throat. I don't know whether it's longing, regret, or gratitude."

"And it has something to do with the little boy giving you his rose?"

"It's a very catching picture. It is very beautiful and very sad at the same time. He's giving me something very precious of himself."

We drop into a long silence. At this point Claire is deeply connected to the feelings of loss and death, the far end of the dark spectrum.

I wait until the mood lets go of Claire so that we may continue. Like a pendulum, emotions come to rest.

We resume. "And now you hear that the younger boy has died?" I ask, to set the tone for the change of atmosphere.

"The new scene," Claire ponders, shifting her attention to this new situation. I have to further encourage her.

"What's it like, this feeling he has died and that this has something to do with you?" This is as far as I'll go in resetting the scene.

"I'm puzzled. I'm curious because I don't understand it and I have to find out what it means! Everybody seems to know except me. The fact that I've had something to do with it makes me feel vulnerable, I guess because I don't know what happened. I only know it has something to do with me, and I want to know what happened."

"What do you feel about the fact he has died, this young boy who has given you this precious gift?"

"In shock, disbelief . . . No," she takes it back. "No, that doesn't ring true. It wasn't shock and disbelief. It just happened. It was supposed to happen and then I just learned about it. It may almost have been like a detachment. I just didn't see him anymore. I was a passenger, a bystander, and I just heard about it." She sounds as if it were all happening to someone else, She's moved light years away from feeling anything but distance.

"Are you still in this detached state?" I ask after a pause.

"Yeah, observation," she replies without interest. She and I feel miles apart.

I look at the paper on my lap on which she has typewritten this dream, an exact copy of her dream notebook. I want to lose the distance and search for an image that might involve her again. We could easily stay removed for the rest of the hour.

"The next sentence I'll read back to you," I remark, fumbling with the paper. " 'I'm lying next to a dark-haired virile handsome man. He had been the father but became the eldest of the two brothers, now the third. He is helping me tell my story to the world. I ask for something. There is a tremendous feeling of closeness between us. Of desire and of sadness about what had happened with the little boy who had given me the rose. We don't speak of this sadness directly. I caress him lovingly. We will soon make love.' Can you go close to the point where you are lying close to this dark-haired handsome man? Where is this taking place?" I ask, emphasizing the word "close."

"On a large bed on the boat I guess. He's lying on his back and I'm more or less lying on my stomach, facing him. I think we are both naked. He looks very handsome. He has a great build, good body, dark hair. In his twenties, I think. Tremendous vitality." She pauses. "I was thinking in how many dreams I'm a bystander. But when I'm with him, I'm not. Never. When I'm with him I can feel things." All previous sense of distance between us is gone. Passion zings through this Wednesday afternoon. Our moods vary as swiftly as the New England weather. The mood spectrum has shifted from the dark melancholy, through the colorless sense of distance, to a passionate red.

"Are you caressing him?" I'm aware of the sensors in my skin.

"I guess so." Her voice drifts again, like a cloud on a hot day. "Right now I'm feeling an intense longing for him. What keeps coming up is that feeling I had in the dream of the man who contacts the boy who had drowned." Claire is referring to a dream in which a little boy–"Tim" had drowned and was found under water by a man who had himself been the recipient of a heart transplant. In the dream she had loved the man because he had been the only one who knew what she had gone through. This man could reach the little boy–"Tim" who had died in the dream a while back, and now again he comes up in a dream where a little boy had died. "He's like a guide," Claire concludes. "I think I'm asking for his advice about how to tell my story to the world. He's telling me what he thinks and what I need to change."

"Does that change your fundamental opinion about your story?"

"No. It's still my story."

At this point I realize how important it is that I don't suggest anything. She has to tell her own story. I also know that this guide may at times be projected onto me, making me function as Claire's guide. But on the deeper interior level this guide is not me. He is the consciousness emerging spontaneously from the transplant. In the dream where he knows how to find the drowned "Tim," he does so because he himself is a transplant. He is the one who knows the intimacy of transplantation. He portrays the meaning emerging from the interior experience of the transplant. From transplantation itself the wisdom emerges. Scarman, the one who has suffered the operation, a guide who Claire first saw behind her back, has returned. We can trace this process through the dreams. The transplant creates a craving to make sense of this profound experience of death and rebirth. This craving for meaning, if paid attention to, engenders a response from the depth of the soul. A new sense of orientation awakens, a new sense of direction that can lead the confused recipient through a maze of baffling experiences to a point of relative clarity.

"He was the eldest of the two brothers but now he is the third. Can you tell me a little bit more about that?" I inquire, wanting to know more about this loved one who knows the lost "Tim."

"Well, I didn't understand that because he wasn't one of the two who I had originally been with. He was older. The original boys were young. Somehow he had transformed. It was the third brother, or it could have been the father. There was all this transformation happening. He was someone in between these young boys and their father. A third person."

The hour is over. Claire leaves. I am left with this third person, this guide who is both me and not-me, the one who is a transformed "Tim." This third is neither "Tim" nor Claire, or he is both "Tim" and Claire. This third consciousness is that of the transplant being itself, a mixture of two, a new guiding spirit. A psychological amalgamation has taken place, much like the images of the alchemy of old where two fundamentally different metals were fused to give birth to a third substance. The alchemists have long descriptions of the "Third," the amalgam of the two. This Third often appears at the end of the alchemical process as the new life form, the stone of wisdom, the profound insight that transforms all experience.

The reality of this new guiding spirit becomes apparent over the next two sessions. Claire begins to emerge from her ambivalence about contacting the family of the young man who was her donor. Her vision becomes clear, she knows what to do, a resolve begins to dawn. Claire decides to contact the family of her heart. This event eventually leads her to a profound understanding of herself with the heart and lungs of this young man.

The trauma of transplantation is one of extreme ambivalence, as can be seen in the experiences of Claire, myself, and the group:

- In Claire's early dreams the image of death and rebirth surfaces often.

- In our transplant group we found both a deep gratitude and a virulent anger toward the medical profession.

- When Claire contacted the donor family, they were at first very grateful for her contact with them. Later they went through a period of anger toward her.

- The transference between Claire and myself vacillated between passionate love and deep feelings of abandonment.

That such an ambivalence is experienced is not surprising. The old heart dies and the new heart lives, the donor dies and the recipient lives. Often the age difference between donor and recipient is significant, so that two fundamentally different vital energies have to learn to live together. We have observed activity-craving teenage hearts wearing out middle-aged recipients.

Often the difficult side of this ambivalence is repressed. The medical profession assists in this repression. Claire was told, right after her transplant, that when she experienced profound emotional distress, she should just forget about it and act normal. Normal!

Experiencing this ambivalence, this inner conflict, is essential. Eventually it may lead to a new understanding of life as the two vitalities who have been thrown together merge into a new person. After a heart transplant one will never be the same, even if one insists that nothing fundamental has happened. The task of psychotherapy is to facilitate the interaction between the old self and the new self. It is the great advantage of psychotherapy, moreover, that this merging process can be experienced in the transference as the vicissitudes of the transferential relationship. In this way the process taking place in the deep interior becomes visible and manageable.

CHAPTER SEVENTEEN

Recurrent Dreams:
Their Relation to Life Events

ANTONIO L. ZADRA

This book has described a wide variety of traumatic events that can cause nightmares. Recurrent dreams and repetitive dream themes are similar in many respects to traumatic nightmares. Most recurrent dreams have negative content, arise during periods of stress, and dissipate once the stressor has been successfully dealt with. Although the continuity between nightmares and other forms of dream recurrence is not a new idea, much of the data that supports this continuity is new.

The Prevalence and Content of Recurrent Dreams

Relatively little is known about the prevalence and content of recurrent dreams. Until recently, what appeared in the clinical literature was mainly passing mention that recurrent dreams had been noted in some patients. For instance, Freud's ([1900] 1931) only comment on the prevalence of recurrent dreams was that "dreams that recur periodically have often been observed" (p. 44).

Almost all of the studies that have used questionnaires to assess the prevalence of recurrent dreams have done so by simply including a question such as "Have you ever had a recurrent dream?" Thus these studies did not evaluate the length of time that the subjects had experienced their recurrent dreams. Moreover, with the exception of data presented by Brown and Donderi (1986), these studies have failed to differentiate between true recurrent dreams (in which the dream content is always identical) from repetitive dream themes that occur across dreams with varying contents. In addition, the literature on the content of recurrent dreams has been largely impressionistic. Only two studies have used well-established, quantitative dream content scales to evaluate recurrent dream content (Larue, 1970; D'Andrade, 1985), and these are undergraduate research papers by students of Domhoff.

In terms of the prevalence of recurrent dreams, 60 to 75 percent of college students and older adults report having had one or more "recurrent dreams" at some point in their lives on questionnaire surveys (Cartwright and Romanek 1978; Cartwright, 1979; Browman and Kapell, 1982; D'Andrade, 1985; Robbins and Houshi, 1983; Robbins and Tanck, 1991–92; Webb and Fagan, 1993). Seventy to 80 percent of adults who take part in dream studies report having had a recurrent dream in early childhood (Brown and Donderi, 1986; Zadra and Donderi, 1992). In some cases, recurrent dreams that emerge during childhood may persist into adulthood (D'Andrade, 1985; Robbins and Houshi, 1983). Questionnaire and home dream diary data collected by Zadra and Donderi (1992) showed that 80 of 217 nonstudent adults reported experiencing an ongoing recurrent dream, or ongoing recurrent themes, of at least one year's duration. There is also some evidence to indicate that recurrent dreams are more prevalent in women than they are in men (Cartwright and Romanek, 1978; Browman and Kapell, 1982; Robbins and Houshi, 1983).

In terms of dream content, 60 to 85 percent of recurrent dreams are described as being unpleasant by the subjects who report them (Cartwright and Romanek, 1978; D'Andrade, 1985; Zadra and Donderi, 1992). In one female sample, 46 percent of the recurrent dreams reported were rated as being highly unpleasant (Cartwright, 1979). Dream content is described as being pleasant in approximately 10 percent of recurrent dreams (Cartwright, 1979; D'Andrade, 1985); about 8 percent of recurrent dreams are rated as containing a mixture of both positive and negative emotions (D'Andrade, 1985).

Cartwright (1979) and Robbins and Tanck (1993) examined retrospective accounts of childhood recurrent dreams. These studies show that between 86 percent and 90 percent of childhood recurrent dreams are unpleasant or of a threatening nature. In approximately 70 percent of the childhood recurrent dreams, external agents (for example, monsters, witches) were responsible for the unpleasant content. Both studies also showed that as people grow older, fewer recurrent dreams are reported as having threatening content. Furthermore, in recurrent dreams from people's second and third decade of life, the dreamer and not an external agent becomes increasingly responsible for the dream action (Cartwright, 1979).

Although the precise content of recurrent dreams is invariably idiosyncratic, themes common across individuals who report recurrent dreams have been noted (for example, Delaney, 1991). These include recurrent dreams of flying, falling, being chased, taking an examination, losing one's teeth, and nudity. These themes are similar to typical dreams or nonrecurrent dreams that many people report having had at least once (for example, Griffith, Miyago, and Tago, 1958; Ward, Beck, and Rascoe, 1961; Kramer, Winget, and Whitman, 1971). Although several studies have investigated the content of typical dreams, no systematic classification of the thematic content of recurrent dreams has appeared in the literature.

A Content Analysis of Childhood and Adult Recurrent Dreams

The goal of this study was to obtain more detailed data on the content of recurrent dreams than had been previously reported. In particular, the study establishes a classification of the thematic content of childhood and adult recurrent dreams.

Method

The data presented in this study is based on the content analyses of 163 recurrent dreams. These dreams were collected from the dream reports of 352 subjects who completed the McGill Sleep/Dream Questionnaire as part of our studies on dreams between 1990 and 1992. These 163 recurrent dreams were selected from a pool of over 250 recurrent dreams and represent all of the dreams that met the following inclusion criteria: the recurrent dream must have occurred over a period of at least six months; the content of the recurrent dream had to be rated by the subject as being "always" or "almost always" identical; and the recurrent dream had to be described in sufficient detail to allow a content analyses of the dream's setting, its affective tone, and the type of characters present. The recurrent dreams were classified as being from adulthood if they first occurred after the age of eighteen, and from childhood if they ceased to recur before the age of twelve.

Dream content was evaluated using the objective content analysis system developed by Hall and Van de Castle (1966). The measures of dream content are described below.

Dream affect. Dream affect was scored using the Emotions scale of Hall and Van de Castle (1966). Negative affect includes classes of emotion such as anger, apprehension, sadness, and confusion. One class of emotions, labeled happiness, encompasses all the adjectives that describe positive affect (for example, pleased, relieved, relaxed, elated).

Success and failure. Success and failure were scored according to Hall and Van de Castle's scales for Achievement Outcomes. Success consists of an expenditure of energy and perseverance in pursuit of a goal, resulting in goal attainment. Failures occur when there is expenditure of energy and perseverance in pursuit of a goal but the result is failure to attain the goal because of personal limitations and inadequacies.

Good fortune and misfortune. Good fortune and misfortunes were scored according to Hall and Van de Castle's scales of Environmental Press. Misfortunes are defined as "any mishap, adversity, harm, danger, or threat which happens to a character as a result of circumstances over which he has no control" (p. 103). Good fortune is scored when "there is an acquisition of goods or something beneficial happens to a character that is completely adventitious or the result of a circumstance over which no one has control" (p. 105).

Categories for the classification of the thematic content of childhood and adult recurrent dreams were not determined a priori. They were constructed following the content analysis of the recurrent dreams and were based on the most frequently reported themes contained in the childhood and adult recurrent dreams.

Results and Discussion

Table 17.1 presents the percentage of recurrent dreams from adulthood and childhood that contain the dream content categories described above.

The percentage of adult and childhood recurrent dreams that were found to contain either negative affect, positive affect, or a mixture of both positive and negative emotions is consistent with the previously reviewed findings. Approximately 5 percent of all the recurrent dreams in this sample were described as containing no affect. Data on the absence of affect in recurrent dreams have not been previously reported.

Among recurrent dreams containing negative affect, fear or apprehension was the most frequently reported emotion, occurring in 67 and 79 percent of the adult and childhood recurrent dreams respectively. The rest of these recurrent dreams contained other negative emotions, including sadness, anger, confusion, and guilt. This finding is of particular interest, because there is evidence suggesting that approximately 20 percent of nightmares contain emotions other than fear and that a significant percentage of individuals cite emotions such as sadness and anger to be primary in their nightmares (Belicki, Altay, and Hill, 1985; Dunn and Barrett, 1988; Zadra and Donderi, 1993).

In terms of Achievement Outcomes, adult recurrent dreams were nine times more likely than childhood recurrent dreams to contain one or more failures. Success was rare in both groups, occurring in less than 3 percent of all recurrent dreams.

Approximately 42 percent of the adult and childhood recurrent dreams contained one or more misfortunes. The dreamer was the recipient of the misfortune in 70 percent of the adult recurrent dreams and in 74 percent of

Table 17.1   Recurrent dream content

	Percentage of RD from adulthood (n = 110)	Percentage of RD from childhood (n = 53)	Percentage of total RD (n = 163)
Emotion			
Negative affect	77.3	81.1	78.5
Positive affect	10.0	7.6	9.2
Mixture of both positive and negative emotions	7.3	5.7	6.7
No affect	5.5	5.7	5.5
Total	100.1	100.1	99.9
Dream Content Scales			
Failure	17.3	1.9	12.3
Success	1.8	3.8	2.5
Misfortune	41.8	43.4	42.3
Good fortune	4.6	3.8	4.3
Total for Achievement and Environmental Press	65.5	52.9	61.4

Note: RD = Recurrent dreams. Totals for emotion dream content scales do not equal 100 owing to rounding. Totals for Achievement and Environmental Press scales do not add up to 100 as several dreams did not contain one or more of these dream content categories.

childhood recurrent dreams. Thus for both groups of recurrent dreams, misfortunes were about three times more likely to happen to the dreamer than to any other character. The other Environmental Press category, good fortune, occurred in less than 5 percent of the adult and childhood recurrent dreams.

Table 17.2 presents the most frequently reported types of themes in the current sample of recurrent dreams from adulthood and childhood. For both adult and childhood recurrent dreams, the most frequently reported theme is one in which the dreamer is being chased. The nature of the threatening agent, however, differs between childhood and adulthood recurrent chase dreams. In nineteen of the twenty-two (86 percent) chase dreams from childhood, the dreamer was being pursued by monsters, wild animals, witches, or ghoulish creatures. By contrast, such threatening agents appeared in only three of the sixteen (19 percent) adult chase dreams. The

Table 17.2 Thematic content of adult and childhood recurrent dreams

Thematic content	Percentage of RD from adulthood (*n* = 110)	Percentage of RD from childhood (*n* = 53)	Percentage of total RD (*n* = 163)
Being chased	14.6	41.5	23.3
Problems with house maintenance	10.9	0.0	7.4
Being alone and stuck or trapped	6.4	3.8	5.5
Facing natural forces	5.5	3.8	4.9
Teeth falling out	4.6	0.0	3.1
Discovering/exploring new rooms in a house	4.6	1.9	3.7
Death of family members	4.6	9.4	6.1
Not knowing why or to whom one is getting married	3.6	0.0	2.5
Unable to use a telephone during an emergency	3.6	0.0	2.5
Unable to find a private toilet	3.6	0.0	2.5
Being late or lost	2.7	1.9	2.5
Driving a car that is out of control	2.7	0.0	1.8
Flying	2.7	3.8	3.1
Other	30.0	34.0	31.2
Total	100.1	100.1	100.1

Note: RD = recurrent dreams. Totals do not add up to 100 owing to rounding.

latter contained predominantly human characters, including burglars, strangers, mobs, and shadowy figures. These findings are consistent with those reported by Robbins and Tanck (1991–92).

Next to chase and pursuit dreams, the second most frequently reported theme in the adult recurrent dreams was one in which the dreamer is having difficulties with house maintenance. In these recurrent dreams, the dreamer may be overwhelmed by an inordinate number of household chores that must be quickly completed, discover that the house is falling apart or in ruins, or have to choose between maintaining one or the other of two houses. Other common themes include being alone and trapped (for example, in an elevator or container), facing natural forces such as volcanic eruptions or tidal waves, and losing one's teeth.

In the childhood recurrent dreams, the second most frequently reported theme was one involving the death of family members. All of these recurrent dreams involved the murder or accidental death of the dreamer's parents. By comparison, the five adult recurrent dreams from the same content category were either dreams in which a distant relative had died or dreams about people who were already dead in actual life (for example, mourning dreams).

Themes in which the dreamer is in danger (for example, threatened with injury, death, or chased) have been found to characterize approximately 40 percent of recurrent dreams (Cartwright and Romanek, 1978; Robbins and Houshi, 1983). Using the same broad content category, 42 percent of the adult recurrent dreams and 65 percent of the childhood recurrent dreams could be classified as containing themes in which the dreamer is in danger. In most of these dreams with threatening content, the subject is either fleeing, attempting to hide, or helplessly watching.

Relatively little is known about the content of pleasant recurrent dreams, because they occur infrequently. In the present sample, five of the six dreams that involved "discovering and exploring new rooms in a house" and four of the five flying dreams were described as containing positive emotions. Other examples of pleasant recurrent dreams included excelling at a particular task (for example, figure skating), finding oneself in a bountiful environment, and being involved in sexual activities.

These results demonstrate key differences between adult and childhood recurrent dreams. For instance, adult recurrent dreams were nine times more likely than the childhood recurrent dreams to contain one or more failures. Because failures in dreams result from a character's "personal limitations and inadequacies," these data suggest that recurrent dreams from adulthood are more likely to reflect issues of personal competence than do recurrent dreams from childhood. This hypothesis is consistent with Cartwright's (1979) suggestion that "as the subject grows, the responsibility in the repetitive dreams with an unpleasant tone is less often attributed to things beyond her control" (p. 135). Although the thematic content category "being chased" was common in both the adult and childhood recurrent dreams, the threatening agents in the former usually were human characters, whereas monsters, wild animals, or ghoulish creatures were predominant in the latter. Several of the thematic content categories reported in adult recurrent dreams are noticeably absent from the childhood recurrent dreams. These include themes involving problems with house maintenance, teeth falling out, and being unable to find a private toilet.

These findings indicate that the content of recurrent dreams changes with age and suggest that the dream symbols or metaphors believed to depict current problems or concerns that underlie recurrent dreams also change with age.

Theories of Recurrent Dreams

Dream theorists generally agree that recurrent dreams are related to unresolved difficulties in the dreamer's life (Fosshage and Loew, 1987). For example, in Gestaltist dream theory, recurrent dreams are viewed as depicting an individual's current state of psychic imbalance. Presenting this psychic state to consciousness allows for a possible restoration of self-balance (Perls, 1969; Fantz, 1978). Neo-Freudian, object-relations, and ego-psychology dream theorists believe that the dream repetition of emotionally painful events allows the ego to attempt to master or assimilate the painful event (Bibring, 1943; Silverberg, 1948; Stewart, 1967; Renik, 1981). Freud viewed recurrent (traumatic) dreams as expressions of a neurotic repetition compulsion (Freud, [1920] 1955; Cavenar and Sullivan, 1978). Jung believed that recurrent dreams not only indicated the presence of psychological conflict, but were also "of specific importance for the integration of the psyche" (Jung, in Adler, 1973, p. 93). Culturalist dream theory (Bonime, 1962) maintains that recurrent dreams indicate a lack of positive change or development in one's personality. In recurrent dreams "people continue to reflect unresolved personality difficulties with the identical symbols" (Bonime, 1962, p. 41). Thus many kinds of dream theories converge in their view that recurrent dreams are associated with a lack of progress in recognizing and resolving conflicts in the dreamer's life.

If recurrent dreams signal the presence of an unresolved conflict, then the cessation of a recurring dream should indicate that the conflict has been successfully dealt with. Dream theorists from many different perspectives have suggested that this is the case (Bonime, 1962; Weiss, 1964; Jung, cited in Mattoon, 1978, p. 84; Sharpe, 1978; Cartwright, 1979; Ullman and Zimmerman, 1979; Delaney, 1991).

Recurrent dreams, however, are not a unitary phenomenon. The repetition of dream symbols or themes over a series of dreams is not the same thing as a recurrent dream, in which the dream content is always identical from beginning to end. Domhoff (1993) has argued that repetitive dream themes and recurrent dreams are related experiences in that they are both part of a "repetition dimension." In the next section, a summary of the types of dreams which make up this dimension will be presented.

The Dream Repetition Continuum

Bonime (1962) distinguished between recurrent dreams in which "the patient reiterates, again and again, his symbolic statement of the core problem" (p. 41) and dreams in which repetitive themes are depicted over a range of symbols. Domhoff (1993) defined a continuum of repetition. At one extreme are the traumatic dreams that repeatedly reproduce overwhelming experiences. Almost any event that is perceived as being traumatic by an individual can produce traumatic dreams, and their occurrence is recognized as a symptom of Post-Traumatic Stress Disorder (APA, 1987). As trauma victims begin to deal successfully with their difficulties, there are often positive changes in the content of their traumatic dreams (for example, Hartmann, 1984). Domhoff (1993) iterates this point by stating "to the degree that the experience gradually is assimilated, to that degree the dreams decrease in frequency and become altered in content" (p. 297).

Next on the continuum is the recurrent dream. The content of recurrent dreams, like that of many traumatic dreams, is replayed in all (or almost all) of its entirety. As noted earlier, recurrent dreams are frequent in both children and adults, and are primarily unpleasant. Although recurrent dreams do not always seem to be directly tied to any particular experience, the evidence suggests that they occur during times of stress and that they cease to recur once the problem has been resolved (Cartwright, 1979; D'Andrade, 1985; Brown and Donderi, 1986). Unlike many traumatic dreams, however, most recurrent dreams do not reflect a conflict or stressor directly, but rather depict it in a metaphorical manner.

Further along the repetition continuum are recurrent themes within a long dream series. In these dreams, the theme is always the same (for example, being late or lost), but the content is not. Finally, the repetition of mundane characters, activities, and objects that occurs in every-day dreams consistently over decades lies at the other end of the continuum. Several examples of repetitive themes and repeated dream elements are presented by Domhoff (1993). He maintains that the dreams which constitute the "repetition dimension" all reflect attempts at resolving emotional preoccupations. Empirical data that support both the validity of the dream repetition continuum and its proposed association with emotional preoccupations will now be reviewed.

Recurrent Dreams and Well-Being

A number of case reports have described positive changes in repetitive dream elements as a function of successful psychotherapy (for example, Bonime, 1962; Maultsby and Gram, 1974; Rossi, 1985). Bergin (1970) presented the case of a client who lacked self-assertion skills and who was excessively intimidated by authority figures. Following an improvement in his condition, the client spontaneously reported that both the negative content and affective tone of a previously recurrent dream had changed in a positive manner. This case is especially interesting because the therapy involved behavioral techniques, and the client's dreams had never been discussed during therapy. The changes reported are consistent with Bonime's (1962) assertion that "to the extent that these alterations of the same symbol take place in accordance with alterations of the personality during therapy, the symbol changes become important indicators of clinical progress" (p. 45).

In addition to anecdotal and clinical case reports, research data support the theory that the repetition of negative dream content is associated with the presence of unresolved conflicts or stressors.

Robbins and Houshi (1983) found that undergraduate students who reported having a recurrent dream had moderately significantly higher scores on the Beck Depression Inventory and reported a significantly greater number of problems in their daily lives than did undergraduate students who did not have recurrent dreams.

Brown and Donderi (1986) published the only study to have specifically investigated the relation of recurrent dreams (as opposed to repetitive dream elements) to well-being. Recurrent dreamers, former recurrent dreamers, and nonrecurrent dreamers were asked to complete a battery of well-being measures and record a fourteen-day sample of their own remembered dreams. People in the recurrent dream group were currently experiencing a recurrent dream. The former recurrent dream group was composed of individuals who had experienced a recurrent dream in adulthood, but for whom the dream had not recurred for at least one year. The recurrent dreams reported by the subjects in both of these groups had persisted over at least a six-month period. Subjects in the nonrecurrent dream group had never experienced a recurrent dream as adults. Recurrent dreams were differentiated from dream series that contained repetitive themes or repeated dream elements and were defined as dreams which "are distinguished by their complete repetition as a remembered experience" (p. 612).

The recurrent dream group scored consistently lower on measures of well-being than both the past-recurrent dream group and the nonrecurrent dream group. For example, recurrent dreamers had the least adaptive scores on measures of anxiety, depression, personal adjustment, and life-events stress. Moreover, content analyses of the dream reports showed that the recurrent dreamers experienced more anxious, dysphoric, and conflict-oriented dream content than either of the other two groups. Past-recurrent dreamers scored consistently higher than the nonrecurrent dreamers on indices of well-being and positive dream content. This latter finding is of particular interest, since it suggests that the maintained cessation of a recurrent dream is associated with a positive rebound effect on well-being.

Several of Brown and Donderi's (1986) findings have been replicated in a younger adult population by Zadra, O'Brien, and Donderi (1993). Using the same methodology as in Brown and Donderi (1986), Zadra, O'Brien, and Donderi (1993) found that recurrent dreamers scored consistently lower on measures of well-being than nonrecurrent dreamers. Specifically, recurrent dreamers reported significantly higher levels of neuroticism, anxiety, depression, somatic symptomatology, and life-events stress and significantly lower levels of personal adjustment. This study also replicated Brown and Donderi's (1986) finding that the dreams of recurrent dreamers contain significantly more negative dream content than those of nonrecurrent dreamers. For example, the dreams of the recurrent dream group contained significantly greater proportions of anxiety, hostility, failure, and misfortune. This finding cannot be attributed to the presence of negative recurrent dreams in the recurrent dream group's two-week dream log reports. Only 2 of the 187 dreams reported by the recurrent dream group were recurrent dreams.

A past-recurrent dream group was also included in Zadra, O'Brien, and Donderi's (1993) study. This group was composed of individuals who had experienced a recurrent dream in early childhood, but for whom the dream had ceased to recur between the approximate ages of ten and twelve. Participants in this group had not experienced any other recurrent dreams since then. The authors found that these past-recurrent dreamers did not differ from nonrecurrent dreamers on the measures of well-being or on any of the dream content measures.

Taken together, these studies provide support for the following conclusions. In both late teenagers and older adults, recurrent dreams: (1) occur in times of stress; (2) are accompanied by negative dream content in everyday dreams; and (3) are associated with a relative deficit in psychological well-being. Furthermore, the cessation of a previously recurrent dream in adulthood is associated with increased psychological well-being. The cessation of a recurrent dream in early childhood, however, does not appear to have any long-term psychological benefits. These conclusions are consistent with the clinical dream theories reviewed earlier.

Zadra, Miller, and Donderi (1994) extended some of the aforementioned findings on recurrent dreams to dreams with recurrent themes. Specifically, they compared individuals who reported repetitive themes in their dreams with people who did not have such dream patterns. Recurrent themes fall lower on Domhoff's (1993) continuum of repetition than do recurrent dreams. For this reason, Zadra, Miller, and Donderi (1994) predicted that, relative to nonrecurrent dreamers, people with repetitive dream themes would show deficits in well-being and negative dream content, but not to the extent shown by recurrent dreamers in their previous studies.

As in the studies by Brown and Donderi (1986) and Zadra, O'Brien, and

Donderi (1993), group membership was based on responses to several questions on the McGill Sleep/Dream Questionnaire as well as on the subjects' written descriptions of any type of "recurrent dream" they remembered. Inclusion criteria for the repetitive theme group consisted of having "recurrent dreams" in which the content was "rarely" or "never" identical but in which the theme was "always" or "often" identical. Furthermore, the repetitive dream themes had to be currently experienced and have persisted for at least twelve months. The nonrecurrent theme group was composed of people who reported never having experienced recurrent dreams or recurrent dream themes in their adult life.

People with repetitive dream themes were found to score significantly lower than people without repetitive dream themes on four of the six measures of well-being. What is more, the scores of the repetitive theme group on these four measures were higher (more adaptive) than the scores obtained by the recurrent dreamers in both the Brown and Donderi (1986) and the Zadra, O'Brien, and Donderi (1993) samples.

A content analysis of dream diary reports revealed that the dreams of the repetitive theme group contained more negative dream elements than did the dreams of the control group (for example, more anxiety, negative affect, hostility-toned content). The frequency and intensity of these negative dream elements, however, were not as great as that found in the everyday dream reports of people with recurrent dreams.

The results from the studies reviewed in this section support both the validity and the heuristic value of Domhoff's (1993) repetition continuum. The data indicate that people who experience recurrent themes show a deficit on measures of well-being, but not to the extent shown by those with recurrent dreams. These results form a pattern which suggests that scores on measures of psychological well-being are inversely related to the position of a dreaming experience on the repetition continuum. If this is correct, we would expect that people with recurrent traumatic dreams would score lower on measures of well-being than people with either recurrent dreams or repetitive dream themes. Similarly, the data from the dream content analyses suggest that, as one moves toward the traumatic dream end of the continuum, people's everyday dreams should contain greater proportions of negative dream elements (for example, aggressive, anxious, and dysphoric dream content).

Domhoff (1993) argues that the dreams which make up his repetition dimension (that is, traumatic dreams, recurrent dreams, repeated themes, and frequent dream elements) all reflect attempts at resolving emotional preoccupations. If this hypothesis is correct, then the cessation of any of these types of "recurrent dreams" should indicate that the emotional issue has been resolved. Consistent with this view, Brown and Donderi (1986) presented evidence that the cessation of recurrent dreams in adulthood was correlated with an elevation in well-being. Whether or not the cessation of previously recurring themes or dream elements in adulthood is also associated with increases in well-being remains to be determined.

A possible exception to these conclusions concerns positive recurrent dreams. As was noted earlier, approximately 10 percent of recurrent dreams are described as being pleasant. Because positive recurrent dreams occur infrequently, their association to measures of well-being has not been investigated. Thus we do not know if people who report positive recurrent dreams also show a relative deficit on measures of well-being. Similarly, we do not know whether the maintained cessation of pleasant recurrent dreams is correlated with positive, negative, or no change in well-being.

The theories and data on recurrent dreams presented here are consistent with a broader view of the dream as an attempt to resolve current emotional concerns, one of the possible function of dreams as proposed by contemporary dream theory (for example, Hall, 1953; French and Fromm, 1964; Breger, 1967; Greenberg and Pearlman, 1975; Cartwright, 1977; Fiss, 1986; Baylor and Deslauriers, 1986–87; Delaney, 1991). However, the data do not show that emotional concerns are resolved by incorporating them in dreams. Given the correlational nature of the data, the direction of causality between dream content and waking emotional states cannot be inferred. In other words, dream content may either reflect or influence waking adjustment. At the present time, no firm conclusions regarding which of these possibilities is correct can be drawn. The nature of the association between dream content and waking state personality may also vary with the individual and the life circumstances. It may turn out that dreams can both influence and reflect waking state personality, albeit at different points in one's life.

The causality issue cannot be resolved until dream content is manipulated as an independent variable. For example, one could attempt to alter recurrent dream content using lucid dream induction techniques or waking imagery exercises. Case studies have shown such treatments to be effective in the treatment of recurrent nightmares (for example, Marks, 1978; Halliday, 1982; Tholey, 1988). In a controlled treatment study, it may be possible to demonstrate a causal relationship between the experimental manipulation of dream content and pre- to post-manipulation changes in objective personality measures, including measures of psychological well-being. Such a study has been undertaken in Donderi's laboratory. The clinical applications of lucid dreaming in altering recurrent dream content will now be briefly reviewed.

Lucid Dreaming and Repetitive Dream Content

Several authors have suggested that there are psychological benefits from lucid dreaming (for example, Kelzer, 1989; LaBerge, 1985; Tholey, 1988).

Lucid dreams occur when one becomes aware that he or she is dreaming while still in the dream state. Sometimes lucid dreamers can recall events from their waking life, can reason, and can move their dream bodies as desired. Some lucid dreamers can change the dream scenery at will. It is now known that lucid dreams occur during unequivocal REM sleep (for example, LaBerge and Dement, 1982; LaBerge, Greenleaf, and Kedzierski, 1983; Schatzman, Worsley, and Fenwick, 1988).

A number of case studies have described the successful use of lucid dreaming in the treatment of recurrent nightmares (for example, Halliday, 1982, 1988; Tholey, 1988; Zadra, 1990). Dream lucidity can also give rise to positive psychological elements that carry over into waking life (for example, Brylowski, 1990; Tholey, 1988). Lucid dreaming may operate through a number of mechanisms to achieve positive therapeutic outcomes. For example, LaBerge and Rheingold (1990) have suggested that what a person expects to happen next in a dream can play an important role in dream construction or the manner in which the dream will unfold. It is possible that individuals who have recurrent dreams (including recurrent nightmares) may be locked into a fixed way of responding to the dream's imagery and of anticipating what will happen next. This in turn leads the dreamer to reexperience the same imagery, which is often threatening in nature. Lucid dreaming may provide such individuals with new responses and expectations concerning the dream's progression, thereby altering the repetitive nature of such dreams. Galvin (1990) suggests that by turning nightmare sufferers into lucid dreamers, the sufferers may develop "a more coherent psychological sense of self through the experience of a degree of mastery in the dream state and possibly resolve their nightmare condition" (p. 78).

When working with recurrent nightmares, I have often combined lucid dreaming with exercises in relaxation and guided imagery. In this treatment approach, subjects are first asked to close their eyes and to make themselves comfortable. If a subjects is unable to relax, he or she may be trained in progressive muscle relaxation (Bernstein and Borkovec, 1973). Once the subjects are relaxed, they rehearse (that is, imagine) their recurrent dream in as much detail as possible while describing it to the therapist. The therapist guides this rehearsal, for example, asking about various dream elements (for example, emotions, settings, characters) or bringing particular details to the subject's attention. Once the dream has been described, the subject is asked to select a part of the recurrent dream that is emotionally and/or visually salient and is instructed to carry out a particular task at this salient point in the dream. The subject imagines performing this task in the dream while saying that he or she is dreaming (that is, that the dream is now a lucid dream). When performed during the actual dream, this action is a cue that the experience is a dream. Typically, this task is as simple as looking at one's hands or calling out a word. Once the relaxation and imagery exercises have been completed, subjects are instructed to practice them at home, especially just before going to sleep.

The rationale for this treatment is as follows: by repeatedly rehearsing the recurrent dream, together with a task which is intentionally carried out at a preselected salient point in the dream, the subject will remember to carry out the task when the recurrent dream occurs. The task serves as a prerehearsed cue to remind the subject that the experience is a dream. At this point, the subject is dreaming lucidly and can consciously choose the manner in which he or she wants to respond to and interact with the dream imagery. This treatment is a variation of Tholey's (1983) intention technique for lucid dream induction.

The therapist then consults with the subject to find an appropriate way to modify the recurrent dream once lucidity is achieved. Various approaches include Garfield's (1974) suggestion to "confront and conquer" the feared scene, Halliday's (1982, 1988) suggestion to alter some small aspect of the dream, and Tholey's (1988) suggestion to have the dream ego engage in conciliatory dialogue with hostile dream figures. Some subjects may be tempted to use lucid dreaming to fly away from threatening agents in their recurrent dreams. I believe that this kind of approach should be discouraged or used only as a last resort. Compared with other methods of dealing with repetitive dream content when lucid, running or flying away from an aversive dream environment is not a constructive act. Moreover, such an approach may deprive both the subject and the therapist of a unique opportunity to gain new insights into the possible significance of the recurrent dream.

Although the ability to become lucid in one's dreams can be of therapeutic value, it remains unclear whether the principal factor responsible for the alleviation of recurrent dreams and nightmares is lucidity itself or the ability to exert some control over the dream. For example, some of my subjects have never become lucid in their recurrent dreams but nevertheless have "remembered" to carry out their rehearsed actions with positive results. Conversely, both Zadra (1990) and Halliday (1988) have reported case studies in which lucidity without the element of control actually worsened the nightmare. The dreamer's ability to alter some detail in the otherwise repetitive dream, either through new responses or through altered expectations during the dream, may therefore represent a key factor in the elimination of recurrent dreams.

General Comments and Conclusion

A question of interest to some dream researchers and to most clinicians who work with clients' dream reports is whether people with similar life events report similar recurrent dreams. The answer to this question has implications for the way in which specific dream content may be constructed across individuals. Clinicians' interests lie in their desire to understand the possible significance of specific dream content for the dreamer and the possible metaphorical expressions represented by specific dream content. In the large sample of recurrent dreams we have reviewed, different people never reported the same recurrent dream, but different life events have produced the same type of recurrent dream content. For example, two people in Zadra, O'Brien, and Donderi's (1993) recurrent dream group reported recurrent dreams involving the loss of their teeth. However, there was no overlap in any of the life events or difficulties reported by these two people. The opposite scenario has also been noted. People reporting the same life events (for example, major financial difficulties, divorce, unwanted pregnancies) were found to have very different content in their recurrent dreams. Thus the same dream themes or symbols may represent different things to different people.

Some adults who have experienced the same recurrent dream since childhood report that the content of the dream changes gradually over the years. Although the thematic content of the dream remains the same, the dream's setting or characters has become altered in ways that often reflect changes in the person's life.

One such example came from a twenty-three-year-old student who reported a recurrent dream in which someone she cared about would hurt her emotionally and show no consideration for her feelings. During this women's childhood, the recurrent dream consisted of her mother giving away belongings that the subject cherished to other children. In early adolescence, she also began to have recurrent dreams in which her older brother would be verbally abusive toward her while damaging her personal belongings. These dreams began to decrease in frequency around the age of eighteen. From that point onward, she began to have recurrent dreams about her boyfriend, who would say hurtful things to her. In these recurrent dreams, the setting was always the subject's home, while the feelings were always ones of extreme sadness and frustration. Invariably, the subject would cry and beg the other characters to stop what they were doing, but her appeals were always ignored. These dreams were described as emotionally intense and extremely vivid. Frequently the feelings experienced in the recurrent dream would persist upon awakening. The subject reported that at times these feelings were so strong that on several occasions over the previous two years, she had made her boyfriend apologize to her in real life.

Some of our recurrent dreamers also report that their recurrent dreams cease for a period of years, only to resurface when a new stressor is encountered. One thirty-eight-year-old woman, who had kept a dream diary since the age of fifteen, reported having had the same recurrent dream intermittently for over twenty years. The dream was an "examination dream" in which she found herself unprepared for an important college exam. This dream had first appeared at the age of nineteen when she had been in college. She reported that this dream reappeared every seven to ten days for several months prior to her getting married, but that it stopped recurring shortly after her wedding. Although she had not had the dream for over five years, she stated that the dream had recurred with varying frequency in the previous eighteen months. During this period she had lost her job and had been actively looking for a new one. This case is similar to the examples described by Kramer, Schoen, and Kinney (1987) in their work with Vietnam veterans. Many veterans reexperience their old traumatic dreams when dealing with marital crises, demonstrating that old recurrent dreams can reappear when one is faced with new stressors. The same phenomenon can take place in individuals who have nontraumatic recurrent dreams.

The data reviewed in this chapter support the generic psychological position that dreams are related to waking states. It has been shown that the link between people's dream content and their current levels of well-being is particularly evident in dreams that make up Domhoff's (1993) repetition continuum. Moreover, it has been shown that the cessation of a recurrent dream in adulthood is associated with an elevation in self-reported levels of well-being. This suggests that changes from repetitive to progressive dream patterns may be important indicators of how well people are adapting to their life circumstances.

These findings underscore the importance of examining series of dreams instead of focusing solely on individual dreams. There is much to be gained from the study of repetitive dream content. This is equally true for clinicians seeking to better understand their clients and for researchers interested in the possible psychological functions of dreaming.

References

Introduction

Barrett, D., and Behbehani, J. 1995. Post-traumatic nightmares in Kuwait following the Iraqi invasion. Paper presented at the Twelfth International Conference of the Association for the Study of Dreams, New York, June.

Domhoff, G. W. 1993. The repetition of dreams and dream elements: A possible clue to a function of dreams. In A. Moffitt, M. Kramer, and R. Hoffmann, eds., *The Functions of Dreaming*. Albany: SUNY Press.

Freud, S. [1900] 1965. *The Interpretation of Dreams*. New York: Avon.

Hall, C., and Van de Castle, R. 1966. *The Content Analysis of Dreams*. New York: Appleton-Century-Crofts.

Hartmann, E. 1984. *The Nightmare: The Psychology and Biology of Terrifying Dreams*. New York: Basic Books.

Jung, C. G. [1916] 1974. General aspects of dream psychology, reprinted in *Dreams*, Bollingen Series. Princeton, N.J.: Princeton University Press.

Ross, R. J., Ball, W. A., Sullivan, K. A., and Caroff, S. N. 1989. Sleep disturbances as the hallmark of posttraumatic stress disorder. *American Journal of Psychiatry*, 146: 697–707.

Terr, L. C. 1990. Repeated dreams, in *Too Scared to Cry*. New York: Basic Books, pp. 207–235.

Van der Kolk, B., Blitz, R., Burr, W., Sherry, S., and Hartmann, E. 1984. Nightmares and trauma: A comparison of veterans. *American Journal of Psychiatry*, 141: 187–190.

Williams, L. M. 1995. Recovered memories of abuse in women with documented child victimization histories. *Journal of Traumatic Stress*, 8: 649–673.

1. Children's Traumatic Dreams

Anthony, E. J. 1986. Terrorizing attacks on children by psychotic parents. *Journal of the American Academy of Child Psychiatry*, 25(3): 326–335.

Baker, A. M. 1990. The psychological impact of the Intifada on Palestinian children in the occupied West Bank and Gaza: An exploratory study. *American Journal of Orthopsychiatry*, 60(4): 496–505.

Bilu, Y. 1989. The other as a nightmare: The Israeli-Arab encounter as reflected in children's dreams in Israel and the West Bank. *Political Psychology*, 10(3): 365–387.

Burgess, A. W. 1975. Family reaction to homocide. *American Journal of Orthopsychiatry*, 45(3): 391–398.

Foulkes, D. 1990. Dreaming and consciousness. *European Journal of Cognitive Psychology*, 2(1): 39–55.

Foulkes, D., Hollifield, M., Sullivan, B., Bradley, L. and Terry, R. 1990. REM dreaming and cognitive skills at ages 5–8: A cross-sectional study. *International Journal of Behavioral Development*, 13(4): 447–465.

Gislason, I. L., and Call, J. 1982. Dog bite in infancy: Trauma and personality development. *Journal of the American Academy of Child Psychiatry*, 2: 203–207.

Hanford, H. A., Mayes, S. D., Mattison, R. E., Humphery II, F. J., Bagnato, S., Bixler, E. O., and Kales, J. D. 1983. Child and parent reaction to the Three Mile Island nuclear accident. *Journal of the American Academy of Child Psychiatry*, 25(3): 346–356.

Horowitz, M. J. 1970. *Image Formation and Cognition*. New York: Appleton-Century-Crofts.

Kashani, J. H., Rosenberg, T. K., and Reid, M. A. 1989. Developmental perspectives in child and adolescent depressive symptoms in a community sample. *American Journal of Psychiatry*, 146(7): 871–875.

Kiser, L. J., Heston, J., Millsap, P. A., Pruitt, D. B. 1991. Physical and sexual abuse in childhood: Relationship with Post-Traumatic Stress Disorder. *Journal of the American Academy of Child Psychiatry*, 30(5): 776–783.

Levine, J. B. 1991. The role of culture in the representation of conflict in dreams. *Journal of Cross-Cultural Psychology*, 22(4): 472–490.

Levy, D. M. 1945. Psychic trauma of operations in children. *American Journal of Diseases of Children*, 69: 7–25.

MacFarlane, A. C. 1987. Posttraumatic phenomena in a longitudinal study of children following a natural disaster. *Journal of the American Academy of Child and Adolescent Psychiatry*, 26(5): 764–769.

McLeer, S. V., Deblinger, E., Atkins, M. S., Foa, E. G., Ralphe, D. L. 1988. Post-Traumatic Stress Disorder in sexually abused children. *Journal of the American Academy of Child Psychiatry*, 27: 650–654.

Nader, K. 1994. Countertransference in the treating trauma and victimization in childhood. In J. Lindy and J. Wilson, eds., *Countertransference in the Treatment of Post-Traumatic Stress Disorder*. New York: Guilford.

Nader, K., and Fairbanks, L. 1994. The suppression of reexperiencing: Impulse control and somatic symptoms in children following traumatic exposure. *Anxiety, Stress, and Coping: An International Journal,* 7: 229–239.

Nader, K., and Pynoos, R. 1991. Play and drawing techniques as tools for interviewing traumatized children. In C. E. Schaefer, K. Gitlin, and A. Sandgrund, eds., *Play Diagnosis and Assessment.* New York: John Wiley and Sons, pp. 375–389.

———— 1993a. School disaster: Planning and initial interventions. *Journal of Social Behavior and Personality,* 8(5): 299–320.

———— 1993b. The children of Kuwait following the Gulf Crisis. In L. Lewis and N. Fox, eds., *Effects of War and Violence in Children.* Hillsdale, N.J.: Laurence Erlbaum Publishers.

Nader, K., Pynoos, R., Fairbanks, L., Al-Ajeel, M., and Al-Asfour, A. 1993. Acute post-traumatic stress reactions among Kuwait children following the Gulf Crisis. *British Journal of Clinical Psychology,* 32: 407–416.

Nader K., Pynoos R., Fairbanks, L., and Frederick, C. 1990. Childhood PTSD reactions one year after a sniper attack. *American Journal of Psychiatry,* 147: 1526–1530.

Nader, K., Stuber, M., and Pynoos, R. 1991. Posttraumatic stress reaction in preschool children with catastrophic illness: Assessment needs. *Comprehensive Mental Health Care,* 1(3): 223–239.

Newman, C. F. 1976. Children of disaster: Clinical observations at Buffalo Creek, *American Journal of Psychiatry,* 133: 312–316.

Nir, Y. 1985. PTSD in children with cancer. In S. Eth and R. Pynoos, eds., *PTSD in Children.* Washington, D.C.: American Psychiatric Press.

Pruett, K. D. 1979. Home treatment for two infants who witnessed their mother's murder. *American Journal of Child Psychiatry,* 18: 647–657.

Punamaki, R. 1987. Psychological stress responses of Palestinian mothers and their children in conditions of military occupation and political violence. *Quarterly Newsletter of the Laboratory of Comparative Human Cognition,* 9(2): 76–84.

Pynoos, R., Frederick, C., Nader, K., Arroyo, W., Steinberg, A., Eth, S., Nunez, F., and Fairbanks, L. 1987. Life threat and posttraumatic stress in school-age children. *Archives of General Psychiatry,* 44: 1057–1063.

Pynoos, R., and Goenjin, A. 1992. The 1988 Armenian earthquake. Paper presented at the World Conference of the International Society for Traumatic Stress Studies, Amsterdam, June.

Pynoos, R., and Nader, K. 1988a. Children who witness the sexual assaults of their mothers. *Journal of the American Academy of Child and Adolescent Psychiatry,* 27(5): 567–572.

———— 1988b. Psychological first aid and treatment approach for children exposed to community violence: Research implications. *Journal of Traumatic Stress,* 1(4): 445–473.

———— 1989. Children's memory and proximity to violence. *Journal of the American Academy of Child and Adolescent Psychiatry,* 28(2): 236–241.

———— 1990. Children's exposure to violence and traumatic death. *Psychiatric Annals,* 20(6): 334–344.

———— 1993. Issues in the treatment of Post-Traumatic Stress Disorder in children and adolescents. In J. Wilson and B. Raphael, eds., *The International Handbook of Traumatic Stress Syndromes.* New York: Plenum, pp. 535–539.

Pynoos, R., Nader, K., Frederick, C., Gonda, L., and Stuber, M. 1987. Grief reactions in school-age children following a sniper attack at school. *Israeli Journal of Psychiatry and Related Sciences,* 24(1–2): 53–63.

Schetky, D. H. 1978. Preschooler responses to murder of their mothers by their fathers: A study of four cases. *Bulletin of the American Academy of Psychiatry and the Law,* 6: 45–57.

Sebold, J. 1987. Indicators of chid sexual abuse in males. *Social Casework: The Journal of Contemporary Social Work,* 68(2): 75–80.

Stillwell, B. M., Galvin, M., and Kopta, S. M. 1991. Conceptualization of conscience in normal children and adolescents, ages 5 to 17. *Journal of the American Academy of Child and Adolescent Psychiatry,* 30(1): 16–21.

Stuber, M., Nader, K., Yasuda, P., Pynoos, R., and Cohen S. 1991. Stress responses after pediatric bone marrow transplantation: Preliminary results of a prospective, longitudinal study. *Journal of the American Academy of Child and Adolescent Psychiatry,* 30(6): 952–957.

Terr, L. C. (1979. Children of Chowchilla: A study of psychic trauma. *Psychoanalytic Study of the Child,* 34: 547–623.

———— 1983. Chowchilla revisited: The effects of psychic trauma four years after a school-bus kidnapping. *American Journal of Psychiatry,* 140(12): 1543–1550.

Westerlund, B., and Johnson, C. 1989. DMT defences and the experience of dreaming in children 12 to 13 years old. *Psychological Research Bulletin,* 29(6): 1–23.

2. Dreams and Nightmares of Burned Children

Ablon, S. E., and Mack, J. E. 1980. Children's dreams reconsidered. *Psychoanalytic Study of the Child,* 35: 212.

American Psychiatric Association. 1993. *Diagnostic and Statistical Manual of Mental Disorders.* 4th ed.—Final Draft. Washington, D.C.: American Psychiatric Association.

American Psychiatric Association. 1994. Sleep disorders. In *Diagnostic and Statistical Manual of Mental Disorders.* 4th ed. Washington, D.C.: American Psychiatric Association, pp. 551–607.

Becker, T. E. 1992. Dream analysis in child analysis. In J. Glenn, ed., *Child Analysis and Therapy.* Northvale, N.J.: Jason Aronson.

Blank, K., and Perry, S. 1984. Relationship of psychological processes during delirium to outcome. *American Journal of Psychiatry,* 141: 843–847.

Hanford, H. A., Mattison, R. E., and Kales, A. 1991. Sleep disturbances and disorders. In M. Lewis, ed., *Child and Adolescent Psychiatry: A Comprehensive Textbook.* Baltimore: Williams and Wilkins.

Hartmann, E. 1984. *The Nightmare: The Psychology and Biology of Terrifying Dreams.* New York: Basic Books.

Honig, R. G., Grace, M. C., Lindy, J. D., Newman, C. J., and Titchener, J. L. 1993. Portraits of survival: A twenty-year follow-up of the children of Buffalo Creek. *Psychoanalytic Study of the Child,* 48.

Keener, M. A., and Anders, T. F. 1985. New frontiers of sleep-disorders medicine in infants, children, and adolescents. In J. O. Cavenar and R. Michels, eds., *Psychiatry,* Philadelphia: Lippincott, 2.52.

Kravitz, M., McCoy, B. J., Tompkins, D. M., Daly, W., Mulligan, J., McCauley, R. L., Robson, M. C., and Herndon, D. N. 1993. Sleep disorders in children after burn injury. *Journal of Burn Care and Rehabilitation,* 14: 83–90.

Piaget, J. 1975. The Child's Conception of the World. Totowa, N.J.: Littlefield, Adams.

Sarnoff, C. A. 1987a. *Psychotherapeutic Strategies in the Latency Years.* Northvale, N.J.: Jason Aronson.

—— 1987b. *Psychotherapeutic Strategies in Late Latency through Early Adolescence.* Northvale, N.J.: Jason Aronson.

Saxe, G. N., van der Kolk, B. A., Berkowitz, R., Chinman, G., Hall, K., Lieberg, G., Schwartz, J. 1993. Dissociative disorders in psychiatric inpatients. *American Journal of Psychiatry,* 150(7): 1037–1042.

Stoddard, F. J. 1982. Coping with pain: A developmental approach to treatment of burned children. *American Journal of Psychiatry,* 139(6).

Stoddard, F. J., Norman, D. K., Murphy, J. M., and Beardslee, W. R. 1989. Psychiatric outcome of burned children. *Journal of the American Academy of Child and Adolescent Psychiatry,* 28(4): 589–595.

Terr, L. C. 1985. Remembered images and trauma: A psychology of the supernatural. *Psychoanalytic Study of the Child,* 40: 493–533.

3. Identifying Sexual Trauma Histories from Patterns of Sleep and Dreams

American Psychiatric Association. 1987. Diagnostic and Statistical Manual of Mental Disorders. 3d ed., rev. Washington, D.C.: American Psychiatric Association.

Attias, R., and Goodwin, J. 1985. Knowledge and management strategies in incest cases: A survey of physicians, psychologists, and family counselors. *Child Abuse and Neglect,* 9: 527–533.

Barry, M., and Johnson, A. 1958. The incest barrier. *Psychoanalytic Quarterly,* 27: 485–500.

Belicki, K., Cuddy, M., Pariak, D., and Weir, C. 1992. Applying research findings to identify sexual abuse from nightmare content. Paper presented to the annual meeting of the Association for the Study of Dreams, Santa Cruz, Calif., June.

Bloom, E. S. 1990. *Secret Survivors: Uncovering Incest and Its Aftereffects in Women.* New York: John Wiley and Sons.

Breger, L. 1969. Dream function: An information processing model. In L. Breger, ed., *Clinical-Cognitive Psychology,* pp. 182–227. Englewood Cliffs, N.J.: Prentice-Hall.

Briere, J., and Runtz, M. 1987. Post-sexual abuse trauma: Data and implications for clinical practice. *Journal of Interpersonal Violence,* 2: 367–379.

—— 1988. Symptamatology associated with childhood sexual victimization in a nonclinical adult sample. *Child Abuse and Neglect,* 12: 51–59.

Burgess, A., and Holmstrom, L. 1978. Accessory to sex: Pressure, sex, and secrecy. In A. Burgess, A. Groth, L. Holmstrom, and S. Sgroi, eds., *Sexual Assault of Children and Adolescents,* Lexington, Mass.: Lexington Books.

Carmen, E., Rieker, P., and Mills, T. 1984. Victims of violence and psychiatric illness. *American Journal of Psychiatry,* 141: 378–383.

Cartwright, R. 1986. Affect and dream work from an information processing point of view. *Journal of Mind and Behavior,* 7, 411–427.

Crick, F., and Mitchison, G. 1983. The function of dream sleep. *Nature,* 304: 111–114.

Cuddy, M. 1990. Predicting sexual abuse from dissociation, somatization, and nightmares. Doctoral dissertation, York University.

Cuddy, M., and Belicki, K. 1989. Characteristics of nightmares in sexually abused and nonabused women. Paper presented at the annual meeting of the Association for the Study of Dreams, London, June.

——— 1990. Predicting a history of sexual abuse from nightmares. *Canadian Psychology,* 31: 384.

——— 1992. Nightmare frequency, night terrors, and related sleep disturbance as indicators of a history of sexual abuse. *Dreaming,* 2: 15–22.

Dunlop, A., Cuddy, M., Belicki, K., and Belicki, D. 1987. Brief group therapy with adult women survivors of childhood sexual abuse. Paper presented at the annual meeting of the Ontario Psychological Association, Toronto, Canada.

Eisenberg, N., Owens, R., and Dewey, M. 1987. Attitudes of health professionals to child sexual abuse and incest. *Child Abuse and Neglect,* 11: 109–116.

Ellenson, G. 1985. Detecting a history of incest: A predictive syndrome. *Social Casework,* 66: 525–532.

Fernandez, M. 1992. Alterations in dream and nightmare patterns among sexually abused women who also disclosed past physical abuse. Paper presented to the annual meeting of the Ontarion Psychological Association, Toronto, February.

Fernandez, M., Cuddy, M., Hoffman, R., and Moffitt, A. 1991. Dreams and nightmares among university women with a history of sexual abuse. Paper presented to the annual meeting of the Association for the Study of Dreams, Charlottesville, Va., June.

Finkelhor, D. 1987. The trauma of child sexual abuse: Two models. *Journal of Interpersonal Violence,* 2: 348–366.

Finkelhor, D., and Browne, A. 1985. The traumatic impact of child sexual abuse: A conceptualization. *American Journal of Orthopsychiatry,* 55: 530–541.

Garfield, P. 1987. Nightmares in the sexually abused female teenager. *Psychiatric Journal of the University of Ottawa,* 12(2): 93–97.

Gelinas, D. 1983. The persisting negative effects of incest. *Psychiatry,* 46: 312–332.

Greenberg, R., and Pearlman, C. 1975. REM sleep and the analytic process: A psychophysiologic bridge. *Psychoanalytic Quarterly,* 44: 392–403.

Greenson, G., and Samuel, S. 1989. Self-cutting after rape. *American Journal of Psychiatry,* 146: 789–790.

Hall, C., and Van de Castle, R. 1966. *The Content Analysis of Dreams.* New York: Meredith Publishing Co.

Herman, J. 1981. *Father-Daughter Incest.* Cambridge, Mass.: Harvard University Press.

———— 1992. *Trauma and Recovery.* New York: Basic Books.

Horowitz, M. 1976. *Stress Response Syndromes.* New York: Jason Aronson.

Jehu, D., Gazan, M., and Klassen, C. 1985. Common therapeutic targets among women who were sexually abused. *Journal of Social Work and Human Sexuality,* 3: 25–45.

Kavaler, S. 1987. Nightmares and object relations theory. In H. Kellerman, ed., *The Nightmare: Psychological and Biological Foundations.* New York: Columbia University Press.

LaBarbera, J., Martin, J., and Dozier, J. 1980. Child psychiatrists' view of father-daughter incest. *Child Abuse and Neglect,* 4: 147–151.

Litz, B., and Keane, T. 1989. Information processing in anxiety disorders: Application to the understanding of post-traumatic stress disorder. *Clinical Psychology Review,* 9: 243–257.

Maltz, W. 1991. *The Sexual Healing Journey.* New York: HarperCollins.

Mannarino, A., and Cohen, J. 1986. A clinical-demographic study of sexually abused children. *Child Abuse and Neglect,* 10: 17–23.

Prince, P. 1992. Trauma survivors: Cases for reconceptualizing the chronic psychiatric inpatient. Paper presented at the annual meeting of the Ontario Psychological Association, Toronto, February.

Robinson, L. 1982. Nursing therapy of an incest victim. *Issues in Mental Health Nursing,* 4: 331–342.

Roth, S., and Newman, E. 1992. The role of helplessness in the recovery process for sexual trauma survivors. *Canadian Journal of Behavioural Science,* 24: 220–232.

Siegal, D., and Romig, C. 1990. Memory retrieval in treating adult survivors of sexual abuse. *American Journal of Family Therapy,* 18: 246–256.

Summit, R. 1983. The child sexual abuse accommodation syndrome. *Child Abuse and Neglect,* 7: 177–193.

Weiss, J., Rogers, E., Darwin, M., and Dutton, C. 1955. A study of girl sex victims. *Psychiatric Quarterly,* 29: 1–27.

Wood, J., and Bootzin, R. 1990. The prevalence of nightmares and their independence from anxiety. *Journal of Abnormal Psychology,* 99: 64–68.

4. The Use of Dreams with Incest Survivors

Axelroth, E. 1991. Retrospective incest group therapy for university women. *Journal of College Student Psychotherapy,* 5(2): 81–100.

Blume, E. S. 1990. *Secret Survivors: Uncovering Incest and Its Aftereffects in Women.* New York: John Wiley and Sons.

Bonime, W. [1962] 1988. *The Clinical Use of Dreams.* New York: Basic Books.

Briere, J. N. 1992. *Child Abuse Trauma: Theory and Treatment of the Lasting Effects.* Newbury Park, Calif.: Sage Publications.

Briere, J., and Runtz, M. 1988. Symptomatology associated with childhood sexual victimization in a nonclinical adult sample. *Child Abuse and Neglect,* 12: 51–59.

Brod, C. 1991. The girl who was afraid to dream: A case presentation. Paper presented at the meeting of the Association for the Study of Dreams, Charlottesville, Va.

Brown, S. 1988. The dreams of women molested as children. Doctoral dissertation, The Wright Institute.

Cartwright, R. 1992. *Crisis Dreaming: Using Your Dreams to Solve Your Problems.* New York: HarperCollins.

Courtois, C. A. 1988. *Healing the Incest Wound: Adult Survivors in Therapy.* New York: W. W. Norton.

Cuddy, M. A., and Belicki, K. 1992. Nightmare frequency and related sleep disturbances as indicators of a history of sexual abuse. *Dreaming,* 21: 15–22.

Delaney, G. 1991. *Breakthrough Dreaming: How to Tap the Power of Your 24-Hour Mind.* New York: Bantam Books.

——— 1992. Manuscript on dreams and sexuality.

Freud, A. 1982. A psychoanalyst's view of sexual abuse by parents. In P. B. Mrazek and C. M. Kempe, eds., *Sexually Abused Children and Their Families.* New York: Pergamon.

Freud, S. [1900] 1965. *The Interpretation of Dreams.* New York: Avon Books.

Garfield, P. 1987. Nightmares in the sexually abused female teenager. *Psychiatric Journal of the University of Ottawa,* 12(2): 93–97.

Herman, J. 1992. *Trauma and Recovery.* New York: Basic Books.

Ratican, K. L. 1992. Sexual abuse survivors: Identifying symptoms and special treatment considerations. *Journal of Counseling and Development,* 71(5): 33–38.

Signell, K. A. 1990. *Wisdom of the Heart.* New York: Bantam Books.

Terr, L. C. 1990. *Too Scared to Cry.* New York: Basic Books.

5. Dreams in Multiple Personality Disorder

Barrett, D. L. 1994a. The dream character as a prototype for the multiple personality "alter." In S. J. Lynn and J. Rhu, eds., *Dissociation.* Washington, D.C.: American Psychological Association Press.

——— 1994b. Dreams in dissociative disorders. *Dreaming,* 4(3): 165–175.

Breuer, J., and Freud, S. [1883–85] 1955. Studies on hysteria. In *The Standard Edition of the Complete Psychological Works of Sigmund Freud,* vol. 2, pp. 3–305. London: Hogarth.

Coleridge, S. T. 1816. Anima poetae. In *The Collected Poetical and Dramatic Works,* ed. J. D. Campbell, pp. 360–398. London.

Gabel, S. 1989. Dreams as a possible reflection of a dissociated self-monitoring system. *Journal of Nervous and Mental Disease,* 177(9): 560–568.

——— 1990. Dreams and dissociation theory: speculations on beneficial aspects of their linkage. *Dissociation,* 3(1): 38–47.

Gruenwald, D. 1971. Hypnotic techniques without hypnosis in the treatment of multiple personality. *Journal of Nervous and Mental Disease,* 153: 41–46.

Janet, P. 1929. *The Major Symptoms of Hysteria.* 2nd ed. New York: Macmillan.

Jeans, R. 1976. An independently validated case of multiple personality. *Journal of Abnormal Psychology,* 85: 249–255.

Jung, C. G. [1916–45] 1974. *Dreams.* Trans. R. Hull. Princeton, N.J.: Princeton University Press.

Kluft, R. 1992. Hypnotherapy of PTSD and dissociative disorders. Workshop presented at the Twelfth Conference of the International Society for Hypnosis, Jerusalem, July.

Lancaster, E. (pseud.). 1958. *The Final Face of Eve.* New York: McGraw-Hill.

Marmer, S. S. 1980a. The dream in dissociative states. In J. M. Naterson, ed., *The Dream in Clinical Practice,* pp. 163–175. New York: Jason Aronson.

———— 1980b. Psychoanalysis of multiple personality. *International Journal of Psychoanalysis,* 61: 439–459.

Paley, K. S. 1991. Dream wars: A case study of a woman with multiple personalities. Talk given at the Association for the Study of Dreams Eighth International Conference, Charlottesville, Va., June.

Perls, F. 1969. *Gestalt Therapy Verbatim.* Moab, Utah: Real People Press.

Prince, M. [1905] 1978. *The Dissociation of a Personality.* Originally published by Longmans, Green and Co., reprinted by Oxford University Press, Oxford.

———— 1910. The mechanism and interpretation of dreams. *Journal of Abnormal Psychology,* 5: 139–195.

Putman, F. W. 1989. *Diagnosis and Treatment of Multiple Personality Disorder.* New York: Guilford Press.

Salley, R. D. 1988. Subpersonalities with dreaming functions in a patient with multiple personalities. *Journal of Nervous and Mental Disease,* 176(2): 112–115.

———— 1991. Dream work with dissociated patients and a self-curative programming function of dreams. In J. Gackenbach and Anees Sheikh, eds., *Dream Images: A Call to Mental Arms,* pp. 147–159. New York: Baywood.

Schreiber, F. R. 1974. *Sybil.* New York: Warner Paperbacks.

Sizemore, C. C. 1989. *A Mind of My Own.* New York: William Morrow.

Sizemore, C. C., and Pittillo, E. S. 1977. *I'm Eve.* Garden City, N.Y.: Doubleday.

Stoller, R. J. 1973. *Splitting.* New York: Quadrangle Books.

Thigpen, C. H., and Cleckley, H. M. 1957. *The Three Faces of Eve.* New York: McGraw-Hill.

6. *The Healing Nightmare: War Dreams of Vietnam Veterans*

Chamberlain, T. C. 1965. The method of multiple working hypotheses. *Science,* pp. 754–760. Reprinted from *Science,* 1890.

Jung, C. G. 1966. *The Practice of Psychotherapy.* Princeton, N.J.: Princeton University Press.

Stevens, A. 1982. Shadow: The archetypal enemy. In *Archetypes: A Natural History of the Self*. New York: William Morris, pp. 210–243.

White, T. H. 1977. *The Book of Merlin*. Austin: University of Texas Press.

7. Who Develops PTSD Nightmares and Who Doesn't

Blitz, R. 1983. Nightmares and the self. Doctoral dissertation, Boston University.

Broughton, R. 1988. Sleep disorders: Disorders of arousal?, *Science*, 159: 1070–1078.

Everstine, D. S., and Everstine, L. 1993. *The Trauma Response*. New York: W. W. Norton.

Fisher, C., Kahn, E., Edwards, A., Davis, D. M., and Fine, J. 1974. A psychophysiological study of nightmares and night terrors. III. Mental content and recall of stage 4 night terrors. *Journal of Nervous and Mental Disease*, 15: 174–189.

Fox, R. 1974. Narcissistic rage and the problem of combat aggression. *Archives of General Psychiatry*, 31: 807–11.

Hartmann, E. 1970. A note on the nightmare. In E. Hartmann, ed., *Sleep and Dreaming*. Boston: Little, Brown.

—— 1973. *The Functions of Sleep*. New Haven: Yale University Press.

—— 1984. *The Nightmare: The Psychology and Biology of Terrifying Dreams*. New York: Basic Books.

—— 1991a. *Boundaries in the Mind: A New Psychology of Personality*. New York: Basic Books.

—— 1991b. Dreams that work or dreams that poison? What does dreaming do? *Dreaming*, 1: 23–25.

Hartmann, E., Russ, D., Oldfield, M., Sivan, I., and Cooper, S. 1987. Who has nightmares? The personality of the lifelong nightmare sufferer. *Archives of General Psychiatry*, 44: 49–56.

Hartmann, E., Russ, D., van der Kolk, B., Falke, R., and Oldfield, M. 1981. A preliminary study of the personality of the nightmare sufferer: Relationship to schizophrenia and creativity? *American Journal of Psychiatry*, 138: 794–797.

Hefez, A., Metz, L., and Lavie, P. 1987. Long-term effects of extreme situational stress on sleep and dreaming. *American Journal of Psychiatry*, 144: 344–347.

Herman, J. L. 1992. *Trauma and Recovery*. New York: Basic Books.

Kramer, M., and Kinney, L. 1988. Sleep patterns in trauma victims with disturbed dreaming. *Psychiatric Journal of the University of Ottawa*, 13: 12–16.

Kramer, M., Schoen, L., and Kinney, L. 1984. The dream experience in dream disturbed Vietnam veterans. In B. van der Kolk, ed., *Post-Traumatic Stress Disorders: Psychological and Biological Sequelae*. Washington, D.C.: American Psychiatric Press.

Stoddard, F. 1982. Body image development in the burned child. *Journal of American Academy of Child Psychiatry*, 21: 502–507.

van der Kolk, B., Blitz, R., Burr, W., Sherry, S., and Hartmann, E. 1984. Nightmares and trauma: A comparison of veterans. *American Journal of Psychiatry,* 141: 187–190.

van der Kolk, B., Hartmann, E., Burr, A., and Blitz, R. 1980. A survey of nightmare frequencies in a veterans outpatient clinic. *Sleep Research,* 9: 229.

Wilmer, H. A. 1982. Vietnam and madness: Dreams of schizophrenic veterans. *Journal of the American Academy of Psychoanalysis,* 10: 47–65.

8. *Sleep, Dreaming, and Coping Style in Holocaust Survivors*

Barron, F. 1977. An ego strength scale which predicts response to psychotherapy. *Journal of Consulting Psychology,* 17: 327–333.

Breznitz, S. *The Denial of Stress.* New York: International University Press, 1983.

Burke, H., and Mayer, S. 1985. The MMPI and the posttraumatic stress syndrome in Vietnam veterans. *Journal of Clinical Psychology,* 41: 152–155.

Butcher, J. N., and Gur, R. 1976. Translation and standardization of the Hebrew MMPI. In N. Y. Butcher and P. A. Pancheri, eds., *Handbook of Cross-Cultural MMPI Research.* Minneapolis: University of Minnesota Press.

Byrne, D. 1961. The Repression-Sensitization Scale: Rational reliability, and validity. *Journal of Personality,* 29: 334–349.

Chodoff, P. 1963. Late effects of the concentration camp syndrome. *Archives of General Psychiatry,* 8: 323–333.

Cohen, D. B. 1974. Effect of personality and presleep mood on dream recall. *Journal of Abnormal Psychology,* 83: 151–156.

Danieli, Y. 1988. Confronting the unimaginable: Psychotherapists' reaction to victims of Nazi Holocaust. In J. Wilson, Z. Harel, and B. Kahana, eds., *Human Adaptation to Extreme Stress: From Holocaust to Vietnam,* pp. 219–237. New York: Plenum Press.

Derogatis, L. R. 1977. *The SCL-90 Manual F: Scoring, Administration, and Procedures for the SCL-90.* Baltimore: Johns Hopkins University, School of Medicine, Clinical Psychometrics Unit.

Eaton, W., Sigal, J., and Weinfield, M. 1982. Impairment in Holocaust survivors after thirty-three years: Data from an unbiased community struggle. *American Journal of Psychiatry,* 139: 773–777.

Figley, C. K., ed. 1978. *Stress Disorders among Vietnam Veterans.* New York: Brunner/Mazel.

Freud, S. 1900. The interpretation of dreams. In J. Strachey and A. Freud, eds., *The Standard Edition of the Complete Psychological Works of Sigmund Freud,* vol. 4. London: Hogarth Press.

—— [1915] 1957. Repression. In J. Strachey and A. Freud, eds., *The Standard Edition of the Complete Psychological Works of Sigmund Freud,* vol. 14, pp. 146–158. London: Hogarth Press.

Goldstein, G., van Kammen, W., Shelly, C., Miller, D., and van Kammen, D. 1987. Survivors of imprisonment in the Pacific Theater during World War II. *American Journal of Psychiatry,* 144: 1210–1214.

Gurland, B. J., Yorkston, N. J., Stone, A. R., and Frank, J. D. 1974. *Structured and Scaled Interview to Assess Maladjustment.* New York: Springer.

Hackett, T. P., Cassem, N. Y., and Wishnie, H. A. 1968. The coronary care unit: An appraisal of its psychological hazards. *New England Journal of Medicine,* 279: 1365–1370.

Hefez, A., Metz, L., and Lavie, P. 1987. Long-term effects of extreme situational stress on sleep and dreaming. *American Journal of Psychiatry,* 144: 345–347.

Hersen, M. 1971. Personality characteristics of nightmare sufferers. *Journal of Nervous and Mental Disease,* 153: 27–31.

Horowitz, M., Wilner, N., and Alvarez, W. 1979. Impact of events scale: A measure of subjective stress. *Psychological Medicine,* 41(3): 209–218.

Kaminer, H., and Lavie, P. 1991. Sleep and dreaming in Holocaust survivors: Dramatic decrease in dream recall in well-adjusted survivors. *Journal of Nervous and Mental Disease,* 179: 664–669.

Klonoff, H., McDougall, G., Clark, C., et al. 1976. Neuropsychological, psychiatric, and physical effects of prolonged and severe stress: Thirty years later. *Journal of Nervous and Mental Disease,* 163: 247–252.

Kluznik, J. C., Speed, N., and Van Valkenburg, P. 1986. Forty year follow-up of United States prisoners of war. *American Journal of Psychiatry,* 143: 1443–1446.

Lavie, P., and Kaminer, H. 1991. Dreams that poison sleep: Dreaming in Holocaust survivors. *Dreaming,* 1: 11–21.

Lazarus, R. S. 1966. *Psychological Stress and Coping Process.* New York: McGraw-Hill.

Marmar, C. R., and Horowitz, M. 1988. Diagnosis and phasic oriented treatment of PTSD. In J. Wilson, Z. Harel, and B. Kahana, eds., *Human Adaptation to Extreme Stress: From Holocaust to Vietnam,* pp. 81–101. New York: Plenum Press.

Nichols, M. P., and Zax, M. 1977. *Catharsis in Psychotherapy.* New York: Gardner.

Rofe, Y., and Lewin, I. 1979. Who adjusts better: Repressors or sensitizers? *Journal of Clinical Psychology,* 35: 875–879.

Rosen, J., Reynolds, C. F., Yeager, A. L., Houck, P. R., and Hurwitz, L. F. 1991. Sleep disturbances in survivors of the Nazi Holocaust. *American Journal of Psychiatry,* 148: 62–66.

Ross, R. J., Ball, W. A., Sullivan, K. A., Caroff, S. N. 1989. Sleep disturbances as the hallmark of posttraumatic stress disorder. *American Journal of Psychiatry,* 146: 697–707.

Shapiro, D., Surwit, R. S. 1979. Biofeedback. In O. F. Pomerleau and J. P. Brady, eds., *Behavioral Medicine: Theory and Practice.* Baltimore: Williams and Wilkins.

Stern, M. J., Pascale, L., and Mcloone, J. B. 1976. Psychological adaptation following a myocardial infarction. *Journal of Chronic Diseases,* 29: 513–524.

Taylor, M. A. 1953. A personality scale of manifest anxiety. *Journal of Abnormal and Social Psychology,* 48: 258–259.

Van Dyke, C., Zilberg, N., and McKinnon, J. 1985. PTSD: A thirty-year delay in World War II veterans. *American Journal of Psychiatry,* 2: 1070–1073.

9. Dreaming Well: On Death and History

M. Casey. 1972. "On death." In *Obscenities*. New Haven: Yale University Press.

H. Kohler. 1972. "Victory." In Larry Rottman, Jan Barry, and Basit Paguet, eds., *Winning Hearts and Minds: War Poems by Vietnam Veterans*. Brooklyn: First Casualty Press.

R. M. Laughlin. 1976. *Wonders Wild and New—Dreams from Zinacantan*. Washington, D.C.: Smithsonian Institution Press.

R. J. Lifton. 1986. *The Nazi Doctors: Medical Killing and the Psychology of Genocide*. New York: Basic Books.

10. The Collective Nightmare of Central American Refugees

Abrams, Elliot, to Jessica Savitch on *Frontline*, July 12, 1983, cited in Golden and McConnell, 1986, p. 45.

Cernovsky, Z. Z. 1988. Refugees' repetitive nightmares. *Journal of Clinical Psychology*, 44(5): 702–707.

Golden, R., and McConnell, M. 1986. *Sanctuary: The New Underground Railroad*. Maryknoll, N.Y.: Orbis Books.

Larrabee, Peter, former director of El Centro, the California INS Detention Center, cited in Golden and McConnell, 1986, p. 45.

11. Jasmine: Dreams in the Psychotherapy of a Rape Survivor

Bradshaw, J. 1992. *Creating Love: The Next Great Stage of Growth*. New York: Bantam.

Burgess, A. W., and Holmstrom, L. L. 1974. *Rape: Victims of Crisis*. Bowie, Md.: Robert J. Brady Co.

Colum, P. [1918] 1958. *The Boy Who Knew What the Birds Said*. New York: Macmillan Company.

12. Dreams of Firestorm Survivors

Dale Westbrook, Ph.D., and Robert Wagner, Ph.D., participated in the early stages of the research. Bryna Siegel, Ph.D., assisted with statistical analysis. The content analysis was performed by Katharine Kibira, Penelope Russell, and Douglas Armstrong, graduate students at the California School of Professional Psychology.

Adler, P. 1992. *Fire in the Hills: A Collective Remembrance*. Berkeley, Calif.: Patricia Adler.

Beck, A. T. 1967. *Depression: Clinical, Experimental, and Theoretical Aspects*. New York: Harper and Row.

Breger, L., Hunter, J., and Lane, R. 1971. *The Effects of Stress on Dreams*. New York: International Universities Press.

Brenneis, C. B. 1975. Theoretical notes on the manifest dream. *International Journal of Psychoanalysis*, 56(197), 197–206.

Gihvan, R. 1992. Studying dreams from the East Bay inferno. *San Francisco Chronicle,* July 1.

Hall, C., and Van de Castle, R. 1966. *The Content Analysis of Dreams.* New York: Apple-Century-Crofts.

Hartmann, E. 1984. *Nightmares: The Psychology and Biology of Terrifying Dreams.* New York: Basic Books.

Horowitz, M. J., Wilner, N., and Alvarez, W. 1979. Impact of events scale: A measure of subjective stress. *Psychological Medicine,* 41: 209–218.

Jones, R., and Ribbe, D. 1991. Child, adolescent, and adult victims of residential fire. *Behavior Modification,* 15(4): 560–580.

Myers, L., and Associated Press. 1992. Nightmares still plague survivors. *Detroit News,* June 25.

Rufus, A. 1992. Interpreting dreams of fire. *East Bay Express,* Berkeley, Calif., June 26, pp. 2–3.

Siegel, A. 1983. Pregnant dreams: Developmental processes in the manifest dreams of expectant fathers. Dissertation Abstracts International, Ann Arbor.

——— 1992a. Dreams and the East Bay fire. *The California Psychologist,* November, pp. 1, 28–29.

——— 1992b. *Dreams That Can Change Your Life: Navigating Life's Passages through Turning Point Dreams.* New York: Berkley/Putnam.

Warren, J. 1992. New lives take root amid ashes. *Los Angeles Times,* January 16, pp. A1, A24.

Winget, C., and Kramer, M. 1979. *Dimensions of Dreams.* Gainesville: University Presses of Florida.

13. *Dreams and Adaptation to Divorce*

Bonime, W. 1962. *The Clinical Use of Dreams.* New York: Basic Books.

Breger, L., Hunter, I., and Lane, R. 1971. The effect of stress on dreams. *Psychological Issues Monograph,* 7(27): 3.

Cartwright, C., Bernick, N., Borowitz, G., and Kling, A. 1969. The effect of an erotic movie on the sleep and dreams of young men. *Archives of General Psychiatry,* 20: 262–271.

Cartwright, R., and Kaszniak, A. 1991. "The Social Psychology of Dream Reporting." In S. Ellman and J. Antrobus, eds., *The Mind in Sleep: Psychology and Psychophysiology,* pp. 251–264. New York: John Wiley and Sons.

Cartwright, R., and Lamberg, L. 1992. *Crisis Dreaming: Using Your Dreams to Solve Your Problems.* New York: HarperCollins.

Cartwright, R., Monroe, L., and Palmer, C. 1967. Individual differences in response to REM deprivation." *Archives of General Psychiatry,* 16: 297–303.

Cohen, D., and Cox, C. 1975. Neuroticism in the sleep laboratory: Implications for representational and adaptive properties of dreaming. *Journal of Abnormal Psychology,* 84: 91–108.

Endicott, J., and Spitzer, R. 1978. A diagnostic interview: The schedule for affective disorders and schizophrenia." *Archives of General Psychiatry,* 35: 837–844.

Fiss, H. 1979. Current dream research: A psychobiological perspective." In B. Wolman, ed., *Handbook of Dreams*, pp. 20–75. New York: Van Norstrand Reinhold.

French, T., and Fromm, E. 1964. *Dream Interpretation: A New Approach.* New York: Basic Books.

Freud, S. [1900] 1965. *The Interpretation of Dreams.* New York: Avon Books.

Garma, A. 1946. The traumatic situation in the genesis of dreams. *International Journal of Psychoanalysis,* 27: 134–139.

Greiser, E., Greenberg, R., and Harrison, R. 1972. The adaptive function of sleep: The differential effects of sleep and dreaming on recall. *Journal of Abnormal Psychology,* 80: 280–286.

Hallam, F., and Weed, S. 1896. Study of dream consciousness. *American Journal of Psychology,* 7: 405.

Jones, R. 1970. *The New Psychology of Dreaming.* New York: Grune and Stratton.

Rechtschaffen, A., and Foulkes, D. 1965. Effects of visual stimuli on dream content. *Perceptual and Motor Skills.* 20: 1149–1160.

Spitzer, R., Endicott, J., and Robins, E. 1978. Research diagnostic criteria: Rationale and reliability. *Archives of General Psychiatry,* 35: 733–782.

Winget, C., and Kapp, F. 1972. The relationship of the manifest content of dreams to duration of childbirth in primipare. *Psychosomatic Medicine,* 34: 313–319.

Witkin, H., and Lewis, H. 1967. Presleep Experiences and Dreams. In H. Witkin and H. Lewis, eds., *Experimental Studies of Dreaming,* pp. 148–201. New York: Random House.

14. Dreams in Bereavement

Barrett, D. 1988. Dreams of death. In Robert Kastenbaum, ed., *Omega: Journal of Death and Dying,* 19: 95–101.

——— 1992. Through a glass darkly: Images of the dead in dreams. In Robert Kastenbaum, ed., *Omega: Journal of Death and Dying,* 24: 97–108.

Bellin, H. 1988. "Opposition is true friendship": Swedenborg's influences on William Blake. In Robin Larsen, ed., *Emanuel Swedenborg: A Continuing Vision.* New York: Swedenborg Foundation.

Coolidge, F., and Fish, C. 1988. Dreams of the dying. In Robert Kastenbaum, ed., *Omega: Journal of Death and Dying,* 14: 1–8.

Evans, A. 1992. Personal communication. Several of Evans's poem are published in *Fireweed;* see, for example, the October 1989 issue.

Freud, S. [1917] 1959. Mourning and melancholia. In Joan Riviere, ed., *Sigmund Freud: Collected Papers,* vol. 4. New York: Basic Books.

Garfield, P. 1988. *Women's Bodies; Women's Dreams.* New York: Ballantine.

——— 1992. *The Healing Power of Dreams.* New York: Simon and Schuster.

Hilton, M. 1992. Personal communication. Unpublished material from Hospice Volunteer training at Sacred Heart Hospital, Eugene, Oregon.

James, J., and Cherry, F.. 1988. *The Grief Recovery Handbook.* New York: Harper.

Jung, C. G. 1963. *Memories, Dreams, Reflections.* New York: Vintage.

Kast, Verena. 1982. *A Time to Mourn: Growing through the Grief Process.* Einsiedeln, Switzerland: Daimon Verlag.

Keelin, Patricia. 1991. Ghost dreams. Paper presented at the meeting of the Association for the Study of Dreams, Santa Cruz, Calif.

—— 1992. Personal communication on unpublished collection of bereavement dreams from 101 survivors.

Kennedy, A. 1991. *Losing a Parent: Passage to a New Way of Living.* San Francisco: Harper.

Kirven, R., and Larsen, R. 1988. Emanuel Swedenborg: A pictorial biography. In Robin Larsen, ed., *Emanuel Swedenborg: A continuing vision.* New York: Swedenborg Foundation.

Kubler-Ross, E. 1975. *Death, the Final Stage of Growth.* New York: Prentice Hall.

Linn, E. 1991. *Premonitions, Visitations, and Dreams of the Bereaved.* Incline Village, Nev.: The Publisher's Mark.

Rogo, D. S., and Bayless, R. 1979. *Phone Calls from the Dead.* New York: Berkeley Books.

Smith, R. 1984. A possible biologic role of dreaming. *Psychotherapy and Psychosomatics,* 41: 167–176.

Staudacher, C. 1987. *Beyond Grief.* Oakland, Calif.: New Harbinger.

Tatelbaum, J. 1980. *The Courage to Grieve.* New York: Harper.

Von Franz, M.-L. 1986. *On Dreams and Death.* Boston: Shambhala.

Woolf, V. 1908. In Nigel Nicolson, ed., *The Letters of Virginia Woolf,* vol. 1: *1888–1912 (Virginia Stephen).* New York: Harcourt Brace Jovanovich.

Worden, J. W. 1991. *Grief Counseling and Grief Therapy: A Handbook for the Mental Health Practitioner.* 2nd ed. New York: Springer.

15. Neurological Dreams

Crick, F., and Mitchison, G. 1983. The function of dream sleep *Nature,* 304: 111–114.

Jouvet, M. 1980. Paradoxical sleep and the nature-nurture controversy. In P. S. McConnell et al., eds., *Adaptive Capabilities of the Nervous System,* pp. 331–346. Amsterdam: Elsevier.

Sacks, O. 1984. *A Leg to Stand On.* New York: HarperCollins.

—— 1985a. *The Man Who Mistook His Wife for a Hat.* New York: HarperCollins.

—— 1985b. *Migraine.* Berkeley: University of California Press.

—— 1990. *Awakenings.* Rev. ed. New York: HarperCollins.

Sacks, O., and Wasserman, R. 1987 The case of the colorblind painter. *New York Review of Books,* November 19, pp. 25–34.

17. Recurrent Dreams: Their Relation to Life Events

Adler, G., ed. 1973. *C. G. Jung Letters,* vol. 1: *1906–1950.* Bollingen Series XCV. Princeton: Princeton University Press.

American Psychiatric Association. 1987. *Diagnostic and Statistical Manual of Mental Disorders.* 3rd ed., rev. Washington, D.C.: American Psychiatric Association.

Baylor, G. W., and Deslauriers, D. 1986–87. Dreams as problem solving: A method of study—Part 1. Background and theory. *Imagination, Cognition, and Personality*, 6: 105–118.

Belicki, K., Altay, H., and Hill, C. 1985. Varieties of nightmare experience. Newsletter of the Association for the Study of Dreams, 2: 1–3.

Bergin, A. E. 1970. A note on dream changes following desensitization. *Behavior Therapy*, 1: 546–549.

Bernstein, D. A., and Borkovec, T. D. 1973. Progressive relaxation training. Champaign, Ill.: Research Press.

Bibring, E. 1943. The conception of the repetition compulsion. *Psychoanalytic Quarterly*, 12: 486–519.

Bonime, W. 1962. *The Clinical Uses of Dreams*. New York: Basic Books.

Breger, L. 1967. Function of dreams. *Journal of Abnormal Psychology Monograph*, 72(5): 1–28.

Browman, C. P., and Kapell, L. A. 1982. Repetitive sexual dream content of normal adults. *Sleep Research*, 11: 115.

Brown, R. J., and Donderi, D. C. 1986. Dream content and self-reported well-being among recurrent dreamers, past recurrent dreamers, and nonrecurrent dreamers. *Journal of Personality and Social Psychology*, 50: 612–623.

Brylowski, A. 1990. Nightmares in crises: Clinical applications of lucid dreaming techniques. *Psychiatric Journal of the University of Ottawa*, 15: 79–84.

Cartwright, R. 1977. *Night Life*. Englewood Cliffs, N.J.: Prentice-Hall.

———. 1979. The nature and function of repetitive dreams: A speculation. *Psychiatry*, 42: 131–137.

Cartwright, R., and Romanek, I. 1978. Repetitive dreams of normal subjects. *Sleep Research*, 7: 174.

Cavenar, J. O., and Sullivan, J. L. 1978. A recurrent dream as a precipitant. *American Journal of Psychiatry*, 135: 378–279.

D'Andrade, J. 1985. On recurrent dreams. Term research paper for a course on dreams taught by G. William Domhoff. University of California, Santa Cruz.

Delaney, G. 1991. *Breakthrough Dreaming*. New York: Bantam Books.

Domhoff, G. W. 1993. The repetition of dreams and dream elements: A possible clue to a function of dreaming. In A. Moffitt, M. Kramer, and R. Hoffmann, eds., *The Functions of Dreams*. New York: State University of New York Press.

Dunn, K. K., and Barrett, D. 1988. Characteristics of nightmare subjects and their nightmares. *Psychiatric Journal of the University of Ottawa*, 13: 91–93.

Fantz, M. 1978. Gestalt dream theory. In J. L. Fosshage and C. A. Loew, eds., *Dream Interpretation: A Comparative Study*. New York: Spectrum.

Fiss, H. 1986. An empirical foundation for a self psychology of dreaming. *Journal of Mind and Behavior*, 7: 161–191.

Fosshage, J. L., and Loew, C. A. 1987. *Dream Interpretation: A Comparative Study*. Rev. ed. New York: PMA Publishing Corp.

French, T., and Fromm, E. 1964. *Dream Interpretation*. New York: Basic Books.

Freud, S. [1900] 1931. *The Interpretation of Dreams*. Trans. A. A. Brill. London: Hogarth Press.

——— [1920] 1955. Beyond the pleasure principle. In J. Strachey, ed. and trans.,

The Standard Edition of the Complete Psychological Works of Sigmund Freud, vol. 18. London: Hogarth Press.

Galvin, F. 1990. The boundary characteristics of lucid dreamers. *Psychiatric Journal of the University of Ottawa,* 15: 73–78.

Garfield, P. 1974. *Creative Dreaming.* New York: Ballantine Books.

Greenberg, R., and Pearlman, C. 1975. A psycho-analytic dream continuum: The source and function of dreams. *International Review of Psychoanalysis,* 2: 441–448.

Griffith, R., Miyago, O., and Tago, A. 1958. The universality of typical dreams: Japanese vs. Americans. *American Anthropologist,* 60: 1173–1179.

Hall, C. S. 1953. *The Meaning of Dreams.* New York: Harper.

Hall, C., and Van de Castle, R. 1966. *The Content Analysis of Dreams.* New York: Appleton-Century-Crofts.

Halliday, G. 1982. Direct alteration of a traumatic nightmare. *Perceptual and Motor Skills,* 54: 413–414.

———— 1988. Lucid dreaming: Use in nightmares and sleep-wake confusion. In J. Gackenbach and S. LaBerge, eds., *Conscious Mind, Sleeping Brain: Perspectives on Lucid Dreaming.* New York: Plenum Press.

Hartmann, E. 1984. *The Nightmare: The Psychology and Biology of Terrifying Dreams.* New York: Basic Books.

Kelzer, K. 1989. *The Sun and the Shadow: My Experiment with Lucid Dreaming.* Virginia: A.R.E. Press.

Kramer, M., Schoen, L., and Kinney, L. 1987. Nightmares in Vietnam veterans. *Journal of the American Academy of Psychoanalysis,* 15: 67–81.

Kramer, M., Winget, C., and Whitman, R. 1971. A city dreams: A survey approach to normative dream content. *American Journal of Psychiatry,* 127: 1350–1356.

LaBerge, S. 1985. *Lucid Dreaming.* New York: Ballantine Books.

LaBerge, S., and Dement, W. C. 1982. Lateralization of alpha activity for dreamed singing and counting. *Psychophysiology,* 19: 331–332.

LaBerge, S., Greenleaf, W., and Kedzierski, B. 1983. Physiological responses to dreamed sexual activity during lucid REM sleep. *Psychophysiology,* 20: 454–455.

LaBerge, S., and Rheingold, H. 1990. *Exploring the World of Lucid Dreaming.* New York: Ballantine Books.

Larue, R. 1970. Recurrent dreams. Term research paper for a course on dreams taught by G. William Domhoff, University of California, Santa Cruz.

Marks, I. 1978. Rehearsal relief of a nightmare. *British Journal of Psychiatry,* 133: 461–465.

Mattoon, M. A. 1978. *Applied Dream Analysis: A Jungian Approach.* Washington, D.C.: V. H. Winson and Sons.

Maultsby, M. C., and Gram, J. M. 1974. Dream changes following successful Rational behavior therapy. *Journal of Rational Living,* 9: 30–33.

Perls, F. S. 1969. *Gestalt Therapy Verbatim: A Book of Gestalt Therapy Sessions.* Moab, Utah: Real People Press.

Renik, O. 1981. Typical examination dreams, superego dreams, and traumatic dreams. *Psychoanalytic Quarterly,* 50: 159–189.

Robbins, P. R., and Houshi, F. 1983. Some observations on recurrent dreams. *Bulletin of the Menninger Clinic,* 47: 262–265.

Robbins, P. R., and Tanck, R. H. 1991–92. A comparison of recurrent dreams reported from childhood and recent recurrent dreams. *Imagination, Cognition, and Personality,* 11: 259–262.

Rossi, E. L. 1985. *Dreams and the Growth of Personality.* 2nd ed. New York: Brunner/Mazel.

Schatzman, M., Worsley, A., and Fenwick, P. 1988. Correspondence during lucid dreams between dreamed and actual events. In J. Gackenbach and S. LaBerge, eds., *Conscious Mind, Sleeping Brain: Perspectives on Lucid Dreaming.* New York: Plenum Press.

Sharpe, E. F. [1937] 1978. *Dream Analysis.* New York: Brunner/Mazel.

Silverberg, W. V. 1948. The concept of transference. *Psychoanalytic Quarterly,* 17: 303–321.

Stewart, W. A. 1967. Comments on the manifest content of certain types of unusual dreams. *Psychoanalytic Quarterly,* 36: 329–341.

Tholey, P. 1983. Techniques for inducing and manipulating lucid dreams. *Perceptual and Motor Skills,* 57: 79–90.

———— 1988. A model for lucidity training as a means of self-healing and psychological growth. In J. Gackenbach and S. LaBerge, eds., *Conscious Mind, Sleeping Brain: Perspectives on Lucid Dreaming.* New York: Plenum Press.

Ullman, M., and Zimmerman, N. 1979. *Working with Dreams.* New York: Jeremy P. Tarcher.

Ward, C. H., Beck, A. T., and Rascoe, E. 1961. Typical dreams. *Archives of General Psychiatry,* 5: 606–615.

Webb, D. E., and Fagan, J. 1993. The impact of dream interpretation using psychological kinesiology on the frequency of recurrent dreams. *Psychotherapy and Psychosomatics,* 50: 203–208.

Weiss, F. 1964. Dreaming: A creative process. *American Journal of Psychoanalysis,* 24: 1–10.

Zadra, A. L. 1990. Lucid dreaming, dream control, and the treatment of nightmares. Paper presented at the Seventh Annual Conference of the Association for the Study of Dreams, Chicago, June 26–30.

Zadra, A. L., and Donderi, D. C. 1992. Unpublished data.

———— 1993. Variety and intensity of emotions in bad dreams and nightmares. *Canadian Psychology,* 34:2a, 294.

Zadra, A. L., O'Brien, S., and Donderi, D. C. 1993. Dream content, dream recurrence, and well-being: A replication with a younger sample. Manuscript.

Zadra, A. L., Miller, M., and Donderi, D. C. 1994. Repetitive dream themes and their relation to self-reported well-being. Manuscript.

Contributors

Adrianne Aron, Ph.D., a clinical psychologist in Berkeley, California, works with the Centro Ignacio Martín-Baró, a group providing mental health services to refugees from Central America who are applying for political asylum.

Deirdre Barrett, Ph.D., is Assistant Professor of Psychology at Harvard Medical School and director of the doctoral program in clinical-developmental psychology at Suffolk University. She is president of the Association for the Study of Dreams, 1995–1996.

Kathryn Belicki, Ph.D., is Associate Professor of Psychology at Brock University, St. Catharines, Ontario, and is also in private practice.

Robert Bosnak, J.D., is a Jungian analyst on the faculty of the C. G. Jung Institute in Boston, Massachusetts. He is the author of *A Little Course in Dreams* (1988), *Dreaming with an AIDS Patient* (1989), and *Tracks in the Wilderness of Dreaming* (1996).

Rosalind D. Cartwright, Ph.D., is chairman of the Department of Psychology and director of the Sleep Disorder Center at Rush-Presbyterian-St. Luke's Medical Center, Chicago. She is the author of *Night Life: Explorations in Dreaming* (1977), *A Primer on Sleep and Dreaming* (1978), and, with L. Lamberg, *Crisis Dreaming* (1993).

David S. Chedekel, Ed.D., is a psychologist at the Shriners Burns Institute, Boston, Massachusetts, and is a Clinical Instructor at Harvard Medical School.

Marion Cuddy, Ph.D., is on the staff of Brockville Psychiatric Hospital, Ontario, and is in private practice in Ottawa.

Patricia Garfield, Ph.D., is a psychologist in San Francisco, California. She is the author of several books, including *Creative Dreaming* (1974) and *The Healing Power of Dreams* (1991).

Ernest Hartmann, M.D., is Professor of Psychiatry at Tufts University Medical School and editor of *Dreaming: The Journal of the Association for the Study of Dreams.* His books include *The Functions of Sleep* (1973) and *The Nightmare* (1984).

Hanna Kaminer, Ph.D., is a clinical psychologist at the Sleep Laboratory of the Faculty of Medicine, Technion-Israel Institute of Technology, Haifa, Israel.

Johanna King, Ph.D., served as doctoral internship director at the Counseling Center of California State University, Chico, for over twenty years and has retired to Port Townsend, Washington. She will serve as president of the Association for the Study of Dreams, 1996–1997.

Peretz Lavie, Ph.D., is director of the Sleep Laboratory at the Faculty of Medicine, Technion-Israel Institute of Technology, Haifa, Israel.

Robert Jay Lifton, M.D., is Distinguished Professor of Psychiatry and Psychology at John Jay College and the Graduate Center of City University of New York. His books include *The Nazi Doctors* (1986) and, with G. Mitchell, *Hiroshima in America: Fifty Years of Denial* (1995).

Karen Hagerman Muller, Ph.D., is a psychologist in practice in Haywood, California. She is the former director of training at Bay Area Women Against Rape.

Kathleen Nader, D.S.W., practices in Laguna Beach, California, and consults internationally on children's trauma.

Oliver Sacks, M.D., is Professor of Clinical Neurology at Albert Einstein College of Medicine and the author of many books, including *Awakenings* (1974), *The Man Who Mistook His Wife for a Hat* (1986), and *An Anthropologist on Mars* (1995).

Laura Shakun is a doctoral candidate at the Massachusetts School of Professional Psychology and a training fellow at the Shriners Burns Institute of Boston, Massachusetts.

Jacqueline R. Sheehan, Ph.D., is the director of counseling at Westfield State College in Westfield, Massachusetts.

Alan Siegel, Ph.D., teaches at the California School of Professional Psychology and is the editor of *The Association for the Study of Dreams Newsletter.* He is the author of *Dreams That Can Change Your Life.*

Frederick J. Stoddard, M.D., is chief of psychiatry at Shriners Burns Institute, Boston, Massachusetts, and Assistant Clinical Professor of Psychiatry at Harvard Medical School.

Harry A. Wilmer, M.D., is a Jungian analyst and director of the Institute for the Humanities at Salado, Texas. His books include *Vietnam in Remission* (1985) and *The Understandable Jung* (1994).

Antonio L. Zadra, Ph.D., is a post-doctoral fellow at the Labo Sommeil de l'Hôpital du Sacré-Coeur, Montreal, Quebec.

Index